Garden Trees

By the Editors of Sunset Books and Sunset Magazine

Lane Publishing Co. · Menlo Park, California

Foreword

Few of us realize how much our lives depend on trees. Their leaves convert vast quantities of carbon dioxide into oxygen we breathe. Their wood furnishes raw materials for many essential products, ranging from the humble pencil to fine furniture and houses—even to the paper upon which this book is printed. Aside from wood many trees contain oils or fluids that are vital to medicine, industry, and the home. And, of course, trees produce nutritious, not to mention delicious, fruits. Even the leaves, buds, and seeds of many trees have come to be economically important.

But in everyday living, a tree's most cherished role is as a provider of beauty and comfort. Trees soften the rough edges of cities and towns and glorify nature's mountains, valleys, and watercourses: they can emphasize, enhance, or even hide both natural and manmade features. Just imagine your neighborhood with all its trees removed and you'll begin to appreciate the visual service they perform. Finally, the presence of trees creates cool shade and shelter from wind, making the environment much more pleasant than it would be if it were treeless.

Trees, then, are a complex and highly varied subject, and a comprehensive book about them for the home gardener could hardly be realized without the generously given assistance from knowledgeable horticulturists. For their invaluable aid in preparing the material for this book we would like to thank J. Clark Ballard, Cooperative Extension Service, Utah State University; Wilbur Bluhm, Salem, Oregon; Clifford Collier, Jr., Cooperative Extension Service, West Virginia University; Fred C. Galle, Callaway Gardens, Pine Mountain, Georgia; E. Sam Hemming, Easton, Maryland; W. R. Hildreth, Saratoga Horticultural Foundation, California; Richard Howard, the Arnold Arboretum of Harvard University, Massachusetts; Joseph E. Howland, DuPage Horticultural School (Illinois) and University of Nevada; Warren D. Jones, University of Arizona; Carl J. C. Jorgensen, Colorado State University; Paul J. Mitchell, Cooperative Extension Service, Oklahoma State University; L. K. Smith, Thousand Oaks, California; Robert L. Ticknor, Oregon State University; Joseph A. Witt, University of Washington Arboretum.

Supervising Editor: Richard Osborne

Research and Text: Philip Edinger

Illustrations: E. D. Bills

Design: Roger Flanagan

Cover: Photograph by Ells Marugg

Photography: William Aplin—p.12, back cover; Glenn Christiansen—p. 62; Philip Edinger—p. 14; Ells Marugg—p. 4; Darrow M. Watt—pp. 18, 26, 82.

Executive Editor, Sunset Books: David E. Clark

First Printing February 1975

Contents

Special Features

Choose a tree carefully, considering its characteristics as they relate to your garden.

Before you choose a tree

Careful selection gives you the best chance of success with your new tree. Here are points to consider when making your choice.

Most trees are long term investments. You can expect any tree to need at least a growing season or two to become established in your garden. After that, years may pass before it reaches maturity. But like a vintage wine, a tree's quality increases with age, and the result is worth the wait. Barring any unusual health problems or natural disasters, many trees will live to give pleasure to future generations.

When you contemplate selecting a tree, you'll want to use the same care and forethought you would in actually planting it in your garden.

Each different tree species is an individual with its own set of needs, appeals, and drawbacks. Similarly, each garden is also an individual, having particular advantages and limitations that affect plant growth. Your challenge is to select a tree whose needs and habits will match its intended location in your garden so that, in years to come, the tree will fulfill the pleasure you've anticipated from it. This section presents a number of points to consider before you select a tree for your yard.

UNDERSTANDING SOME BASIC DIFFERENCES

On pages 26-93 you'll find descriptions and illustrations of several hundred different tree species. These trees fall quite naturally into three categories: deciduous trees, broad-leafed evergreen trees, and needle-leafed evergreen trees.

Deciduous trees (pages 26-61) are those that yearly drop all of their leaves at one time. Most do this in the autumn, remain leafless throughout winter, and produce new foliage again in the springtime. (A few tropical deciduous trees growing in the warmest zones may shed all their leaves in winter or spring and then flower or leaf out again immediately.) Deciduous trees often have broad, flattish, supple leaves and may put on a good show of spring or summer flowers or fall foliage color—sometimes both.

Broad-leafed evergreens (pages 62-81) have generally the same flat, often wide leaves as deciduous trees do, though on closer inspection these evergreen leaves often turn out to be thicker and more leathery than deciduous foliage. But the most conspicuous difference is that broad-leafed evergreens keep a full canopy of leaves throughout the year (dropping old leaves a few at a time, usually through winter and spring) rather than shedding all of them at one time.

Needle-leafed evergreens (pages 82-93) are those trees with mostly needlelike or scalelike leaves that persist (with few exceptions) the year round. Often these trees are cone bearing. Like the broad-leafed evergreens (above), these needle-leaf types shed their oldest foliage while the newer remains on the tree. Old foliage is innermost on branches and turns yellow or brown before it drops.

Shall it be deciduous or evergreen?

In many cases, the first question you'll ask when selecting a tree is, "Do I want a tree that holds leaves throughout the year or one that sheds them entirely at some season, leafing out again later on?"

To a great extent, your climate will help determine whether you buy a deciduous or an evergreen tree. For example, broad-leafed evergreens aren't adapted to really cold winter climates. In such regions, your choices will be among the deciduous trees or the needle-leafed evergreens that will take cold weather. But in areas with mild to only moderately cold winters, you can enlarge your field of choice to include many of the broad-leafed evergreen trees, as well as some tropical deciduous species.

Typically, deciduous trees begin the year in spring with a burst of new leaves or flowers and continue through summer fully clothed in foliage. In autumn, leaf color often changes. Later, the leaves drop for the winter to reveal often attractive branch and limb structure, possibly interesting bark color and texture, and on some trees, ornamental fruits that persist through winter.

As a result of their nature, deciduous trees can offer you a broad range of different attractions, whereas both needle-leaf and broad-leaf evergreens retain a more constant appearance throughout the year.

Because of their changes, though, deciduous trees may not be capable of fulfilling one landscape function all year long. For instance, they'll be fine screen, shade, or windbreak trees only while in leaf. Needle-leafed evergreens, on the other hand, will function as screens and windbreaks year-round in such cold-winter climates as Zones 3-7 (see page 96 for a map of the climate zones), whereas most broad-leafed evergreens serve well in warmer areas, such as Zones 8-10. Still, a deciduous tree can be an excellent year-round climate moderator where winters are cool to cold: its foliage canopy will provide shade during warm months, and bare branches in winter will let the sunshine through.

Think carefully about planting a deciduous tree in the warmest zones (9 and 10), where broad-leafed evergreens often dominate the landscape: fully clothed evergreens sometimes can make a deciduous tree look embarrassingly naked in wintertime. Remember, too, if you prefer to keep all fallen leaves raked up, that a deciduous tree drops its foliage in a relatively short time but that evergreen types shed old leaves over an extended period.

THE RIGHT TREE IN THE RIGHT PLACE

What role in your landscape do you want a tree to play? In a patio or terrace, the most satisfactory candidates may be among the small or slow-growing types. But if you're looking for a tree to provide lots of shade, then it may be the larger kinds you'll want to investigate.

Perhaps you'd like a tree to block an objectionable view or to screen a patio. Depending on the situation, you might try something low but spreading, upright and narrow (plant several in a row), or perhaps a tree with low-branching trunks. If a large area needs to be screened, you might get best results by planting a grove of trees.

A focal point in your landscape—such as a view from a featured window—deserves special treatment. There you might plant a tree that presents a smashing burst of spring flowers or a dazzling autumn color display—or both. In the colder zones, you might want to feature a needle-leafed evergreen for a striking winter effect.

A number of specific garden situations and trees that will suit them are presented on pages 6-11. Consulting this section may help you to focus your search for a tree.

Consider the root system

A tree's root structure isn't always important to you, but in some garden situations you will want to avoid trees with certain root systems that will eventually cause problems. For example, poplars have roots that are extremely aggressive and invasive. Planting a poplar near water or sewage lines almost guarantees future problems with clogged pipes. Similarly, to plant any tree with aggressive surface roots next to a paved area is to invite cracked and raised pavement.

If a lawn is to be maintained beneath your tree, you'll want to avoid types having greedy surface roots that will successfully compete with the lawn for water and nutrients. And you don't want large roots rising above the ground to interfere with mowing.

Match its location to its needs

No matter how gorgeous a tree is, it loses much appeal if you have to tend it more than you'd anticipated.

Often a tree may require protracted attention because its location is incompatible with its needs. For example, a moisture-needing tree in an arid climate will constantly need watering; brittle-wooded trees will demand periodic pruning and repair in regions subject to heavy winds or snow and ice storms that will break their limbs. If you select a tree that is too large and aggressive for its allotted space, you'll be faced with repeated pruning—a task that, when overdone, can become tiresome to you and detrimental to the tree.

Some trees may be plagued in certain parts of the country by a particular pest or disease. To avoid an eternal battle, look for another species that isn't likely to be troubled in your area.

Most trees are always shedding something, but some trees shed more than others. Although falling leaves, fruit, or cones, shedding bark, and dead flowers may not bother you in a background or in a "wild" garden, they can be a distinct nuisance in a more formal setting or on a lawn if you feel compelled to keep all litter raked away.

To avoid any of these possible problems, always select a tree by keeping in mind its needs and its advantages and limitations in your garden.

A selection guide to trees

These lists will help you in your search for that elusive "perfect" tree

FLOWERING TREES

Deciduous Trees

Name of tree	Climate zones	Flowering season	Color
Acer pseudo-platanus, p. 29	6-9	Spring	Greenish yellow
Aesculus carnea, p. 29-30	5-9	Spring	Pink to red
Albizia julibrissin, p. 30-31	5-9	Spring	Pink
Amelanchier species, p. 31	Vary	Spring	White
Cassia fistula, p. 33-34	10	Spring	Yellow
Castanea species, p. 34	Vary	Spring	Light yellow
Catalpa species, p. 34	5-10	Spring	White
Cedrela sinensis, p. 34	6-10	Spring	Yellow
Cercidium species, p. 35	8-9	Spring	Yellow
Cercis species, p. 35-36	Vary	Spring	Pink (also dark red, white)
Chionanthus species, p. 36	Vary	Spring	White
Cladrastis lutea, p. 36,	4-9	Spring	White
Cornus species, p. 36-37	Vary	Spring	White, pink
Crataegus species, p. 37-39	Vary	Spring	White, pink
Davidia involucrata, p. 39	6-9	Spring	White
Delonix regia, p. 39	10	Spring	Red
Erythrina species, p. 40	Vary	Spring	Red, pink, yellow
Franklinia alatamaha, p. 41	6-9	Spring	White
Fraxinus ornus, p. 42	6-9	Spring	White
Halesia species, p. 43-44	Vary	Spring	White
Jacaranda acutifolia, p. 44	9-10	Spring	Lavender (also white)
Koelreuteria species, p. 44	Vary	Summer	Yellow
Laburnum watereri, p. 44-45	5-9	Spring	Yellow
Lagerstroemia indica, p. 45	7-9	Summer	Pink (also red, lavender, purple, white)
Liriodendron tulipifera, p. 46	5-9	Spring	Greenish
Magnolia species, p. 46-48	Vary	Spring	Pink, white
Malus species, p. 48-49	Vary	Spring	White, pink
Oxydendrum arboreum, p. 51	6-9	Summer	White
Parkinsonia aculeata, p. 51	8-10	Spring	Yellow
Parrotia persica, p. 51	6-9	Spring	Red
Paulownia tomentosa, p. 51-52	6-10	Spring	Lavender
Prosopis glandulosa torreyana, p. 52-53	8-9	Spring	Greenish yellow
Prunus species, p. 53-55	Vary	Spring	White
Pterostyrax hispida, p. 55	7-9	Summer	White
Pyrus species, p. 55-56	Vary	Spring	White
Robinia species, p. 57	Vary	Spring	White, pink, magenta
Sophora japonica, p. 59	5-10	Summer	White
Sorbus species, p. 59	Vary	Spring	White
Stewartia species, p. 59	6-9	Spring	White
Styrax species, p. 59-60	Vary	Spring	White
Zizyphus jujuba, p. 61	8-10	Spring	Yellow

Broad-leafed Evergreens

Name of tree	Climate zones	Flowering season	Color
Acacia species, p. 63	Vary	Spring	Yellow, cream
Arbutus species, p. 63-64	Vary	Spring	White
Bauhinia species, p. 64	9-10	Spring	Pink, purple, white
Brachychiton acerifolium, p. 64	9-10	Spring	Orange red
Brachychiton bidwillii, p. 64	9-10	Spring	Orange red
Brachychiton discolor, p. 64	9-10	Summer	Pink
Callistemon citrinus, p. 64-65	9-10	Summer	Red
Callistemon salignus, p. 65	9-10	Spring	Cream
Callistemon viminalis, p. 65	9-10	Summer	Red
Castanospermum australe, p. 65	9-10	Summer	Red and yellow
Chorisia speciosa, p. 66	9-10	Winter	Pink purple
Clethra arborea, p. 67	9-10	Summer	White
Crinodendron patagua, p. 68	9-10	Summer	White
Eucalyptus calophylla, p. 69	10	All year	White, pink, red
Eucalyptus ficifolia, p. 69	9-10	All year	Red (also orange, pink, cream)
Eucalyptus leucoxylon, p. 69-70	9-10	Winter	White, pink
Eucalyptus sideroxylon, p. 70	9-10	Fall-spr.	Pink
Lagunaria patersonii, p. 72	9-10	Summer	Pinkish

(Continued on next page)

Name of tree	Climate zones	Flowering season	Color
Leptospermum laevigatum, p. 72-73	9-10	Spring	White
Magnolia grandiflora, p. 73	9-10	Spring	White
Magnolia virginiana, p. 73	7-10	Spring	White
Melaleuca armillaris, p. 74	9-10	Spr.-fall	White
Melaleuca decussata, p. 74	9-10	Summer	Lilac, purple
Melaleuca ericifolia, p. 74	9-10	Spring	Cream
Melaleuca linariifolia, p. 74	9-10	Summer	White
Melaeuca nesophila, p. 74	9-10	All year	Pink
Melaleuca quinquenervia, p. 74-75	9-10	Sum.-fall	Cream

Name of tree	Climate zones	Flowering season	Color
Melaleuca styphelioides, p. 75	9-10	Sum.-fall	Cream
Metrosideros excelsa, p. 75	10	Summer	Red
Photinia serrulata, 77-78	8-10	Spring	White
Prunus laurocerasus, p. 78-79	8-10	Summer	White
Prunus lusitanica, p. 79	8-10	Summer	Cream white
Prunus lyonii, p. 79	8-10	Spring	White
Pyrus kawakamii, p. 79	9-10	Winter	White
Stenocarpus sinuatus, p. 80-81	9-10	Fall	Red and yellow
Tamarix aphylla, p. 81	8-10	Summer	White, pink

TREES FOR AUTUMN COLOR

Here are trees you can count on for autumn color. But remember that fall color on a given plant may not be consistent from year to year because of overall weather conditions, garden location, or the section of the country the tree is growing in. Under certain conditions, color will be less intense: when autumn is warm or wet, if the tree doesn't receive full sunlight, and in mild-winter areas. Good red color, in particular, depends upon sunlight and warm days followed by cool nights.

Name of tree	Climate zones	Color
Acer species, p. 27-29	Vary	Red, orange, yellow
Amelanchier species, p. 31	5-8	Red, orange, yellow
Betula species, p. 32-33	Vary	Yellow
Carpinus species, p. 33	Vary	Yellowish
Carya species, p. 33	Vary	Yellow
Castanea species, p. 34	Vary	Yellowish
Celtis species, p. 34-35	Vary	Yellow
Cercidiphyllum japonicum, p. 35	4-9	Red, yellow
Cercis species, p. 35-36	Vary	Yellow
Chionanthus species, p. 36	Vary	Yellow
Cladrastis lutea, p. 36	4-9	Yellow
Cornus species, p. 36-37	Vary	Red, yellow
Crataegus species, p. 37-39	Vary	Red, orange, yellow
Diospyros species, p. 39	Vary	Red, orange, yellow
Erythrina coralloides, p. 40	8-10	Yellow
Fagus species, p. 40	Vary	Yellowish brown
Ficus carica, p. 40-41	5-10	Yellow
Franklinia alatamaha, p. 41	6-9	Red, orange
Fraxinus species, p. 41-42	Vary	Purple, red, yellow
Ginkgo biloba, p. 42-43	5-10	Yellow
Halesia species, p. 43-44	Vary	Yellow
Juglans species, p. 44	Vary	Yellow
Koelreuteria henryi, p. 44	9-10	Yellow
Lagerstroemia indica, p. 45	7-9	Red, orange, yellow
Larix species, p. 45-46	Vary	Yellow
Liquidambar styraciflua, p. 46	6-10	Purple, red, orange, yellow
Liriodendron tulipifera, p. 46	5-9	Yellow
Maclura pomifera, p. 46	6-10	Yellow
Malus species, p. 48-49	Vary	Yellow
Morus alba, p. 50	5-10	Yellow
Nyssa sylvatica, p. 50-51	5-9	Red

Name of tree	Climate zones	Color
Ostrya virginiana, p. 51	5-9	Yellow
Oxydendrum arboreum, p. 51	6-9	Red
Parrotia persica, p. 51	6-9	Yellow, orange, red
Pistacia chinensis, p. 52	9-10	Red, orange
Populus species, p. 52	Vary	Yellow
Prunus species (most), p. 53-55	Vary	Yellow
Prunus avium 'Plena', p. 54		Red
Prunus sargentii, p. 54-55	4-9	Red
Prunus serrulata 'Ukon', p. 55	5-9	Red
Pyrus species, p. 55-56	Vary	Red
Quercus alba, p. 56	5-10	Red
Quercus bicolor, p. 56	4-9	Red
Quercus coccinea, p. 56-57	5-10	Red
Quercus palustris, p. 57	5-10	Red
Quercus phellos, p. 57	6-9	Yellow
Quercus rubra, p. 57	4-10	Red
Quercus shumardii, p. 57	6-9	Red
Rhus typhina, p. 57	3-9	Red
Salix species, p. 57-58	Vary	Yellow
Sapium sebiferum, p. 58	9	Red
Sassafras albidum, p. 59	5-9	Red, orange, yellow
Sorbus alnifolia, p. 59	6-9	Yellow, orange, red
Sorbus americana, p. 59	3-9	Yellow
Sorbus aucuparia, p. 59	3-9	Yellow, orange, red
Stewartia koreana, p. 59	6-9	Orange red
Stewartia ovata, p. 59		Orange red
Stewartia pseudo-camellia, p. 59	6-9	Brown purple
Styrax species, p. 59-60	Vary	Red, yellow
Tilia species, p. 60-61	Vary	Yellow
Ulmus species, p. 61	Vary	Yellow
Zelkova serrata, p. 61	6-10	Yellow

TREES FOR GROVE PLANTING

Name of tree	Type	Climate zones
Acer palmatum, p. 28	D	6-9
Alnus species, p. 31	D	Vary
Betula species, p. 32-33	D	Vary
Cedrus deodara, p. 84-85	NL	7-10
Eucalyptus citriodora, p. 69	BL	9-10
Eucalyptus sideroxylon, p. 70	BL	9-10
Hymenosporum flavum, p. 71	BL	9-10

Name of tree	Type	Climate zones
Liquidambar styraciflua, p. 46	D	6-10
Pinus species, p. 88-91	NL	Vary
Sequoia sempervirens, p. 92-93	NL	7-10
Tristania conferta, p. 81	BL	9-10

D: *Deciduous*
BL: *Broad-leafed evergreen*
NL: *Needle-leafed evergreen*

TREES FOR CITY GARDENS

All the air pollutants in cities that bother humans also make life difficult for plants. In addition, city soils often are poor, of limited volume, or dry because they are difficult to water. Only an especially tough tree will grow willingly and look good under such trying conditions.

D: *Deciduous*
BL: *Broad-leafed evergreen*
NL: *Needle-leafed evergreen*

Name of tree	Type	Climate zones
Acer campestre, p. 27	D	5-8
Acer negundo, p. 28	D	3-10
Acer platanoides, p. 28-29	D	4-9
Aesculus carnea, p. 29-30	D	5-9
Ailanthus altissima, p. 30	D	5-10
Amelanchier species, p. 31	D	Vary by kind
Betula papyrifera, p. 32	D	3-8
Betula verrucosa, p. 33	D	3-10
Broussonetia papyrifera, p. 33	D	6-10
Carpinus betulus, p. 33	D	6-10
Catalpa species, p. 34	D	5-10
Cedrela sinensis, p. 34	D	6-10
Crataegus species, p. 37-39	D	Vary by kind
Ficus retusa, p. 70	BL	9-10
Fraxinus species, p.41-42, p. 70-71	D, BL	Vary by kind

Name of tree	Type	Climate zones
Gleditsia triacanthos inermis, p. 43	D	5-9
Ilex altaclarensis 'Wilsonii', p. 71	BL	7-10
Ilex aquifolium, p. 71-72	BL	6-9
Laburnum watereri, p. 44-45	D	5-9
Magnolia acuminata, p. 47	D	5-10
Magnolia soulangiana, p. 47-48	D	5-10
Picea omorika, p. 88	NL	5-8
Platanus acerifolia, p. 52	D	5-10
Prunus ceracifera 'Atropurpurea', p. 54	D	4-9
Prunus serrulata, p. 55	D	5-9
Pterocarya stenoptera, p. 55	D	8-10
Quercus ilex, p. 79	BL	7-10
Sophora japonica, p. 59	D	5-10
Tilia cordata, p. 61	D	4-9
Tilia euchlora, p. 61	D	5-9

PATIO TREES

Since a patio or terrace is often used as an outdoor room of the house, you'll usually want it to be neat and presentable with the minimum of maintenance. The trees below fit a patio location well because they are good looking at all times and because they shed relatively little litter—or drop it entirely in a short space of time. In addition, these are the smaller trees, well suited to the more intimate scale of a patio. They may grow slowly or fast but will not explode so aggressively that you'll have to keep them restrained.

Deciduous Trees

Name of tree	Climate zones
Acer buergerianum, p. 27	6-9
Acer davidii, p. 27	6-9
Acer ginnala, p. 27	3-8
Acer griseum, p. 27	6-9

Name of tree	Climate zones
Acer japonicum, p. 27-28	6-9
Acer palmatum, p. 28	6-9
Amelanchier species, p. 31	4 or 5-8
Cassia fistula, p. 33-34	10

Name of tree	Climate zones
Cercidiphyllum japonicum, p. 35	4-9
Cercidium floridum, p. 35	8-9

(Continued on next page)

Name of tree	Climate zones
Cercis species, p. 35-36	5 or 6-9
Chionanthus species, p. 36	Vary
Cladrastis lutea, p. 36	4-9
Cornus florida, p. 36	5-9
Cornus kousa, p. 36-37	6-9
Crataegus species, p. 37-39	Vary
Diospyros kaki, p. 39	7-9
Erythrina crista-galli, p. 40	9-10
Franklinia alatamaha, p. 41	6-9
Halesia carolina, p. 43-44	5-9
Koelreuteria species, p. 44	Vary
Laburnum watereri, p. 44-45	5-9
Lagerstroemia indica, p. 45	7-9
Magnolia species, p. 46-48	Vary
Malus species, p. 48-49	Vary
Oxydendrum arboreum, p. 51	5-9
Parkinsonia aculeata, p. 51	8-10
Parrotia persica, p. 51	6-9
Prunus species, p. 53-55	Vary
Pterostyrax hispida, p. 55	7-9

Name of tree	Climate zones
Rhus typhina, p. 57	3-9
Sapium sebiferum, p. 58	8-9
Sorbus americana, p. 59	3-6
Stewartia species, p. 59-60	6-9
Styrax species, p. 59-60	6 or 7-9
Zizyphus jujuba, p. 61	7-10

Broad-leafed Evergreens

Name of tree	Climate zones
Acacia baileyana, p. 63	9-10
Bauhinia species, p. 64	9-10
Callistemon species, p. 64-65	9-10
Clethra arborea, p. 67	9-10
Corynocarpus laevigatus, p. 67-68	9-10
Crinodendron patagua, p. 68	9-10
Eriobotrya deflexa, p. 68	9-10
Ilex altaclarensis 'Wilsonii', p. 71	9-10
Leptospermum laevigatum, p. 72-73	9-10

Name of tree	Climate zones
Macadamia species, p. 73	9-10
Magnolia grandiflora 'St. Mary', p. 73	7-10
Melaleuca species, p. 74	9-10
Olea europaea, p. 75	9-10
Photinia serrulata, p. 77-78	7-10
Pittosporum phillyraeoides, p. 78	9-10
Pittosporum rhombifolium, p. 78	9-10
Pyrus kawakamii, p. 79	8-10
Schinus terebinthifolius, p. 80	9-10
Stenocarpus sinuatus, p. 80-81	9-10

Needle-leafed Evergreens

Name of tree	Climate zones
Pinus thunburgiana, p. 91	5-9
Podocarpus gracilior, p. 91	9-10
Podocarpus macrophyllus, p. 91	7-10

SHADE TREES

Here are the medium sized to large specimens that will give you pools of refreshing shadow, good sized shaded areas for a lawn picnic, or a screen to place between house and sun for interior cooling in summertime.

Deciduous Trees

Name of tree	Climate zones
Acer macrophyllum, p. 28	7-9
Acer platanoides, p. 28-29	4-9
Acer pseudo-platanus, p. 29	6-9
Acer rubrum, p. 29	4-9
Acer saccharum, p. 29	4-9
Aesculus carnea, p. 29-30	5-9
Albizia julibrissin, p. 30-31	7-10
Broussonetia papyrifera, p. 33	6-10
Carpinus caroliniana, p. 33	3-9
Carya Illinoinensis, p. 33	6-9
Castanea species, p. 34	5-9
Catalpa speciosa, p. 34	5-10
Cedrela sinensis, p. 34	6-10
Celtis species, p. 34-35	Vary by kind
Erythrina caffra, p. 40	9-10
Fagus species, p. 40	Vary by kind
Fraxinus species, p. 41-42	Vary by kind
Gleditsia triacanthos inermis, p. 43	5-9
Juglans species, p. 44	Vary by kind
Koelreuteria henryi, p. 44	9-10
Magnolia acuminata, p. 47	5-10
Magnolia cordata, p. 47	6-9
Malus pumila, p. 49	4-9
Melia azedarach, p. 49-50	7-10
Morus alba, p. 50	5-10
Parkinsonia aculeata, p. 51	8-10

Name of tree	Climate zones
Phellodendron amurense, p. 52	4-9
Pistacia chinensis, p. 52	6-10
Platanus acerifolia, p. 52	5-10
Platanus occidentalis, p. 52	5-10
Populus alba, p. 52	4-10
Prosopis glandulosa torreyana, p. 52-53	7-9
Pterocarya stenoptera, p. 55	8-10
Quercus species, p. 56-57	Vary by kind
Salix alba 'Tristis', p. 57	3-10
Salix babylonica, p. 57	7-10
Salix blanda, p. 57-58	5-10
Salix elegantissima, p. 58	5-10
Sophora japonica, p. 59	5-10
Tilia species, p. 60-61	Vary by kind
Ulmus species, p. 61	Vary by kind
Zelkova serrata, p. 61	6-10

Broad-leafed Evergreens

Name of tree	Climate zones
Acacia pruinosa, p. 63	9-10
Brachychiton populneum, p. 64	9-10

(Continued on next page)

Name of tree	Climate zones
Castanospermum australe, p. 65	9-10
Cinnamomum camphora, p. 66	9-10
Eucalyptus cornuta, p. 69	9-10
Eucalyptus gunnii, p. 69	8-10
Eucalyptus maculata, p. 70	9-10
Eucalyptus melliodora, p. 70	9-10
Eucalyptus robusta, p. 70	8-10
Ficus rubiginosa, p. 70	9-10
Fraxinus uhdei, p. 70-71	9-10

Name of tree	Climate zones
Magnolia grandiflora, p. 73	8-10
Persea americana, p. 77	9-10
Pittosporum undulatum, p. 78	9-10
Prunus caroliniana, p. 78	7-10
Prunus laurocerasus, p. 78-79	7-10
Prunus lusitanica, p. 79	7-10
Prunus lyonii, p. 79	9-10
Quercus species, p. 79-80	Vary by kind
Umbellularia californica, p. 81	7-10

EVERGREEN WINDBREAK AND HEDGE TREES

Some trees have the stamina to withstand constant wind buffeting with no ill effects. Their density deflects the air currents enough to permit comfortable living and gardening in their lee. Ideally, the best plan is gradually to lift the wind with as many as five rows of shrubs and trees—each row 16 feet apart. Lacking this space, a row of shrubs on the windward side with a row of trees behind will do a good job, and even a single or staggered row of bushy trees (branched to the ground) will help considerably. Trees for hedges and screens share with windbreak trees the ability to grow closely together and still retain density. But they may not take strong winds as well. Unlike windbreak trees, though, they can be sheared or trimmed and definitely will hold branches all the way to the ground.

Broad-leafed Evergreens

H: *Hedge trees*
W: *Windbreak*
    f: *freezing winds (central United States)*
    c: *coastal (salty) winds*
    d: *desert (hot, dry) winds*

Name of tree	Climate zones	Hedge or windbreak, type of wind
Acacia melanoxylon, p. 63	8-10	H, W: c
Brachychiton populneum, p. 64	9-10	W: c
Casuarina stricta, p. 65	9-10	W: c
Ceratonia siliqua, p. 65-66	9-10	H, W
Eucalyptus gunnii, p. 69	8-10	W: c
Eucalyptus melliodora, p. 70	9-10	W: c
Eucalyptus robusta, p. 70	9-10	W: c
Eucalyptus sideroxylon, p. 70	9-10	W: c
Ilex altaclarensis 'Wilsonii', p. 71	7-10	H
Lagunaria patersonii, p. 72	9-10	H, W: c, d
Laurus nobilis, p. 72	8-10	H
Leptospermum laevigatum, p. 72-73	9-10	H, W: c
Melaleuca nesophila, p. 74	9-10	H
Myoporum laetum, p. 75	9-10	H, W: c
Olmediella betschleriana, p. 75	9-10	H
Photinia serrulata, p. 77-78	7-10	H
Pittosporum crassifolium, p. 78	9-10	H
Pittosporum eugenioides, p. 78	9-10	H
Pittosporum tenuifolium, p. 78	9-10	H
Pittosporum undulatum, p. 78	9-10	H, W: c
Prunus caroliniana, p. 78	7-10	H, W: c
Prunus laurocerasus, p. 78-79	7-10	H
Prunus lusitanica, p. 79	7-10	H
Prunus lyonii, p. 79	9-10	H, W: c
Quercus ilex, p. 79	7-10	H, W: c
Rhamnus alaternus, p. 80	7-10	H, W: c, d
Syzygium paniculatum, p. 81	9-10	H
Tamarix aphylla, p. 81	8-10	H, W: c, d

Needle-leafed Evergreens

Name of tree	Climate zones	Hedge or windbreak, type of wind
Calocedrus decurrens, p. 84	5-10	H, W: f
Cedrus deodara, p. 84-85	7-10	H, W
Chamaecyparis lawsoniana 'Allumii', p. 85	6-9	H
Cupressocyparis leylandii, p. 86	5-10	H, W
Cupressus glabra, p. 86	7-10	H, W: d, f
Cupressus macrocarpa, p. 86	8-10	H, W: c
Juniperus species, p. 87	Vary by kind	H, W: f
Picea abies, p. 87	3-8	W: f
Picea glauca, p. 88	3-5	W: f
Picea pungens, p. 88	3-8	W: f
Pinus canariensis, p. 89	9-10	W: c
Pinus contorta, p. 89	7-10	W: c
Pinus halepensis, p. 89	8-10	W: c
Pinus nigra, p. 89	5-8	W: f
Pinus ponderosa, p. 90	5-9	W: f
Pinus radiata, p. 90	8-10	W: c
Pinus sylvestris, p. 90-91	3-8	W: f
Podocarpus gracilior, p. 91	9-10	H
Podocarpus macrophyllus, p. 91	7-10	H
Pseudotsuga menziesii, p. 91-92	6-9	W: c
Sequoia sempervirens, p. 92-93	7-10	H, W: c
Thuja occidentalis 'Fastigiata', p. 93	3-8	H
Thuja plicata, p. 93	6-9	H, W: c, f
Tsuga species, p. 93	Vary by kind	H

FAST-GROWING TREES

*All trees listed below should put on three or more feet in height a year
(after they get established) as long as you give them good routine care.
Although not all are long-lived or the most elegant trees, they can at least be planted
to supply quick effect while slower-growing (but perhaps more desirable) trees mature.*

Deciduous Fast Growing Trees

Name of tree	Climate zone	Height, width
Acer negundo, p. 28	3-10	50 ft.; 50 ft.
Acer platanoides, p. 28-29	4-9	90 ft.; 50 ft.
Acer pseudo-platanus, p. 29	6-9	70 ft.; 70 ft.
Acer rubrum, p. 29	4-9	60 ft.; 45 ft.
Acer saccharinum, p. 29	4-9	100 ft.; 75 ft.
Ailanthus altissima, p. 30	5-10	60 ft.; 50 ft.
Albizia julibrissin, p. 30-31	7-10	40 ft.; 50 ft.
Alnus species, p. 31	Vary by kind	Vary by kind
Betula maximowicziana, p. 32	6-10	80 ft.; 30 ft.
Betula nigra, p. 32	5-10	50-90 ft.; 40-60 ft.
Carya illinoinensis, p. 33	6-9	100 ft.; 100 ft.;
Cassia fistula, p. 33-34	10	30 ft.; 30 ft.
Castanea mollissima, p. 34	5-9	60 ft.; 60 ft.
Catalpa species, p. 34	5-10	Vary by kind
Celtis australis, p. 34	7-9	40-70 ft.; 25-50 ft.
Cercidium floridum, p. 35	8-9	25 ft.; 25 ft.
Cercis canadensis, p. 36	5-9	25-35 ft.; 20 ft.
Cornus controversa, p. 36	6-9	40-60 ft.; 40-60 ft.
Delonix regia, p. 39	10	50 ft.; 60 ft.
Fraxinus species, p. 41-42	Vary by kind	Vary by kind
Gleditsia triacanthos inermis, p. 43	5-9	Vary by kind
Gymnocladus dioica, p. 43	5-9	50-70 ft.; 25-35 ft.
Liriodendron tulipifera, p. 46	5-9	60-90 ft.; 30-45 ft.
Maclura pomifera, p. 46	5-9	50-60 ft.; 50-60 ft.
Magnolia acuminata, p. 47	5-10	60-80 ft.; 30
Magnolia cordata, p. 47	6-9	30 ft.; 20 ft.
Magnolia veitchii, p. 48	7-10	40 ft.; 30 ft.
Malus arnoldiana, p. 48	5-9	20 ft.; 30 ft.
Malus 'Hopa', p. 49	5-9	25 ft.; 20 ft.
Melia azedarach, p. 49-50	7-10	50 ft.; 50 ft.
Morus alba, p. 50	5-10	35 ft.; 40 ft.
Paulownia tomentosa, p. 51-52	6-10	50 ft.; 30-40 ft.
Pistacia chinensis, p. 52	6-10	60 ft.; 50 ft.
Platanus species, p. 52	Vary by kind	Vary by kind
Populus species, p. 52	Vary by kind	Vary by kind
Prunus cerasifera 'Atropurpurea', p. 54	4-9	25-30 ft.; 25 ft.
Pterocarya stenoptera, p. 55	8-10	40-90 ft.; 30-60 ft.
Quercus rubra, p. 57	4-10	90 ft.; 60 ft.
Rhus typhina, p. 57	3-9	Variable size
Robinia pseudoacacia, p. 57	4-9	40-75 ft.; 30-50 ft.
Salix species, p. 57-58	Vary by kind	Vary by kind
Ulmus species, p. 61	Vary by kind	Vary by kind

Broad-leafed Evergreens

Name of tree	Climate zone	Height, width
Acacia species, p. 63	Mostly 9-10	Vary by kind
Casuarina species, p. 65	9-10	Vary by kind
Chorisia speciosa, p. 66	9-10	30-60 ft.; 15-30 ft.
Eucalyptus species, p. 68-70	Vary by kind	Vary by kind
Ficus mysorensis, p. 70	9-10	20 ft.; 20 ft.
Fraxinus uhdei, p. 70-71	9-10	70 ft.; 35-40 ft.
Harpephyllum kaffrum, p. 71	10	25-30 ft.; 20-25 ft.
Lagunaria patersonii, p. 72	10	20-40 ft.; 10-20 ft.
Melaleuca ericifolia, p. 74	9-10	15-25 ft.; 15-25 ft.
Pittosporum undulatum, p. 78	9-10	40 ft.; 40 ft.
Prunus laurocerasus, p. 78-79	7-10	30 ft.; 30 ft.
Rhamnus alaternus, p. 80	7-10	20 ft.; 20 ft.
Schinus molle, p. 80	9-10	40 ft.; 40 ft.
Tamarix aphylla, p. 81	8-10	30-50 ft.; 20-40 ft.

Needle-leafed Evergreens

Name of tree	Climate zone	Height, width
Abies grandis, p. 83	6-9	100 plus ft.; 25-40 ft.
Abies procera, p. 83	6-8	75-100 ft.; 25 ft.
Cedrus deodara, p. 84-85	8-10	80 ft.; 40 ft.
Cryptomeria japonica, p. 85-86	7-9	100 ft.; 30 ft.
Cupressocyparis leylandii, p. 86	5-10	50 ft.; 10 ft.
Picea abies, p. 87	3-8	100-150 ft.; 30-40 ft.
Picea sitchensis, p. 88	6-9	100-150 ft.; 50-60 ft.
Pinus species, p. 88-91	Vary by kind	Vary by kind
Sequoia sempervirens, p. 92-93	8-10	70-90 ft.; 15-30 ft.
Sequoiadendron giganteum, p. 93	6-10	75 ft.; 15-30

__Pruning__ and thinning older trees is made easier by use of pole saw with cutting attachment.

Planting techniques and care

How to get your new tree into the ground and off to a good start and–later–how to keep it healthy.

Since a tree can live on for many decades—often beyond your own lifetime—you owe it the best possible attention. Particularly if you plant a new tree, the first step to success begins with understanding your soil. With established trees, your attention will turn to watering, fertilizing, pruning, and possibly pest and disease control.

UNDERSTANDING YOUR SOIL

All soils consist of much more than just simple earth. Soils are a dynamic combination of mineral particles, organic matter, air, water, and micro-organisms. The ratios and arrangement of these components determine a soil's quality and how successfully a plant will grow in it.

What is a good garden soil?

In the best soils, 30 to 50 per cent of a given volume consists of pore space between particles of soil and organic matter. Roughly 20 per cent of that pore space is filled with air; the remaining space is filled with water. Around each soil particle is a microscopic film of water containing nutrients in solution.

This good garden soil (often referred to as loam) contains enough oxygen for roots to respire normally; it allows carbon dioxide to escape easily; it holds enough water and dissolved nutrients to sustain the tree and yet drains rapidly enough that it doesn't become waterlogged. Not all soils are ideal, though. In varying degrees, many garden soils are described as either "heavy" or "light."

Soil can be heavy or light

"Heavy" soils (a word often used to describe soils with a high clay content) are made up of exceedingly small, platelike mineral particles that fit together very closely like a pile of playing cards. If you squeeze a handful of moist soil and it sticks together (often with a slightly slick feel) and doesn't crumble apart when you press the lump with your finger, you can presume the soil has a high clay content.

Because clay soil particles fit together so closely, the pore spaces between them are very small. These small pore spaces mean that water not only soaks in slowly but also percolates through at an equally slow rate. And small pore spaces also restrict that gaseous exchange that is vital to root growth: oxygen enters the soil with difficulty, and carbon dioxide respired by the roots has equal difficulty escaping.

"Light" or sandy soils represent just the opposite extreme from heavy, claylike soils. Sandy soils are composed of much larger, rounded, and irregularly shaped particles that fit together very loosely, leaving large pore spaces between particles. As a result, water and dissolved nutrients drain through rapidly. Although light soils can supply plenty of air to roots, they often lack fertility (because nutrients have been leached out) and tend to dry out rapidly.

Fortunately, most garden soils are neither completely claylike nor entirely sandy. Instead, they tend toward one or the other condition in varying degrees. A majority of soils are loam—a mixture of sand and clay plus organic matter—and need little if any special treatment in order to grow most trees well.

Steps toward soil improvement

It's both impractical and unnecessary to try to change your entire yard's soil to provide an optimum root environment for one tree. And whatever improvements you make to the planting soil, you can be sure that the tree's roots are going to outgrow that soil in a few years' time. For these reasons, it's important to select a tree that is likely to grow well in the sort of soil you have. At planting time you're most concerned with supplying a good soil around the tree's root system so that the new roots it forms will be encouraged to grow vigorously and establish the tree well.

As discussed earlier, the key to a healthy soil is the amount of pore space between soil particles. One agent for improving soil is organic matter. In clay soil the organic material acts as wedges to help separate the closely packed soil particles; the result is improved drainage and aeration. In sandy soils whose pore space already is large, organic matter acts as "sponges" to absorb water and nutrients; this helps counteract the fast drainage and nutrient leaching.

Even good loamy soils can profit from the addition of organic material at planting time because soil micro-organisms are constantly at work breaking down its organic matter into forms that plants can absorb.

A few familiar organic soil amendments are peat moss, compost, nitrogen-fortified sawdust, bark dust, ground bark, buckwheat and rice hulls, and leaf mold from a forest floor.

Additional help to clay soils can come from applying agricultural gypsum or lime. Both of these compounds cause

clay

sand

Soil structure depends on particle size: clay soils have tiny particles, sand has large ones, loam contains a mixture of large and small.

loam

soil particles to group together into larger units, improving drainage and aeration. Gypsum and lime actually can provide *primary* help whenever soil is extremely dense or compacted. Many homeowners in new housing developments, for example, are left with soil that has been compressed by trucks and other heavy equipment used during construction. And whenever extensive grading has been done prior to building, the topsoil often has been scraped away, leaving the poorer quality, denser subsoil on the surface. In both these situations, gypsum or lime can help to aerate the compacted soil (see following paragraphs).

Use lime only if you *know* your soil is too acid for what you want to grow: it will help neutralize an acid soil but only increases the alkalinity of a neutral or an alkaline soil. Your county or university agricultural extension agent can tell you if your soil is acid and how much lime you might apply if it is.

Since gypsum does not appreciably affect the acidity or alkalinity of soil, it is useful whenever you just want to improve soil structure. For helping heavy soils that already support healthy plant life, the usual recommendation is to scatter it on the surface so that it looks like a light snowfall and then dig it in. But for compacted soils, your county or university agricultural extension agent can suggest more specific application rates based on his knowledge of soils in your area.

HOW TO PLANT A TREE

Trees are sold in three ways for the gardener to plant: bare-root, balled-and-burlapped, or growing in containers such as 1, 5, or 15-gallon cans (depending on tree size). Which of these forms your tree comes in depends mostly on the season and on whether the tree is deciduous or evergreen. The planting methods for bare-root, balled-and-burlapped, and containerized trees are somewhat different; each is described below. But for planting all trees, you'll first need to dig a planting hole and, after setting the tree in the ground, follow up with a few important procedures.

Digging the planting hole

The planting hole you dig for your tree should be larger than you need just to accommodate its root system: dig a hole with vertical sides that is approximately twice as broad and twice as deep as the tree's root spread. This will provide plenty of loosened soil for roots to spread easily into during the tree's first few growing seasons in your garden. By the time roots grow to the perimeter of the planting hole, they should be strong enough to continue pressing into the undisturbed native soil beyond.

At the same time you dig the planting hole, your chance arrives to condition and improve the soil by mixing in organic matter, as well as gypsum or lime if needed (see pages 12-13). Mix the conditioners with the soil you've removed from the planting hole. Then return the improved soil to the hole after you set the tree in position.

If you are planting in a sandy or loamy soil that drains well, be generous with organic amendments. To the soil you've removed from the planting hole, add from 25 to 50 per cent by volume of the organic matter. In easy-to-remember terms, that means mixing anywhere from one to two shovelfuls of organic matter to each two shovelfuls of soil.

For clay soils there's one note of caution in soil preparation and planting: don't add too much organic matter. Although organic materials can improve the structure and permeability of any soil, if you add a large quantity to a planting hole in clay soil you can create, in effect, an underground "container" for your new tree's roots. Upon reaching the outskirts of the planting hole and its soft, permeable, conditioned soil, roots will run into the dense native clay and have some difficulty penetrating it; their tendency will be to remain in the softer conditioned soil, even to the point of becoming twisted and rootbound. Then, too, water won't drain into the native clay as fast as it is absorbed by the prepared soil around the roots. Excess water then collects in the planting hole, waterlogging the root zone and possibly killing the tree from lack of air in the soil.

In clay soils the safest procedure is to place only soil that's been generously amended with organic matter right around the tree's roots. (This conditioned soil will encourage development of new feeder roots.) Fill the rest of the planting hole with native clay soil to which you've added only a small amount of organic matter—no more than about 25 per cent of the total volume.

You needn't mix any fertilizer into the soil at planting time. An overabundance of fertilizer added to the planting soil raises the possibility of burning new feeder roots as they begin to grow. (But for fertilizing young trees, see suggestions on page 18.)

Planting bare-root trees

During their dormant season (fall through winter), many deciduous trees are sold "bare-root." In this condition, all soil is removed from around their root systems. The only trees available in bare-root form are species that can tolerate total uprooting while dormant without suffering damage as long as the roots are protected from drying. Nurseries hold these plants with their roots carefully covered by a lightweight, moist material (such as sawdust) so that roots will stay in good condition and be cushioned from breaking.

Where winters are relatively mild or usually are not continually below freezing for extended periods, planting

1
Mound *soil in bottom of planting hole. Mix organic soil amendments with soil removed from hole.*

2
Spread *roots over mound, check planting depth with stick.*

3
Fill in *around roots with soil prepared in step 1.*

4
Flood *soil thoroughly to insure complete contact between roots and soil.*

bare-root trees in autumn before soil freezes (if it does freeze at all) has several advantages over later planting. Winter rains will settle roots into the soil and may even encourage some root growth. Certainly the roots will be able to begin growth just as soon as soil begins to warm up in spring. Waiting until early spring to plant may put you in conflict with rainy weather and delay planting until later than desirable.

Even in some colder climates (where frozen soil and plenty of winter snow are the norm), fall planting may be successful. But the most reliable advice on planting time in cold winter areas will come from the county or university agricultural extension agent (or a reputable local nursery person) who will be familiar with local conditions.

In planting a bare-root tree, follow the advice on organic amendments and planting hole sizes page 14). Prepare the hole and mix conditioners into the backfill soil (soil removed from the hole that will be returned to it when the tree is in position).

While you are digging, soak the tree's roots in water or keep them in a moist plastic bag. If roots are even slightly dry, soaking them (but for no longer than half a day) will restore moisture to their tissues. Never leave bare roots exposed to dry air.

Firm a mound or cone of soil in the center of the planting hole. Place the roots of the tree upon this mound, carefully spreading them out at their natural angles. (Most bare-root trees will have roots projecting out and down from the base of the trunk.) Be sure the hole is more than large enough to accommodate the outspread roots without your having to bend or cut them. You should, though, trim back any roots that have been broken. Make the cut just behind the break.

It's imperative that you plant a tree at the same depth that it has been growing previously—or even slightly higher. Look for a distinct color change in the bark low on the trunk and just above the point where roots begin. That marking indicates the former soil level. Position the tree in the planting hole so that this point is about an inch above the soil surface—this allows for some settling during planting. A straight stick or tool handle placed across the hole enables you to position the tree quite accurately.

With the tree positioned on the cone of soil in the hole, fill in about half to two thirds of the hole with the prepared backfill soil and then thoroughly soak the soil. When the water has drained away, fill in the rest of the hole with more prepared backfill soil and thoroughly water it in. Watering as you plant puts roots and soil in complete contact, eliminating any air pockets. If the tree settles too low in the process, you can raise it to the proper depth while the soil is flooded. Grasp the base of the trunk and *gently* lift up with some side-to-side rocking motion until the tree is raised as much as necessary. Then apply more water (and add more soil if needed) to be sure all the roots are covered by soil.

Next, build up a ring of earth around the rim of the filled-in hole to form a watering basin. Slowly flood the basin with water so that the soil throughout the root zone becomes saturated.

After you have thoroughly watered the tree, apply a loose mulch to the soil surface within the watering basin. A mulch will prevent the soil from drying out rapidly and also will keep it cooler in warm weather and warmer in cool weather. If you live where hard winter freezes are commonplace, though, remove the soil ring before cold weather sets in so water won't collect in the basin and freeze, possibly damaging the trunk. You might wait until late spring to make a watering basin if your soil is not too well drained and winter rains are plentiful: heavy rains collecting in a basin may just accentuate any drainage problems and waterlog the tree's roots. (After your tree has been planted, be sure to follow up with the post-planting procedures outlined on page 16-17.)

Planting balled-and-burlapped trees

Many needle-leafed, scale-leafed, and broad-leafed evergreen trees are dug out of the ground with a ball of earth around their roots. This root ball is then wrapped securely in burlap and the tree offered for sale as "balled-and-burlapped" ("B and B" in the nursery trade language). With a few special considerations, preparation of the planting hole and the planting procedures for balled-and-burlapped trees are the same as for bare-root trees. Be sure to follow the post-planting procedures outlined on page 17.

When you plant balled-and-burlapped trees, set the still-wrapped root ball on a mound of earth in the planting hole (just as you would a bare-root tree—only don't try to spread out the roots). Check the level of the trunk in the hole with a stick placed across the hole, as described for planting bare-root trees on page 14, making sure that the top of the root ball rests 1-2 inches higher than the level of the surrounding soil. The inevitable settling that occurs when you soak the backfill soil should bring the ball down to the proper level.

Only after the tree is surely positioned in the planting hole should you untie the burlap wrapping. Remove the twine that ties the burlap around the trunk's base and pull the burlap a few inches away from the trunk. You needn't remove the burlap wrapping from the root ball. Just fill in around the burlap with the prepared backfill soil; the burlap will disintegrate within a few years. Note: some nurseries sell balled-and-burlapped trees with the root ball wrapped in heavy plastic or plastic coated burlap. When you plant one of these, *carefully* remove the wrapping from the root ball before you add the backfill soil.

Most balled-and-burlapped trees are grown in fairly heavy or at least loamy soils so that they can be dug, wrapped, and handled with little danger of the soil breaking away from the roots. Planting them in a comparable soil type presents no problem. But if your garden soil is sandier than the soil in the root ball, the root ball of heavier soil will absorb water much more slowly than the sandy soil around it. As a result, what may seem to you like a thorough watering of the tree actually may just barely moisten the outside of the root ball.

A little bit of special attention, though, can minimize this problem. First, soak the root ball in water for an hour or so to make sure it is thoroughly moistened. Then, after the tree is planted, pay close attention to watering during the first year or two. Be sure to keep the soil moist (but not soggy) so roots will move out into surrounding soil as fast as possible. Where garden soil is very light, you can give water a better opportunity to penetrate the root ball if you punch holes *carefully* in the root ball. Use a pointed (not blunt) instrument, such as a sharpened ¼ to ½-inch dowel, so you won't damage the roots. After several years, when roots have grown into surrounding soil, the difference in soil density will be insignificant.

Planting container-grown trees

Available for planting in spring, summer, fall, and, in mild climates, even in winter, are trees growing in containers. Most frequently used are 1, 5, and 15-gallon cans. Alternatives to balled-and-burlapped specimens, container-grown trees are easier for nurserymen to care for until they are sold. And in contrast to balled-and-burlapped specimens, you get all of a container-grown tree's root system. Some broad-leafed evergreen trees and many needle-leafed evergreens are sold only as container-grown plants. Deciduous stock unsold at the end of the bare-root planting months also may be "canned up" for planting during the growing season.

Dig a planting hole (see page 14) and, after removing the tree from its container, set it on a mound of earth in the hole, adjusting the level as desired for planting bare-root trees, page 14.

You may find some trees growing in "knock out" containers, particularly those in 1 or 2-gallon cans. These cans have tapered or fluted sides. Just set the can on its side and give the rim a sharp rap; the can should easily slide away from the root and soil mass. With straight-sided, cylindrical cans, removing a tree involves cutting the can apart. If you intend to plant the tree within a day or so after bringing it home from the nursery, ask the nurseryman to cut the can open for you. But if planting is more than about two days away, leave the can intact and cut it open yourself just before planting. Use tin snips to make two cuts down opposite sides of the can. Cans over 5 gallons may need three or four cuts. Try to remove the tree from its can without breaking up the soil around the roots. Caution: Handle a cut can with extreme care, for the cut edges are *very* sharp and can inflict serious cuts or gashes. The soil you return to the planting hole may need special preparation. Trees in nursery containers are often grown in a very light soil composed chiefly of sand and/or organic materials—with or without actual soil. This can present a problem just opposite to that posed by the balled-and-burlapped tree: unless your garden soil also is fairly sandy, excess water can collect around the tree's roots because it can't be absorbed quickly by the heavier native soil that surrounds the newly planted tree. The smaller the container size, the less of a problem this will be, but for trees in 5-gallon containers or larger, the possibility of a waterlogged root zone becomes more serious.

The solution is to make a transition zone of an intermediate-density soil. Mix sand (or a sandy soil and organic amendments) with the heavier garden soil and use this mixture to fill in the planting hole around the root ball.

Reputable nurseries that do a brisk business usually sell their trees before they outgrow their can size. But even in the best of nurseries, you occasionally may encounter a rootbound plant. Tip-off signs are reduced vigor (you can tell by the amount and length of new or most recent growth),

small leaf size, dull leaf color, decaying containers, and, in some cases, evidence of girdling roots at soil level.

Unless given special treatment (see below), roots of can-bound stock won't actively move out into surrounding soil; years later, the tree may fail or decline because its roots are still restricted to a very small area and may actually be strangling one another. Unless the tree is especially rare and you can find no other source, it would be better to pass it by and choose another specimen.

If you must buy a rootbound tree (or you discover upon removing it from the container that many large roots are spiraling around the outside of the root ball), here's a planting technique that can go far toward remedying the situation. Thoroughly soak the root ball; then wash as much soil away from roots as necessary in order for you to see how badly the roots are entangled. *Carefully* unsnarl as many major roots as possible so that they can be directed *outward* and *downward* instead of in the spiral created by container restriction. If you discover any two roots that are tightly wrapped around one another, try to unwind them. Should that fail, cut out the smaller one at its point of origin. Then plant the tree quickly (so roots won't dry out) as you would a bare-root tree (see pages 14-15).

After planting, what?

Now that your tree is in the ground, much of your work is finished. But a few items still need attention.

Pruning. In most transplant operations—planting a new bare-root or balled-and-burlapped tree really is a transplant —some of the specimen's root system is left behind in its original growing location. Since a tree's roots and crown grow in proportion to one another, this means that the crown will be too large for the roots to support comfortably. If the bare-root tree has not been pruned by the nursery (if you can't easily tell if branches have been cut, ask the nurseryman), remove about one-third of the tree's top growth. Eliminate weak, twiggy growth and shorten lateral branches somewhat.

Don't cut the tree's leader or terminal bud: it must continue growing if the tree is to increase in height. (Exceptions to this rule are some fruit trees that need specialized pruning to promote a strong lateral branching system and keep fruit-producing limbs from growing too high for easy picking.) Always cut off broken branches to the first strong side branch behind the break. Or cut just behind the break if

Balled-and-burlapped *planting: place root ball on soil mound a few inches higher than final level should be; loosen burlap, fill in with soil, flood thoroughly to settle tree in.*

Container-grown *tree is removed from container, set on soil mound in hole, then hole is filled in with mixture of garden soil and sandy soil or organic matter.*

there are no branches further back on the limb; then when new growth emerges on that limb, cut the branch back to that growth. (See pages 21-22 for more information on pruning young trees.)

Trunk protection. The trunk of a newly planted tree is its most vulnerable area. It is exposed to drying winds, searing sunlight, freezing winter weather in many zones, and the onslaught of any chewing animals in the neighborhood (dogs included) or scratching cats. You take fewer chances with the whims of nature if you wrap the trunk with burlap or, even better, with one of the special wrappings made especially for tree trunks. Such wrappings usually will expand as the trunk diameter increases, a worthwhile feature since the wrap should remain on the trunk throughout the first year and, ideally, through the second year as well. Wrappings are available at nurseries.

If nibbling rodents or gnawing canines are likely to sample your new planting, encircle the trunk with a cylinder of woven wire, such as poultry netting.

Extra support. Until the tree's root system is well established in your soil and its trunk diameter is large enough to hold the crown erect, your new tree will need some additional anchorage. Smaller trees can get by with simple staking; larger specimens require guying for greatest stability. The drawing at right illustrates the best staking method.

Remember that whenever a trunk or limb is encircled with a non-expanding material (either for staking or protection), you should check the tie several times during the growing season. In less time than you might expect, a tree can grow to the point where it becomes girdled and possibly damaged by the tie.

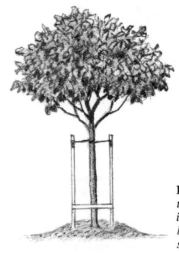

Proper staking *holds tree upright but leaves it flexible. Crossbar at bottom braces two stakes, tie (looped around trunk just below branches) lets tree bend a bit in wind.*

WATER TO MEET YOUR TREE'S NEEDS

Your aim in watering is to create a root zone that will be moist enough to encourage growth of new roots but not so soggy that air is excluded and growth actually hampered.

The first point to realize is that you can't partially dampen soil. Frequent light sprinklings or irrigation on the surface (such as a lawn watering) will moisten only the surface. To benefit a tree, you must soak the soil for a period of time so that water will penetrate down to and beyond the roots. Deep watering encourages deep root penetration that can sustain a tree in dry periods.

The second point to keep in mind is that water travels through soil almost straight downward with very little lateral movement. Because of this, it's important that the watering basin include the entire area of the planting hole: the tree's roots extend—or soon will—throughout that space. A loose surface mulch (such as straw, leaf mold, or pine needles) placed on the soil in the watering basin will help conserve moisture and lessen fluctuations in soil temperature.

No hard and fast rule exists that will tell you precisely how often to water. Frequency is influenced by the kind of tree you have, weather conditions (light intensity, temperature, humidity, and wind), soil type, root competition from other plants, and how well established the tree is.

Some trees like constantly moist soil; others prefer soil to dry out between waterings. Warm days and windy or dry weather will dry out surface soil and cause trees to lose water rapidly through their leaves—sometimes more rapidly than roots can replenish it. If your newly planted tree will be subjected to frequent drying winds from one direction, you should protect it during its first year with some sort of wind screen.

Sandy soils without much organic matter will drain water rapidly, not retaining very much for the tree's use. Clay soils, on the other hand, take longer to absorb moisture but will stay moist for a long time. Older trees may not need as much supplemental watering as young ones since their roots spread farther and deeper. Depending on the species and the climate, some established trees may thrive with no more water than what nature provides.

As a *general* guide to watering, remember that the more claylike a soil is, the more water you'll have to apply to moisten it deeply. But since clay soils retain water longer, you'll apply water less frequently than you would in a sandy soil. Let the soil surface dry slightly between waterings. This enables soil to take in a good supply of air as the water drains out of the pore spaces. For newly planted trees and young trees still getting roots established, water thoroughly when no more than the top inch of soil has dried; for most established trees you can wait longer—until the top 2-4 inches of soil have lost moisture. If you're in doubt as to how deep your waterings are penetrating, use a soil sampling tube to check (see photo p. 18). This same instrument can help you determine when to apply more water if you take samples from the root zone and surrounding soil and observe how moist the soil is at various depths.

Sandy soils, as opposed to clay ones, absorb moisture quickly but do not retain it for long periods. So, to keep them damp you'll have to water them more frequently than you would a heavy soil.

Leaves, as well as roots, can absorb water, although not a major quantity of it. On a cloudy day you can help along newly planted trees—particularly evergreens—by sprinkling the foliage. (Watering leaves on a hot, sunny day introduces the possibility of burning the leaves.)

If you plant a tree in a lawn, keep a 3-foot-diameter circle free of grass around it until the tree becomes well established (usually about 3 years). This keeps the lawn from competing with the tree for water and nutrients.

FERTILIZING GIVES NECESSARY NUTRIENTS

You may rightly wonder why fertilizing is recommended for garden trees when obviously healthy specimens grow wild with no helping hand. The answer is that the wild trees *are* being fertilized but in ways that are usually eliminated when we cultivate a garden. Dead leaves from forest trees fall to the ground and decompose, releasing small but vital amounts of nutrients each year. Generally, the gardener rakes up and disposes of fallen leaves. Forest animals leave their droppings and eventually their bodies to decompose into nutrient sources; any droppings or dead animals in a garden most often are scrupulously removed.

You may think that a tree growing in lawn gets fertilized whenever the lawn does. The truth is that the average fertilizer application to a lawn is extremely meager by a tree's standards, and the lawn has first call on the nutrients because its roots are closer to the surface.

All trees don't always need fertilizer, but in the following paragraphs you'll find the instances when fertilizing may be necessary, descriptions of various kinds of fertilizers, and how to apply them.

Remember that there are drawbacks to overfertilizing. Branches that have grown rapidly tend to be more brittle than is normal for the species and are more subject to breakage by wind, snow, and ice storms.

Fertilizing newly planted trees

During its first year in your garden, a tree's major effort is to establish roots. The new soil and organic amendments you used at planting time will supply some nutrients to get the tree on its way, but to help along the establishment process, you may want to fertilize, too.

Though most dry, inorganic fertilizers (see page 20) are helpful to established trees, some may burn tender new roots if applied too liberally or if roots and fertilizer come into direct contact with one another. Because new roots are so

Soil sampling *tube removes plug of soil, can show how deep water penetrates and can indicate when more is needed.*

vital to establishing a tree, refrain from using these fertilizers during a tree's first year after planting. (An exception is the timed or slow-release fertilizer that releases nutrients gradually in small amounts and so is not likely to burn if you follow directions.) Dry organic fertilizers are safe enough to use on the soil surface because, like the inorganic timed-release types, they release their nutrients gradually (see page 20).

Foliar fertilizing (a method of spraying liquid fertilizer solution directly onto the leaves, see page 21) will give a quick additional boost to new trees. Try it in spring when leaves on deciduous trees are half grown or when new growth on broad-leafed evergreens is half to fully formed but not yet hardened.

Liquid fertilizer (page 20), applied to the soil in recommended dilution, also can be used on young trees during their first year   Let the tree get its new roots established during spring; then apply a liquid fertilizer in the tree's watering basin in early summer. Don't fertilize later than midsummer unless you live in a near frost-free climate. New growth produced after the middle of summer may not have a chance to ripen and harden before freezing autumn or winter weather arrives, making it a prime target for damage.

Fertilizing mature trees

As mentioned earlier, most garden trees don't receive the natural fertilizing through decaying organic matter dropped on the ground that trees in the wild may get. Still, many trees will continue to grow healthily with no direct assistance. You must judge whether or not an established tree appears to need a helping hand. If your tree seems healthy and vigorous, fertilizing may be an unnecessary expenditure of time, effort, and materials. Even professional arborists and scientists don't agree completely on the amount of fertilizer trees should receive or how often fertilizer should be applied.

Signs of need. A prominent display of strong new growth having good color is the sign of a healthy tree. But weak or little growth, an unusual amount of die-back, and paler than normal leaves tell you to get out the fertilizer sack. (Note: In most cases, new growth is paler than the mature leaves.) Other times of need will occur following periods of stress: a severe insect attack, especially one that partially or entirely defoliates the tree; treatment for a diseased condition; and repair of physical damage to the tree. Fertilizer will promote more rapid regeneration and healing of wounds. One application may be enough to bring the tree back to health, or you may need to fertilize annually for several years. The tree's appearance, rate and health of its new growth, and how well wounds heal over will be your guides to whether continued fertilizing is necessary.

Best times to fertilize. To do the most good, fertilizer must be available during the period when new growth is most active. For most trees this time is early spring. Gardeners in cold-winter areas (where snow covers the ground during winter) fertilize either in the fall or in earliest spring. An advantage of fall application is that the fertilizer will become available as soon as the soil warms up in spring and growth begins. (And even during winter, if soil isn't frozen to great depth, roots will absorb some of the nutrients in preparation for spring growth.)

Where winters are warmer and rainy or wet, much nitrogen applied in fall or winter may be leached by rain water through the root zone by the time spring comes. In these

GUARD THOSE ROOTS

The health of a tree's roots is vital to the tree's well being. To be growing well means that an established tree's roots are receiving satisfactory amounts of moisture and air in order to function properly. Anything that alters the moisture and air relationship that the roots need poses an adjustment problem for them. The bigger the alteration, the greater the adjustment required and the greater the risk of tree failure.

Four potentially damaging situations are common enough to mention in detail, and each is most often associated with construction activities or landscape installation: soil compaction, soil covering, addition of soil over roots, and removal of soil from the root zone.

Soil compaction happens frequently at building sites where heavy equipment is used for grading or construction work. Trucks driving repeatedly over the same piece of ground can cause it. Compacted soil makes it difficult or impossible for air and water to penetrate into the root zone, resulting in a tree's impaired growth or actual death by suffocation.

If you know in advance that heavy equipment will be operating anywhere near valued established trees, construct sturdy barricades around the trees to divert the traffic. The more area around a tree the barricade can enclose, the better is the tree's chance for continuing health.

Soil covering is serious when the paving material—whether for a patio or parking lot—is laid solidly over the soil beneath a tree. Unbroken pavement accomplishes the same end result as soil compaction because it, too, cuts off free penetration of air and moisture to the roots. You may see trees flourishing in paved areas where they have only a small patch of soil around their bases, but it's almost certain that those trees were planted *after* the paving was done. Their roots have established themselves in relation to the existing restriction.

Whenever you decide to install a paved surface beneath an established tree (or even under just part of a tree), make sure you don't put in a solid surface. First, leave as much open soil around the tree as you possibly can. Then, choose a material that can have portions open to the soil beneath. Just bricks set in sand with spaces between bricks (or between groups of bricks) will let small amounts of water and air through. If it is a modular paving—for example, 4-foot squares of concrete in a grid pattern—try to leave some parts of the grid unpaved and fill these squares with gravel instead. These should be well-distributed through the covered area for maximum benefit to the roots.

Addition of soil over established roots poses no real problem if you plan to spread it to a depth no greater than about 4 inches and you refrain from packing it down solidly. Enough moisture and air will get to the established roots so that the ones closest to the old surface will grow up into the new soil. Try to get a sandy, porous type of soil for any grade-raising work.

If you plan an addition of from 4 to 12 inches of soil, you should do two things. First, build a wall around the tree's trunk that will be the height of the soil fill and will leave at least a 3-foot radius of soil at the original level around the trunk. Then cover the soil outside the wall to within about 4 inches of the intended new surface level with coarse gravel and add a 1-inch layer of fine gravel on top of that. A 3-inch layer of new soil spread over the area finishes the job. Water (and air) can percolate through a shallow soil layer and the gravel to reach the roots in the soil below.

Any time a grade change involves 1-2 feet of soil, you should amplify the preceding operation with installation of drainage pipes. Before spreading the gravel, place a network of about 8 perforated pipes (with the holes on the ground) or drainage tile radiating out from the well around the trunk and extending at least to the drip line of the tree's foliage. The inner ends of the pipe should open into the tree well and the outer ends should either be sealed off (to prevent clogging with soil) or be connected to an upright section of pipe or tile that will vent them to slightly above the new soil surface. (Venting allows air and moisture to enter at both ends.) When the pipes are in place, fill in with the gravel layers and soil as described above.

Should you want to raise the soil level more than 2 feet, you should seek professional advice. You may learn that the cost of the operation would be prohibitive or even that the work would be futile. If you find that raising the soil level is possible, though, you'd be wise to let a professional tackle it.

Removing soil from around a tree can be the trickiest proposition because you will remove roots that not only keep the tree alive but that also help anchor it.

The simplest jobs are those that remove soil only on one side of a tree and to a depth of no greater than 2 feet. If at all possible, limit the removal to outside the tree's drip line; the farther under a tree you go, the greater are the risks. When you have carefully dug soil away from the point where the level is to change, build a retaining wall to separate the two levels. Fill in behind it (on the tree's side) with good soil liberally enriched with organic material; this will encourage new roots to grow where you have disturbed the established ones. Be sure the wall has enough drainage holes in it to let water seep through instead of collecting behind it.

climates, it's better to fertilize about a month before the flush of spring growth will begin.

Except in the mildest winter regions, where frost damage is not a problem and growth on some trees may occur in more than one spurt per year, it's best to stop fertilizing in early summer. New growth stimulated by later fertilization probably won't have enough time to mature and harden before frosts hit; as a result, the growth can be damaged or destroyed by freezing.

Exceptions to these guidelines are severely weakened or damaged trees. These trees should be fertilized whenever the damage occurs or as soon as the weakness is detected.

What fertilizer should you use?

The goal of fertilizing is better growth. Of the three major fertilizer components — nitrogen, phosphorus, and potassium—nitrogen is the one most responsible for increased vegetative growth. So you'll want to use a fertilizer containing more nitrogen than other ingredients. The percentages of these three major nutrients are listed on fertilizer containers: nitrogen always appears first, and the second and third numbers always represent phosphorus and potassium, in that order. For general tree use, look for a fertilizer that has these elements in approximately a 3-2-1 ratio. A 10-6-4 formula (10 per cent nitrogen, 6 per cent phosphorous, 4 per cent potassium), for example, should supply enough nitrogen in relation to the other two major elements.

Fertilizers come in many forms and are composed of materials ranging from organic to synthetic. For how to apply each of these types, see pages below.

Dry organic fertilizers generally don't contain as much nitrogen by volume as commercial fertilizers do. But the nitrogen they do have is released gradually as micro-organisms in the soil break down the fertilizer elements. For trees, cottonseed meal and blood meal are good choices of organic fertilizers.

Slow-release inorganic fertilizers make their components available, particularly nitrogen, over a long period of time. They will give plants a steady supply of nutrients throughout the growing season from only one application. Some slow-release fertilizers are prepared to last for more than one year; their release of nutrients is controlled by soil temperature and/or moisture and the activity of soil micro-organisms.

Standard dry inorganic fertilizers not specifically in the slow-release category are numerous. You'll find the longest lasting are those that derive half or more of their nitrogen from urea formaldehyde (urea form). This information usually is stated on the back of a fertilizer package where the percentages of the nutrients are listed.

Liquid fertilizers are special fertilizers that are to be diluted in water before application. They aren't as long lasting as fertilizers that are applied in dry form, but their nutrients usually are more quickly available to roots.

Foliar fertilizers are specially made to be sprayed onto the tree's leaves in solution with water.

How to fertilize

For a tree to get the most from a fertilizer application, the nutrients must be applied where roots can get them easily. With an established tree, this is within a general zone that usually occupies the outer two-thirds of the branch spread plus a distance beyond that's equal to one-third the radius of total branch spread.

Applying dry fertilizers. Scattering dry fertilizer on the soil surface may reach some feeder roots, but it also encourages surface rooting. Shallow roots, in turn, discourage growth of lawn or other plants beneath the tree and also make the tree susceptible to drought and less stable because of poor anchorage.

A better method of dry fertilization involves boring small holes into the ground and pouring fertilizer down them. (See the diagram at right.) These holes should be 1-2 inches across, about 10-12 inches deep, and go into the soil at an angle rather than straight down, so that nutrients will leach into a wider area.

Use a soil auger or a soil sampling tube to make the holes; both make holes by removing soil. (Just poking the holes with a sharp stick or rod only compacts the soil around the hole, making it more difficult for nutrients to penetrate.)

Space fertilizer holes evenly within the feeder root zone Make the holes about 2 feet apart and in concentric rings around the tree—each ring 4 feet larger in diameter than the previous ring.

Calculating the amount of dry fertilizer you need to apply usually is based upon the trunk's diameter measured at a point about 4 feet above the ground. But tree experts differ in their opinions of how much fertilizer to use. Here is a simple formula for calculating a moderate application: multiply the trunk's diameter (at 4 feet from ground level) by itself and divide that figure by 3. The result gives you the number of pounds to apply of a 10 per cent nitrogen fertilizer. Example: A 2-inch-diameter tree trunk times itself (2 times 2) equals 4; 4 divided by 3 gives 1⅓—the number of pounds to apply of a dry, 10 per cent nitrogen fertilizer.

Mix the dry fertilizer with an approximately equal amount of dry sand, soil, peat moss, or a combination of these materials to reduce its concentration. Then distribute the fertilizer mixture as evenly as possible among the holes. After pouring in the fertilizer, water thoroughly so that the fertilizer will begin to dissolve and become available to roots.

Applying liquid fertilizers. To apply liquid fertilizers, you can use a special root feeder available at nurseries and hardware stores. The root feeder is a hollow, pointed tube several feet long with a chamber at one end that holds special dry fertilizer that dissolves easily and quickly in water. Attach the end of your garden hose to the fertilizer chamber; then turn on the tap. The water will dissolve the fertilizer, and the mixture will flow through the tube and out the holes in the pointed end. For fertilizing trees, insert the root feeder about 18 inches into the soil and at the same spacing described above for dry fertilizer applications.

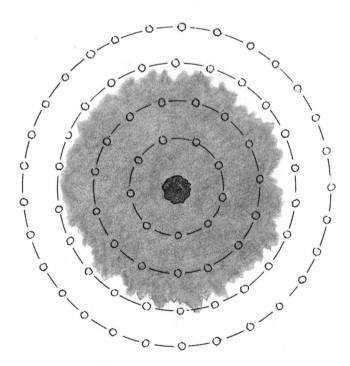

Fertilizer holes *two feet apart in concentric rings around tree; each ring is four feet wider than previous one.*

Foliar fertilizing. A number of fertilizers are made to be sprayed in solution with water directly onto a tree's leaves. Known as foliar fertilizing, this is a fine, quick tonic for young trees and for those in poor health. Foliar fertilizing will be safe if practiced according to directions.

Foliar fertilizing should be done on a cloudy day to avoid sunscalding the leaves. Be sure to spray both upper and under sides of leaves, since both surfaces can absorb nutrients.

Note that foliar fertilizing and dry fertilizing serve quite different purposes. One foliar fertilization doesn't have the long-term effect of dry fertilizers in the soil. Soil fertilizers are released over a period of time as water dissolves them, so their nutrients are continually made available. But foliar fertilizers are immediately absorbed by the tree to give quick results.

PRUNING CAN BE PAINLESS

All too often the word "pruning" evokes visions of a tedious, routine chore, often made even more unpleasant by the pruner's sense of inadequacy. But unless you are pruning certain fruit trees for high crop yield, there is little you need to know and often no need to put all of that knowledge into practice on a regular basis.

On a mature tree, pruning's objective is to direct growth. More specifically, you prune to maintain an established tree's health by removing broken and diseased parts and excess growth, to improve its appearance, and to remove weak growth that might break, causing damage to the tree, your property, or a passerby. On young saplings of deciduous and broad-leafed evergreen trees, your pruning efforts for the first several years will be directed at training the tree to grow in a desirable form. The needle-leafed evergreens seldom need early training unless they develop more than a single leading shoot when you want only one.

Pruning to train young trees

Look at the illustration on this page of a model tree with several types of "bad" growth. During a tree's early years, you have a chance to eliminate such growth—weak V-shaped crotches, double leaders, cross branches, water-sprouts—without resorting to any major surgery. In fact, if you catch undesirable growth early enough, you can just pinch, break, or cut it out without causing any significant wound to the tree. Below are some pruning pointers for deciduous and broad-leafed evergreen trees that will hasten your new tree's progress toward a good mature form.

The first fact of tree life to remember is that branches do not move up as the tree trunk grows. A branch on a young tree that is 3 feet from the ground always will be 3 feet from the ground unless it is removed. But *do not* cut off at one time all side growth up to the height at which you want the tree to branch. Young trees need all the leaves they can produce in order to manufacture food for growth. And leaves shading the trunk will protect it from sunburning. In addition, the trunk thickness will increase faster with branches along its length than it will if you meticulously strip them all off up to what you are encouraging as the tree's crown. If you want your tree to grow rapidly and sturdily, leave lateral branches along the trunk. There will be time enough later to cut off those you don't want.

If lower lateral branches appear to be growing too rapidly at the expense of the rest of the tree, you should pinch or

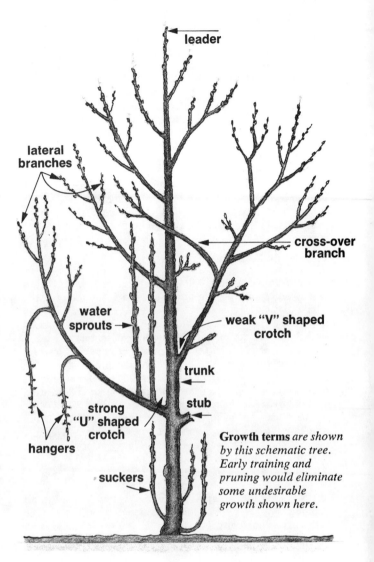

Growth terms are shown by this schematic tree. Early training and pruning would eliminate some undesirable growth shown here.

head them back; but don't remove them entirely. Headed back, they will branch out and provide still more leaves to help the tree along.

For trees of moderate to rapid growth rate (1 foot or more of terminal growth per year), some tree experts suggest you leave trunk branches on for 3 years. This gives the branches higher up a chance to develop and produce plenty of foliage so that you then can remove the trunk branches. Any lateral branch along the trunk should be removed before its diameter begins to approach that of the trunk.

After about the third year, your best training guide will be the tree itself. By then you will begin to notice its inherent form and can guide its development accordingly. If a particular lateral branch begins to dominate the tree's growth to the detriment of the desired shape, cut it back far enough that the tree retains a symmetrical outline. Should too many lateral branches develop in the crown, remove some. Aim for an even branch spacing, both vertically along the trunk and radiating horizontally out from it.

Always remember to prune to retain the natural form of the species you have selected. A well pruned tree is one you wouldn't know had been pruned.

Pruning mature trees

If you begin with a young tree and train it as it grows, you should have little need for real pruning expertise unless, of course, the tree becomes damaged or ill. But what do you do if you've inherited a tree that's been neglected or badly handled in the past?

The first act should be to assess your own capabilities. Removing old limbs in large oaks, maples, or elms, for example, is not a job for a novice with a saw in one hand and pruning instructions in the other. Even experienced gardeners shy away from removing thick limbs and from most high-up work: the risk to man, tree, and property is too great without professional equipment and safeguards.

But there's no reason why you can't confidently tackle ground level work and branches easily reached from a sturdy ladder. The drawings on this page show you how to make pruning cuts that should heal over well.

How to make a pruning cut

Every pruning manual will caution you to leave no stubs when you remove growth of any size—and for good reason. Think of each twig, branch, and limb as a tube for conveying nutrients. When you cut off a stem very far above a lateral branch or dormant bud, there is nothing in that bare remaining section of cut stem for nutrients to be conveyed toward, so nutrients will cease to move beyond the closest stem or bud below the cut, and the cut stem section will die. Into the dead wood, decay organisms can enter and spread, causing damage to healthy parts of the tree.

But when you make your cuts nearly flush with a living branch or stem (or the trunk), the tree's cambium layer just beneath the bark goes to work immediately after you prune; it grows inward from the edges of the cut to cover it over with new, barklike cells. In time, the wound will be completely sealed over by new bark tissue.

It's a good idea to apply a pruning wound "paint" to all pruning cuts over an inch in diameter. Any cut surface offers an opportunity for disease and decay organisms to enter the tree. The larger the cut, the longer it will take before it will be healed over completely—and the longer it will be open for possible infection.

Most nurseries or garden supply stores will carry preparations made especially for dressing pruning cuts. The most common ones are water soluble asphalt preparations and orange shellac. These compounds provide protection and some disinfection and are not harmful to plant tissues. Don't use any product not specified for plants (such as wood preservatives, paint, roofing asphalt), for it may contain elements that will damage rather than help the wound.

Examine the dressed cuts at least twice a year to check that they appear to be healing well and that the wound dressing hasn't worn away. Cuts that will take more than a year to heal over will need additional applications of the protective compound.

Special pruning situations

Some trees grow too fast for their own good, producing long, soft, brittle growth that may be damaged easily by wind, the weight of water on the leaves, or even the weight of the branch itself. Fruitless mulberries (varieties of *Morus alba*, page 50), provide a good example of this type. To thwart this potential hazard, cut the long, drooping branches back to an upward growing lateral branch. The remainder of the branch you cut back will thicken, and the lateral branch that you cut to will elongate to take the place of the part that was removed, growing upward instead of down. You can repeat this cutting back process—even on any upward pointing branches that droop later—until you achieve a sturdy system of framework branches.

Some mature trees (such as many oaks) have branches that hang lower and lower as growth accumulates. In time, these trees may obscure a view or obstruct a walkway or patio. One solution would be to remove the low-hanging limbs. But this can't always be done without destroying some of the tree's beauty. A simpler remedy that might work is to remove some of the side or bottom branches from the low hanging limbs. Reduction of weight can cause the branches to raise up high enough to restore the view or utility of the area beneath.

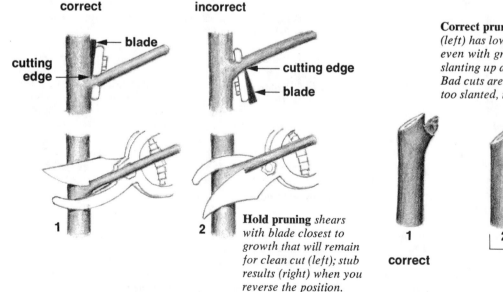

correct   **incorrect**

blade   cutting edge   cutting edge   blade

1   2

Hold pruning *shears with blade closest to growth that will remain for clean cut (left); stub results (right) when you reverse the position.*

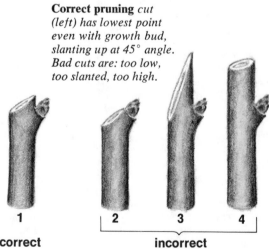

Correct pruning *cut (left) has lowest point even with growth bud, slanting up at 45° angle. Bad cuts are: too low, too slanted, too high.*

1   2   3   4

correct   **incorrect**

CABLING AND BRACING

Sometimes pruning alone won't improve structural problems of mature trees, particularly those that have been neglected. In such cases, cabling or bracing may be the answer. Here are some typical situations in which cabling or bracing might be used instead of pruning:

• To support a V-shaped crotch when removal of one or the other arm of the V would ruin the tree's shape.
• To separate crossing branches that rub together, either of which couldn't be removed without spoiling the tree's appearance.
• To repair a crotch that is split but not completely broken.
• To connect with cables the trunks of a multitrunked tree so that they will help support one another.
• To protect a brittle-limbed specimen tree against storm damage.
• To provide support for limbs of a tree that has had extensive cavity repair.

Most of these jobs require a high degree of skill for good results; they are too formidable for the amateur. If a particular tree with any of the above problems is a valued part of your landscape, call in a professional to shore it up. His repair fee always will be a bargain compared to the cost of replacing it with a tree of similar size.

CAVITY REPAIR

The old "hollow trees" of literature and folklore survived not so much because of their health as because of luck. Hollowness is a result of decay in the interior wood, and the loss of any of a tree's core wood means a loss in structural soundness. Such trees are the types most likely to split apart just because of their own weight and size.

Sometimes, though, a tree with a decaying cavity in the trunk or in major limbs will occupy a position of such prominence in the landscape that you won't want to remove it if there's any hope of saving it. In such cases, cavities often can be cleaned and sometimes filled, but it is a job strictly

PROFESSIONAL HELP

A professional tree worker is your friend. He combines knowledge, skill, experience, and equipment far beyond what can be supplied by most amateur gardeners. Although popularly referred to as "tree surgeons," professional tree people are much more than expert limb removers and wound dressers.

Their first function is as advisors about any tree problem: spraying; fertilizing; moving a tree; changing soil level around a mature specimen; cabling or bracing; cavity repair; thinning, pruning, and complete tree removal; and even an answer to the common question, "What's wrong with my tree and what should I do for it?" Call a professional for consultation and then a cost estimate if he and you decide action is needed.

Look in the classified section of your telephone book for names of individuals and companies that serve your area. You will want to be absolutely sure that they have adequate insurance coverage for any accidents that could happen while your work is being done. Public liability and property damage are standard coverages; reputable professionals won't hesitate to spell out the type and extent of their insurance. In some states, licenses are required before a person can do certain types of tree work. Checking with the state or county agricultural commissioner should tell you if this is so in your state and for what kinds of work. If licensing is required in your area, be sure your worker has it.

for a skilled, experienced worker. And after the cavity is repaired, the live parts of the tree may need cabling or bracing for added insurance against collapse. For help with these trees, call a professional tree person, who will be able to tell you if a cavity repair job is possible.

PESTS AND DISEASES

Pests, diseases, or just plain "bugs"—these are afflictions we like to think of as visiting someone else's garden, not our own. Unfortunately, that's not always the case. But you can greatly minimize having to combat most of nature's pests and diseases if you follow these few simple suggestions.

Only plant trees that are relatively pest and disease free *in your area.* In many regions, one or two diseases and pests are consistently troublesome to specific trees. For example, in the northeastern states the European white birch (*Betula verrucosa*) frequently falls victim to the bronze birch borer, which can prove fatal if not watched for and eradicated. Yet some other birches can be planted there without worry.

Learn to evaluate which problems can be let alone and which should be attended to. Many disease and insect attacks come in short-lived waves triggered by weather and season. The first aphids of spring are a good example. They come in waves at first but fade quickly.

Some insects are migratory, moving on when alerted to do so by a change in temperature or day-length. Others go into a state of dormancy, caused by climate or weather change. Some bacterial and fungal diseases are active only in certain weather (usually damp) and so only appear in particular seasons or even just one particular year.

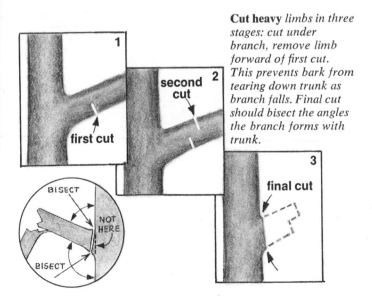

Cut heavy *limbs in three stages: cut under branch, remove limb forward of first cut. This prevents bark from tearing down trunk as branch falls. Final cut should bisect the angles the branch forms with trunk.*

GOOD TREES COME IN SMALL PACKAGES

With few exceptions, dwarf fruit trees aren't simply the runts of their litters. Instead, they are manmade specimens, one of the results of the continuing horticultural quest for something different that will be of value to the gardener. In this case, the "something different" is a size that is suitable to many gardens where a lack of space prevents the planting of full-sized fruit trees.

Most dwarf fruit trees are produced by grafting a standard variety onto a rootstock that causes the resulting tree to grow much smaller than it normally would but leaves fruit size and quality unchanged. Another advantage is that dwarf trees begin fruiting at an earlier age than full-sized forms of the same varieties do. And any pest or disease control is much simpler because you easily can reach the entire tree.

In some cases, fruits have not yet been successfully dwarfed; in others, the attempt has worked with only a few varieties. The most common (and successful) dwarf fruits sold are apple, citrus of various kinds, and peach and nectarine.

Apple. A number of favorite apple varieties are available as dwarf and semi-dwarf trees. True dwarf trees won't exceed 5-6 feet in height and width; they can be grown as trees (really bushes) or trained as espaliers. Semi-dwarfs reach 10-15 feet with a more treelike structure. All dwarf apples are shallow rooted and should always be staked to prevent tipping over. See *Malus* (pages 48-49) and *Malus pumila* (page 49) for general information on apples.

Citrus. Grapefruits, lemons, kumquats, mandarin oranges, oranges, tangelos, and tangors all are available as dwarf trees. These become shrubs or small trees up to 10 feet high (depending on variety) but otherwise require the same culture as the larger forms do (see pages 66-67). Landscape uses are as specimen plants, hedges, espaliers, or as handsome container subjects.

Peach and Nectarine. You won't find your favorite peach and nectarine varieties as dwarf trees. Instead, these dwarfs are special hybrids that grow only to shrub proportions but still bear large, flavorful fruits. Eventually, the largest may reach 6-7 feet high; with the profusion of long, down-curving leaves, the plants resemble large, shaggy dogs. For more information on peaches and nectarines, see pages 54-55.

Usually there's little point in treating a problem that soon will remedy itself. Knowledge of the insect or disease will be your best guide in deciding whether or not to act. Remember, too, that a strong, actively growing tree can fend off or endure insects and disease far more easily than can a struggling, undernourished one.

Don't expect *total* eradication of most problems. A certain amount of pest damage may be inevitable. To strive for an antiseptic garden is to aim for the unnatural. A few chewed leaves may bother *you,* but chances are the tree that bears them isn't suffering from them.

Recognize the limits of your abilities: call a professional whenever the problem is too big for you to handle. Don't attempt to spray your 30-foot oak from atop a ladder using a 5-gallon sprayer. You'll only endanger yourself and probably do a poor job of covering the tree.

Insects

Taking the word "insect" loosely, this would include a wide variety of organisms that, at some stage of their life cycle, crawl.

Sucking insects. These insects bite into and suck the vital juices from a plant. Damage is not immediate, and the culprit is often hard to see.

Aphids are tiny green, yellow, or pink insects—soft and sometimes winged. You'll find them clustered thickly on new growth which they feed on and can stunt. Control: A stream of water from the hose to knock them off; or spray with a soap-and-water solution, nicotine sulfate, pyrethrum/rotenone, malathion, or diazinon.

Mealybugs are small, waxy white, nearly immobile insects that form colonies at stem joints or toward leaf bases (usually on the undersides.) Control: Nicotine sulfate, malathion, or diazinon.

Scale insects begin life as crawlers but later attach themselves to stems and leaves, covering their bodies with protective shells. Usually you'll find them in groups. Control: Nicotine sulfate, malathion, or diazinon during growing season; use dormant oil spray in earliest spring before new growth starts to get mature scales (note: beech, birch, and two maples—Japanese and sugar—are harmed by oil sprays).

Spider mites are active during the warm summer months. Almost too small to see, they do their work on leaf undersides. Evidence is a stippled appearance on the leaf surface with—in heavy infestations—silvery webbing underneath. Control: Malathion, diazinon.

Chewing insects. All kinds of worms and caterpillars belong here, including the leaf miners that chew away the tissue between veins but not the outer surface of the leaves.

Caterpillars and worms can be controlled with sprays of pyrethrum/rotenone, malathion, or diazinon. But the most ingenious (and very effective) control is a spray of *Bacillus thuringiensis,* sold under various trade names. This is a bacteria that proves fatal to the caterpillar, not a toxic substance that could kill other organisms as well.

Leaf miners are the larvae of various sawflies. Control can begin by attempting to kill adults in spring, as the leaves emerge, before flies lay their eggs. Following that, control consists of killing larvae before they are able to tunnel into leaves. Use malathion or diazinon; best results come from three applications spread about ten days apart.

Burrowing insects. These insidious, invisible pests work on trunks, limbs, and twigs of trees. A sign of their presence is small holes in the tree's wood and often a bit of telltale sawdust nearby. Young trees with soft wood are especially vulnerable.

Since these insects lay their eggs on a tree's bark, wrapping the trunk of new trees (see page 17) is one good deterrent. Spraying with diazinon at ten-day intervals from early to midspring may catch newly hatched larvae before they enter the wood. Otherwise, hand kill the worms by sticking a wire into any holes you find in the trunk or major limbs. Smaller branches and twigs that are infested can just be cut off and burned.

Diseases

Foliage, stem, and root problems are covered in the wide-ranging disease category. Some, such as mildew and many leaf-spot organisms, are quite minor league and are easily controlled if they make an unusually heavy appearance. Others (*Armillaria* root rot, for example) signal the beginning of the end for the afflicted tree.

Leaf problems. Ease of recognition is one aid to the cure of any diseases that affect foliage.

Leaf spots. Red, brown, yellow, or almost black spots on leaves; with some types, the spots drop out, leaving a "shot hole" condition. These fungi flourish in a warm, wet spring and during rainy summer weather. The spores live from year to year in plant refuse, dead leaves, or fruit; a thorough cleanup of possibly infected material is a key to combating the problem. Control: Spray as soon as leaves begin to emerge (or as soon as flower buds begin to open, for flowering trees) with ferbam, zineb, maneb, captan, folpet, or ziram; repeat in a few weeks when leaves are half grown and once more when they are full size.

Mildew. This is a white or gray powdery coating on young leaves and stems. It thrives in periods of high humidity rather than in actual wet weather and where plants are too shaded or too crowded. Control: Foliage sprays of benomyl to protect new growth from further infection, of acti-dione PM or of dinocap to eradicate mildew already present.

Stem diseases. These problems are often signaled by die-back of leaves and branch tips (or sometimes of entire branches). Another symptom of stem disease is discolored, oval areas of various sizes on the branches.

Anthracnose. Attacking tender new shoots in spring, this disease causes them to turn brown and die. On older leaves it shows up as large, irregular brown patches, the leaves falling sooner than normal. The disease is severe in wet springs but disappears during warm, dry weather. It lives over winter in cankers on branches and on twigs it has killed; removal of diseased branches is the first step to combat the disease. After each cut, disinfect the pruning shears. Control: Spray emerging leaves with zineb, maneb, captan, folpet, or thiram; repeat the spray one to two weeks later.

Cankers. Although more than one disease can cause cankers, their appearance is generally similar: oval, discolored, and dead spots on branches or even on the trunk. Sometimes cankers are sunken into the surface, but at other times they are flat. Control: If you can do this without drastically altering the tree's appearance, cut out infected branches below the cankered area, disinfecting the pruning shears between each cut. If such treatment would do serious damage to the tree's appearance, your best recourse is to contact a professional tree company for diagnosis and treatment.

Fireblight. Sometimes serious on plants in the rose family, fireblight thrives during moist spring weather when the bacteria begins in the blossoms and progresses down branches, blackening leaves and stems as it works downwards. Affected trees look as if they were scorched by fire. Control: Remove infected branches below the blighted area,

disinfecting shears between each cut. If fireblight has been a problem in the previous year, spray blossoms with strep-tomycin, Bordeaux, or fixed copper.

Root Diseases. As a group these are the most difficult problems to counteract because the roots are hidden from sight and access. By the time damage is evidenced in the top growth, it may be too late for a remedy. If a large and cherished tree appears to be the victim of any of the following root problems, you would be wise to let a professional tree company attempt to save it—if they find that its revival is possible.

Armillaria root rot. Oak root fungus, as it is known in the West, can infect not only oaks but also a good number of other ornamentals as well. The fungus invades the root tissue, forming black, shoestringlike threads just beneath the roots' bark. The final stage of this fungus shows up as clusters of mushrooms at the tree's base. Because no practical remedy exists, removal of the infected tree and as much as possible of its root system is the best course of action.

Texas root rot. This fungus disease occurs in the semiarid Southwest, especially where soils are highly alkaline and content of organic matter is extremely low. In less alkaline soils with more organic materials, the fungus cannot compete with other soil micro-organisms. Symptoms are a sudden wilting of leaves as the fungus destroys the outer portion of the roots, cutting off their ability to absorb water.

Control measures usually consist of adding sulfur to the soil to reduce alkalinity and organic matter to encourage the multiplication of organisms that naturally combat the fungus.

Verticillium wilt. With this disease a fungus invades and plugs the water-conducting tissues in the roots, preventing water from reaching the leaves. Common symptoms are a wilt on one side of the tree only. The leaves yellow, brown, and die upward from the base of the plant or branch. The sapwood (outer layer of tissue in a stem or branch) usually becomes discolored—frequently turning olive green, dark brown or black. Although the fungus develops in cool, moist soil in springtime, foliage wilting may not show until late spring or early summer, when warm sunny days stimulate growth, putting stress on the tree.

Mildly affected trees often recover from an attack. You can aid recovery by deep but infrequent irrigation. If the tree has been in poor health, fertilize it to stimulate new root growth. But don't fertilize an afflicted tree that is growing vigorously—this will just stimulate growth of more leaves to compound the problem.

Cultural problems

A tree's leaves can show abnormalities that may suggest disease but which really indicate some problem associated with culture. These are two common ones:

Scorched leaves, where foliage turns brown from the edges upward, is not a disease but indicates a lack of adequate moisture at the roots. During hot weather, leaves may release more moisture than roots can replace. Newly planted trees are especially vulnerable. The remedy is better watering and moisture conservation. (See page 17.)

Yellow leaves with veins that remain green usually signal an iron deficiency (called *chlorosis*) rather than a foliage disease. This condition occurs most often in alkaline soils where any soil iron is rendered unavailable to plant roots. The most immediate remedy is application of iron chelates to the soil.

White-barked *birches are among the most familiar deciduous trees from coast to coast.*

Deciduous trees

If a tree is deciduous, it loses all of its leaves at one time each year. Many of these trees have spectacular spring flowers, flaming autumn foliage color.

Generally speaking, trees can be classed either as those that lose all their leaves at some point during the year or as those that remain full foliaged year-round.

"Deciduous" describes trees that annually shed all leaves. Trees that keep their leaves throughout the year are known as "evergreens." (You'll find evergreen trees, both those with broad leaves and those with needlelike leaves, described on pages 62-93.)

The most distinguishing feature of deciduous trees is that during part of the year they're fully clothed with leaves and during another part of the year, after leaves have fallen, they present a bare skeleton of branches and trunk. (Of course, evergreen trees also drop leaves during the year — but not all of them at once.)

Deciduous trees may be native either to temperate regions (where winter temperatures dip below freezing) or to tropical areas. With those from temperate regions, total leaf drop is the tree's means of protection against the rigors of cold: all active growth ceases and the tree goes dormant.

For many parts of the country, these temperate-climate deciduous trees are the only trees with broad leaves and/or flowers that can be grown. (Most broad-leafed evergreens are too tender for the freezing winters.)

In contrast to the unchanging, needle-leafed evergreens with which they often associate in cold-winter gardens, deciduous trees are the garden's clothes-horses; a different season brings out a different garb. Typically, the active growth season begins in spring, usually with flowers or at least new leaves. Summer gives the richness of mature foliage and, in some trees, ripening fruit. As the growing season comes to a close in autumn, leaves often exchange green for some other color (purple, red, orange, or yellow), and fruit that didn't mature in summer then ripens. Winter offers a clear view of the tree's structure unencumbered by foliage; and many deciduous trees have decorative, or at least distinctive, bark that lends decoration to the subdued winter scene.

Unlike deciduous trees native to cold-winter areas, tropical deciduous trees do not always drop all their leaves in winter. Many remain fully clothed during winter and then lose their leaves in early spring, just before their flowering season. As flowers fade, they return to leaf.

In choosing a deciduous tree or in deciding on a deciduous tree as opposed to an evergreen, you will want to consider climate, use, size, form, and roots. Be sure to read through the section about choosing a tree on pages 4-5.

The trees in this section are listed alphabetically by their botanical names. Following each botanical name is the tree's common name (or names) and the climate zones in which it will grow well. These zones were prepared by the United States Department of Agriculture; a map of their locations appears on page 96. Each tree's common name is listed in the index (pages 95-96), with a cross-reference to the correct botanical name and the page on which it is described. Each kind of tree is represented by at least one drawing.

In the description of the trees, we've often indicated growth rate as slow, moderate, or fast. Slow growth is less than 12 inches per year; moderate growth is 1-2 feet per year; and fast growth is more than 2 feet per year.

If you are unable to find a description of the tree you want in this section or if you don't know whether it is a deciduous, a broad-leafed evergreen, or a needle-leafed evergreen type (some trees have species that are deciduous and other species that are broad-leafed evergreens), look up its common or botanical name in the index.

Acer (The Maples)

The word "maple" may first bring to mind a big, round-topped tree with broad, sharply lobed leaves. But this image is only a partial picture of the maples, which range in size from short and shrubby to forest patriarchs and whose leaves range from very plain to quite fancy. The easy-to-recognize characteristic common to all species is their fruits: each has two wings (with one exception), one on either side, and looks much like a wing nut you'd buy in a hardware store.

Maples of one species or another will succeed in most regions except southern California (only silver and big-leaf maples there) and the low-elevation, arid Southwest. And unless specified as tough or drought resistant, most maples have difficulty in the lower Midwest. Success in those areas is variable; burned leaf margins are commonplace from midsummer to autumn leaf drop. Most maples are rather shallow and fibrous rooted and provide dense shade — not suitable for cultivating a garden under. They all prefer well-drained (not soggy) soils but must have water available in the root zone at all times during their period of leaf.

A. buergerianum. TRIDENT MAPLE. Zones 6-9 (western states), 6-8 (eastern and southern states). Like a trident, each leaf of this species has three lobes, the reason for its common name. Leaves are glossy green, paler on the underside, and about 3 inches across. New spring growth is red; in the fall leaves turn red but may turn orange or yellow. Natural growth habit is low branching and spreading to form a multitrunked tree up to 25 feet high with a rounded crown. With training, trees can become single trunked and high branching enough to walk under.

A. campestre. HEDGE MAPLE. Zones 5-8. The slow, dense, and compact growth of this species makes it useful for a hedge planting. Allowed to grow naturally, single specimens form rounded heads to no more than about 30 feet high. Leaves are dull green, 3-5 lobed, and 2-4 inches wide. They may turn yellow before falling in autumn, or they may drop without appreciable color change. Hedge maples have high tolerance of city air pollution, and will also grow well in poor soil.

A. cappadocicum. COLISEUM MAPLE. Zones 6-9. A dome shaped tree of moderate size (35-40 feet tall), this species has leaves about 5½ inches across with 5-7 lobes. In autumn, leaves turn pale yellow. (On one variety, 'Rubrum', new growth is red, later turning green.) Leaf stalks exude a milky sap when broken — as do those of the Norway maple (A. platanoides).

A. circinatum. VINE MAPLE. Zones 5-9. (5-8 in eastern regions). In its native coniferous evergreen forests of the Pacific Northwest, this maple has a crooked, sprawling, and vinelike habit when growing in the shade. But in the open or at the forest's edge, it forms a multi-trunked and only slightly irregular small tree to 35 feet high and of variable spread. As leaves unfold in spring, small red, purple, and white flowers appear. Leaves are essentially circular to 6 inches across with 5-11 lobes and a soft, light green color. Autumn color in shade or in warmer zones may be yellow, but in chilly temperatures or with exposure to sun, colors will be orange to bright red. Foliage also fails to color well when trees are watered heavily or fertilized in summer. Where summers are hot and dry, trees need shade during the warmest part of the day. Vine maples are sculptural trees to be viewed at close range or against a darker, denser background to show off their delicate, irregular structure. You might choose to train your specimen to grow fairly flat against a wall.

A. davidii. DAVID'S MAPLE. Zones 6-9 (6-8 in eastern regions). The first distinctive feature of this maple is its white-striped, shining green bark. Next are its leaves: rather than being lobed, they are heart shaped with toothed edges, have a bronze tint when new, and grow 5-7 inches long in maturity. Autumn colors are yellow, red orange, and purple. Growth is round topped to perhaps 50 feet tall, with a rather spreading habit. Branch patterns tend to be in horizontal layers.

A. ginnala. AMUR MAPLE. Zones 3-8. A small tree from Siberia and Manchuria for our cold and wind swept regions, this species is as good looking as it is hardy. Trained to a single trunk, Amur maple can become a 20-foot, upright or spreading (but not straight-trunked) tree; left to its own devices, it grows slowly to a many-stemmed shrub-tree of about the same height. By late summer, its small but fragrant spring flowers develop into red fruits that contrast with the still-green foliage. Leaves are 3-lobed, as in the trident maple (A. buergerianum), and to about 3 inches long but with distinctly longer central lobes. The big show comes when chilly autumn nights turn leaves a blazing red. Amur maples grow well even in poor, dry soils.

A. griseum. PAPERBACK MAPLE. Zones 6-9 (6-8 in eastern regions). This species may not be easy to find in nurseries, but it's worth searching for because no other maple species is like it. Its unique feature is reddish bark that peels away in paper-thin sheets just as does the bark of some birches. Growth is rather open and fairly slow to about 25 feet, with branches that angle out and then up from the main trunk. Leaves consist of three coarsely toothed leaflets, each about 2½ inches long, dark green above but silvery on the underside. In autumn the foliage becomes brilliant red.

A. japonicum. FULLMOON MAPLE. Zones 6-9. This species is similar in overall appearance to the Japanese maple (A. palmatum), but it grows into a slightly larger tree (20-30 feet high, 20 feet wide at maturity) and has a rounded top with foliage held in horizontal tiers. Leaves are nearly round, about 5 inches across and divided

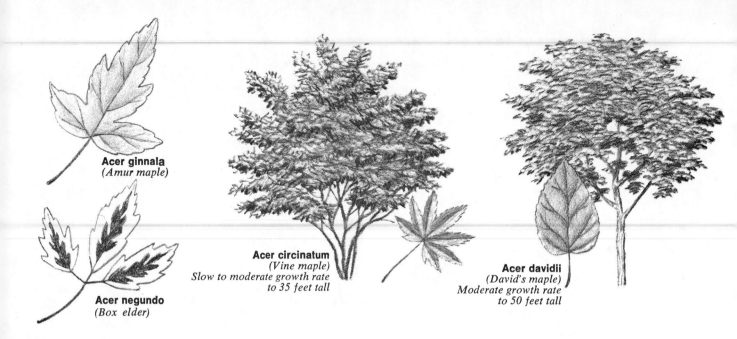

Acer ginnala
(Amur maple)

Acer negundo
(Box elder)

Acer circinatum
(Vine maple)
Slow to moderate growth rate
to 35 feet tall

Acer davidii
(David's maple)
Moderate growth rate
to 50 feet tall

into 7-11 lobes. Autumn color is orange to bright red. The variety 'Aconitifolium' with deeply cut leaves is probably the most easily obtained. These trees are slow growers.

A. macrophyllum. BIGLEAF MAPLE. Zones 7-9 (western states only). For the large garden, this is an impressive tree. Upright and spreading, it can reach 90 feet when mature. Young trees tend to irregular shapes. The leaves are most unusual, with 3-5 lobes up to a width of a foot or more—the largest of the more common maple species. Small yellow flowers are carried in 4-6-inch, drooping clusters. The fruits are different from other maple species listed here in that they often have three wings (instead of two) and hang in long "chains." Native to the West Coast from Alaska down into California, it grows well only within this range. Fall color is yellow.

A. negundo. BOX ELDER. Zones 3-10. For most purposes, this species and its two western subspecies (*A. n. interius* and *A. n. californicum*) have less to offer than other maples except in cold, harsh climates. Not only is the wood weak and easily broken in storms but also the trees seed themselves profusely and are a favorite of the box elder bug. The tree's few virtues are its rapid growth in unhospitable territory where summer heat, dryness, and winter cold limit the choice of better trees, and its usefulness as a quick screen or windbreak tree on larger or country properties.

Individually, the trees grow in a rounded and spreading habit, to about 50 feet high and 40 feet across. Leaves are divided into separate leaflets (each up to 5 inches long) rather than lobes. The species may have up to nine leaflets to a leaf; the western subspecies have three. Autumn color is yellow.

A. negundo 'Variegatum'. VARIEGATED BOX ELDER. Zones 3-10. Because *A. negundo* and its subspecies have so many negative qualities, this cultivated variety is listed separately to emphasize its good

points: moderate, uninvasive growth and colorful foliage. A selected color variation of *A. negundo*, each leaflet of every leaf is irregularly bordered with creamy white, contributing a bright—almost "blooming" —note in the landscape. It is neither so large nor so weedy as *A. negundo*.

A. palmatum. JAPANESE MAPLE. Zones 6-9 (5-8 in eastern regions). Many varieties of the Japanese maple are available in the nursery trade. The differences among them are mostly in leaf color and texture. The basic species is a small, round-topped, and spreading tree that grows to about 20 feet high and wide. It usually branches very low to the ground or has several trunks and often carries its foliage in a horizontally layered fashion. Leaves are 2-4 inches long with 5-9 lobes; their basic green turns to red or yellow in autumn. New growth may be pink or red. The overall effect is airy and graceful—creating probably the most delicate appearance of all maples.

Named selections (usually with Japanese or Latinized names) can be the most refined of all. Some of these have leaves with quite delicately cut lobes. In occasional varieties, lobes are so fine that they really become separate leaflets. In other selections, leaves are colored red, purple, yellowish green, or are variegated white, pink, and green. Types with both colored and finely dissected leaves are also sold. Some of these are not as easy to grow (or are not as vigorous) as the basic species.

Named Japanese maple varieties are always grafted plants. They command a higher price and tend to be slower growing than types started from seed. The dissected-leaf forms may reach what might be considered tree size only after many years— if ever.

Japanese maples will grow in full sun in much of the Pacific Northwest, the Atlantic Seaboard, and coastal northern California—where atmospheric moisture is high

during the growing season. Where summers are hot and dry, the trees require partial shade, at least during the hottest part of the day. Shelter from hot drying wind is also necessary.

You can use Japanese maples a number of different ways in the landscape: as specimen trees in a lawn or patio, in group or grove plantings, and as underplantings beneath taller trees in a woodland garden.

A. platanoides. NORWAY MAPLE. Zones 4-9, but in eastern states the leaves will burn in warmer parts of Zones 7-9. During the growing season, break a leaf from the stem and a milky sap will exude. This characteristic—along with sharply pointed leaf lobes—distinguishes Norway maple from two other similar species: red maple (*A. rubrum*) and sugar maple (*A. saccharum*).

Before leaves unfold in spring, quantities of small, greenish yellow flowers appear. The 4-7-inch-wide leaves have five lobes; fall color is a strong yellow.

The rapid growth produces a broadly rounded tree, ultimately to 90 feet tall and over half as wide, that casts very heavy shade. Roots are both deep and shallow, dense and greedy. This is not a tree to grow other plants under; it is tough competition even for a lawn. But otherwise, Norway maple is very adaptable, tolerating many types of soil and climate conditions. It even thrives in polluted city atmosphere, which usually discourages *A. rubrum* and *A. saccharum*. But like *A. saccharum* its roots are damaged by chemicals used to melt road ice in winter so it is not a good city street tree.

Nurseries also offer a number of named forms of the Norway maple. 'Cleveland' is tall and oval rather than rounded. 'Columnare', a somewhat slow grower, is tall and slender, spreading not more than half its height (but not so rigidly narrow as a Lombardy poplar, page 52). 'Summershade' is narrower than the species and per-

Acer platanoides
(Norway maple)
Fast growth rate
to 90 feet tall

Acer palmatum
(Japanese maple)
Slow to moderate growth rate
to 20 feet tall

Acer griseum
(Paperbark maple)
Slow growth rate
to 25 feet tall

forms better than other maples in the heat and humidity of the southern states (but still not beyond Zone 7). Among the colored-leafed varieties, 'Crimson King' has purplish red leaves throughout the growing season and is much slower growing than the species, reaching only about 50 feet; 'Faassen's Black' leaves are dark and purplish and the tree has a pyramidal growth habit; 'Schwedleri' begins spring with purple red leaves that turn bronzy green during the summer.

A. pseudo-platanus. SYCAMORE MAPLE. Zones 6-9 (only Zones 6-8 in eastern regions). A conspicuous show of greenish yellow flowers precedes the leaves in springtime. When leaves do appear, they have five lobes and are dark green, thick textured, to about 5 inches across; varieties 'Atropurpureum' and 'Spaethii' have leaves that are rich purple on the undersides. In contrast to most other maples, sycamore maple leaves have no real autumn color.

Fairly rapid growth produces a broadly rounded tree to about 70 feet high at maturity with equal spread. It is a particularly fine tree for the seashore because the leaves tolerate high winds and salt spray.

A. rubrum. RED MAPLE. Zones 4-9. This tree gets its common name from the reddish color of its spring growth buds, flowers, leaf stalks, and young fruits and from the foliage, which turns brilliant scarlet in autumn. Best fall color occurs on trees planted in acid soil, but acid soil is not necessary for healthy growth. Some trees turn yellow or orange in autumn; the color of young fruits in spring indicates what the fall color will be. The 5-lobed leaves, 3-5 inches across, are quite similar to those of the sugar maple *(A. saccharum)*, but they are generally smaller and have sharp angles between the lobes, whereas those of sugar maple are rounded. Dense, fast-growing trees, red maples are taller than they are wide, reaching about 50-70 feet tall in a garden and often taller in the wild. Several columnar forms of varying narrowness are available, and some nurseries offer named varieties selected for especially good fall color.

Red maple's native range extends from eastern Canada through the deep South. Trees grown from seed of southern specimens will not be as tolerant of cold weather as those raised from northern stock. In the wild, red maple is frequently associated with moist or even swampy soil. Because of this, it is a good choice for habitually damp garden locations. But it does equally well in normal garden soil, too. Weak wood is its liability; storms and snow or ice often cause limbs to break.

A. saccharinum. SILVER MAPLE. Zones 4-9. Leaf undersides and bark (except on oldest wood) are a silvery gray giving the tree its name. Each leaf is 5-lobed and 3-6 inches wide, and light green on the upper surface; foliage turns yellow or a mixture of yellow and orange in the frosts of autumn. Growth is very rapid, with the main limbs ascending sharply upward but side branches drooping gracefully. Ultimate height may be as much as 100 feet with a spread to 75 feet.

Despite its obvious beauty, silver maple's faults should limit its use to situations where it won't cause problems. For one thing, weak wood and narrow crotches make the tree especially susceptible to breakage by wind, storms, snow, or ice. For another, surface roots can clog pipes, raise pavement, and interfere with growth and maintenance of a good lawn. Aphids and cottony maple scale are especially fond of silver maple, and in alkaline soils the leaves show chlorosis (yellowing between the veins). For the Great Plains states this is a maple that will easily endure the rigors of climate. There, in dry summers, it may show marginal leaf burn.

Several different growth and leaf types may be carried by some nurseries. The narrow *pyramidale* variety is less susceptible to storm damage. A form with finely dissected, lacelike leaves is known variously as 'Laciniatum' or 'Wieri'; though not as tall as the species, its limitations are the same.

A. saccharum. SUGAR MAPLE. Zones 4-9 (4-7 in eastern regions). This is the tree responsible for New England's maple syrup. Stout branches sweep upward from a short, thick trunk to form a rounded to oval outline 60-75 feet high in gardens. Growth rate is moderate. Dense foliage consists of 3-5-lobed leaves (rounded between the lobes), each leaf being 3-6 inches across and paler green on the underside than on the top. Autumn color is spectacular red, orange, or yellow.

Unfortunately, sugar maples do not tolerate city conditions. The shallow roots are particularly sensitive to ice-melting chemicals used on streets in cold-winter regions, so avoid planting a sugar maple along a road that will receive this winter treatment. Shallow and greedy roots plus dense shade make it difficult to grow other plants underneath a sugar maple. 'Newton Sentry' and 'Temple's Upright' are two narrow-growing forms. For the dry-summer regions of Oklahoma and the Southwest, the variety 'Caddo' is best adapted.

Aesculus carnea

RED HORSECHESTNUT. Zones 5-9. Although they have showy flowers and almost tropically dramatic foliage, many horsechestnuts are a poor choice for the garden. Drawbacks are large, poisonous seeds (and sometimes leaves), litter, large size, dense shade and lack of fall color. The red horsechestnut's smaller size and good flower color make it the best of the horsechestnuts for home planting. A round-headed

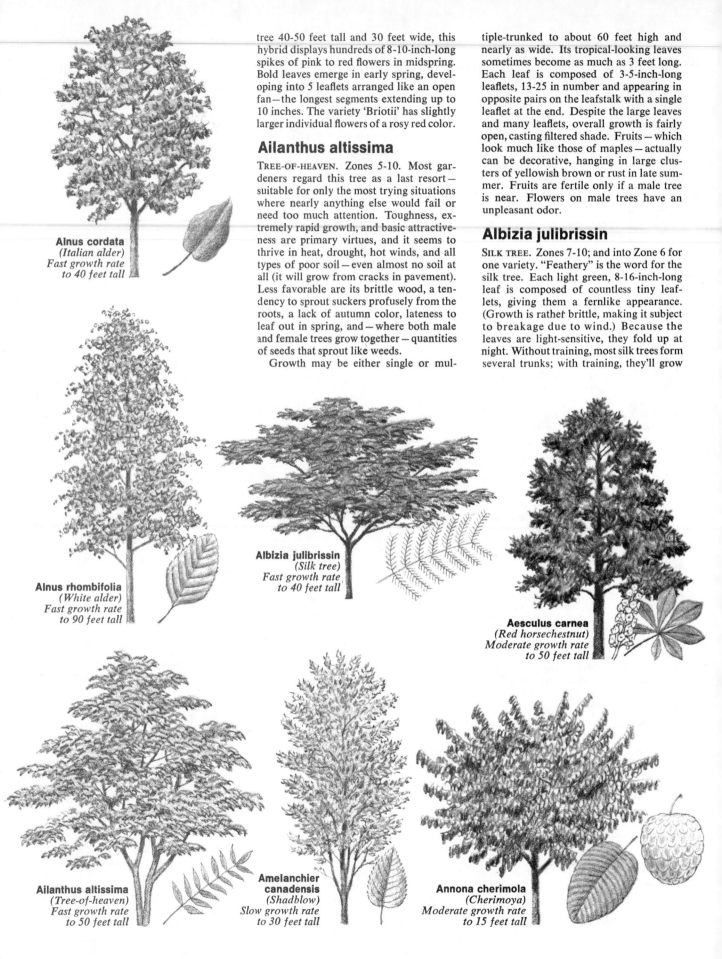

tree 40-50 feet tall and 30 feet wide, this hybrid displays hundreds of 8-10-inch-long spikes of pink to red flowers in midspring. Bold leaves emerge in early spring, developing into 5 leaflets arranged like an open fan—the longest segments extending up to 10 inches. The variety 'Briotii' has slightly larger individual flowers of a rosy red color.

Ailanthus altissima

TREE-OF-HEAVEN. Zones 5-10. Most gardeners regard this tree as a last resort—suitable for only the most trying situations where nearly anything else would fail or need too much attention. Toughness, extremely rapid growth, and basic attractiveness are primary virtues, and it seems to thrive in heat, drought, hot winds, and all types of poor soil—even almost no soil at all (it will grow from cracks in pavement). Less favorable are its brittle wood, a tendency to sprout suckers profusely from the roots, a lack of autumn color, lateness to leaf out in spring, and—where both male and female trees grow together—quantities of seeds that sprout like weeds.

Growth may be either single or mul-

tiple-trunked to about 60 feet high and nearly as wide. Its tropical-looking leaves sometimes become as much as 3 feet long. Each leaf is composed of 3-5-inch-long leaflets, 13-25 in number and appearing in opposite pairs on the leafstalk with a single leaflet at the end. Despite the large leaves and many leaflets, overall growth is fairly open, casting filtered shade. Fruits—which look much like those of maples—actually can be decorative, hanging in large clusters of yellowish brown or rust in late summer. Fruits are fertile only if a male tree is near. Flowers on male trees have an unpleasant odor.

Albizia julibrissin

SILK TREE. Zones 7-10; and into Zone 6 for one variety. "Feathery" is the word for the silk tree. Each light green, 8-16-inch-long leaf is composed of countless tiny leaflets, giving them a fernlike appearance. (Growth is rather brittle, making it subject to breakage due to wind.) Because the leaves are light-sensitive, they fold up at night. Without training, most silk trees form several trunks; with training, they'll grow

Alnus cordata
(Italian alder)
Fast growth rate
to 40 feet tall

Alnus rhombifolia
(White alder)
Fast growth rate
to 90 feet tall

Albizia julibrissin
(Silk tree)
Fast growth rate
to 40 feet tall

Aesculus carnea
(Red horsechestnut)
Moderate growth rate
to 50 feet tall

Ailanthus altissima
(Tree-of-heaven)
Fast growth rate
to 50 feet tall

Amelanchier canadensis
(Shadblow)
Slow growth rate
to 30 feet tall

Annona cherimola
(Cherimoya)
Moderate growth rate
to 15 feet tall

into single-trunked specimens. Both trained and untrained trees have a flat-topped canopy of horizontally layered foliage. During the summer, fluffy, pincushionlike pink to reddish flowers dot the top of the foliage canopy, providing an attractive view from above. Because the shade from this tree is light, just filtering the sunlight, a lawn underneath is possible (so long as you don't mind some litter from fallen flowers, seedpods, and leaves). Silk trees are rapid growers, in maturity reaching about 40 feet tall and spreading even more. Small trees establish faster than ones planted from large containers. Like many other fast-growing trees, they never reach great age.

Best growth is wherever summer heat is high, within the tree's regions of adaptability. Although best performance is in good garden soils, growth also is good in poor, sandy, or alkaline soils. Small trees are more sensitive to cold than are larger trees. Especially if you live in Zone 7 or 8, you should either plant a good-sized specimen (6 or more feet tall) or carefully protect a smaller tree for the first two winters.

Several selected varieties adapted to certain regions are sold. In the South, a wilt disease kills the species, but varieties 'Charlotte' and 'Tryon' are resistant. The mimosa web worm can be a serious pest in the eastern and southern states. In Zone 6, look for variety 'Ernest Wilson' (sometimes sold as *A. j. rosea*); it is more cold tolerant than the species, though a somewhat smaller tree with darker pink flowers.

Alder (see Alnus, p. 31)

Almond (see Prunus, pp. 53-55)

Alnus (Alder)

The different alder species vary in ultimate size, but all have a recognizable similarity and share a liking for water or damp soils. Like their relatives, the birches, alders look good in grove plantings and often grow as multiple-trunked specimens. Autumn color is not remarkable and may be completely absent, but the gray-barked winter silhouette is good looking and in late winter, while branches still are bare, is decorated with tassel-like male catkins and small female cones. Since alder's roots tend to be shallow and invasive, the tree's best use is as background, grove, screening, and stream or pond-side planting. All species are rapid growers.

A. cordata. ITALIAN ALDER. Zones 6-10. The smallest (to about 40 feet high) and neatest-appearing of the alders, this species also is the least demanding of a moist soil. Growth is upright, somewhat wider than half the height, with branches tending to be horizontal. The dense foliage canopy consists of glossy, rich green leaves (paler beneath), heartshaped to about 4 inches. Deciduous period is brief. Leaf miners may be troublesome in Northwest.

A. glutinosa. BLACK ALDER. Zones 4-10. Sticky new growth and upper leaf surfaces distinguish this species from other alders. Leaves are 2-4 inches long, rounded to pear shaped, and coarsely toothed on the edges. Black alder tends to grow several trunks to about 70 feet and can appear as a dense mass of dark green from the ground up. Its best use is as a screen tree in wet soils. The variety 'Laciniata' has deeply lobed leaves and therefore gives a much more finely textured effect than the species.

A. incana. SPECKLED or GREY ALDER. Zones 3-8. This is the hardiest alder and makes a good 60-foot-high by 15-foot-wide screening tree in wet soils. (Also see *A. glutinosa,* the black alder.) It will also grow in normal (not wet) soils. Oval leaf surfaces are dull green; the undersides are gray and downy.

A. oregona. RED ALDER. Zones 7-9. This alder will thrive not only where soils are wet but also where the underground water is brackish (somewhat saline). In its native Pacific Coast range, it is a narrow, tall tree to 100 feet or so, but in cultivation it will be about half that height and have a broad pyramid shape. Smooth, light gray bark is a pleasant contrast to dark green leaves, which are oval, 2-4 inches long, and coated with short rusty hair on the undersides. In the Northwest, tent caterpillars can be a springtime problem while the fall webworm may bother foliage in summer and autumn.

A. rhombifolia. WHITE ALDER. Zones 6-9. Very fast growth carries this gray-barked alder to as much as 90 feet high and about half as wide. Coarsely toothed oval leaves reach 4½ inches long, are dark green above but paler underneath, and appear early in spring. Because of its branching habit, which tends to be spreading with drooping branch tips, this tree possesses a certain gracefulness despite its ultimate size. White alder may be bothered by tent caterpillars in its native territory in the western states.

Amelanchier

SHADBLOW, SHADBUSH, SERVICE BERRY. For beauty in all four seasons, good behavior in the garden, and ease of cultivation, these trees can't be faulted. In some regions, however, they may be bothered by two pests that frequently attack members of the rose family: spider mites and fireblight.

All species are lightweight, delicate, and often multi-trunked trees with a good show of spring flowers (of very short duration if days are hot), edible fruits in summer, glowing autumn foliage color, and good winter branch and twig pattern. Against a dark-foliage background, their seasonal beauty really stands out. The shade they cast isn't heavy and roots aren't invasive, making for easy cultivation of other plants beneath. Neutral or acid soil is preferred.

A. canadensis. SHADBLOW or DOWNY SERVICE BERRY. Zones 4-8. A profusion of slender-petaled, single white flowers mantle the plant in early spring, giving way to conspicuous new growth that is covered with gray down. Mature leaves are small, dark green ovals that turn to a brilliant red, orange, or yellow in fall. In the wild, this tree may reach 60 feet, but garden height usually is no more than a slender 30 feet, often with several trunks (unless trained to one only). Small, maroon red fruits ripen early in summer, to the delight of birds in the neighborhood.

A. grandiflora. APPLE SERVICEBERRY. Zones 5-8. This is a hybrid of the preceding species (*A. canadensis*) and the one that follows (*A. laevis*). It is characterized by being smaller than either of its parent species but with larger flowers. The maximum height is about 20-25 feet, and branch spread is approximately the same. Following the white 1¼-inch blossoms in early spring (there's also a pinkish flowering form), new foliage emerges bronzy red, turning dark green as it matures. Bright fall color varies from yellow to red. Summer fruit is purplish black.

A. laevis. ALLEGANY SERVICE BERRY. Zones 5-8. In the wild, this is a shorter tree than *A. canadensis*, but its garden height is about the same: 30 feet. However, this species does have a spreading rather than upright habit and somewhat showier flowers. After drooping clusters of the fragrant, white, early spring blossoms pass, new bronzy purple leaves emerge. Mature leaves are small and oval with a smooth, green finish. The autumn display is typical of the service berry — yellow to red.

Annona cherimola

CHERIMOYA. Zones 9-10 (but not in desert valleys). From the mountains of South America comes this unusual fruit tree. Although it is tender (about 25° is its low limit), the cherimoya doesn't require steaming tropical heat for good performance. Initially, growth is rapid; but after the first several years it slows, eventually achieving a 15-foot height with equal or somewhat greater spread. Oblong, dull green leaves may reach 10 inches in length. They have velvety undersides and — unlike most deciduous trees — fall in late spring. As the leaves drop, 1-inch yellow to brownish, fleshy, and hairy flowers begin to open; they emit a pleasant, fruity odor and continue to open for several months. The fruit that forms from the flowers will ripen in winter, each weighing ½ to 1½ pounds at maturity. (Some varieties have larger and heavier fruits.) In shape, fruits resemble strawberries but are covered with green, leaflike scales. Creamy white, custardlike flesh contains large black seeds and has a mild flavor likened to bananas, pineapples, and nectarines.

Apple (see Malus, pp. 48-49)

Apricot (see Prunus, pp. 53-55)

Ash (see Fraxinus, pp. 70-71)

Aspen (see Populus, p. 52)

Basswood (see Tilia, pp. 60-61)

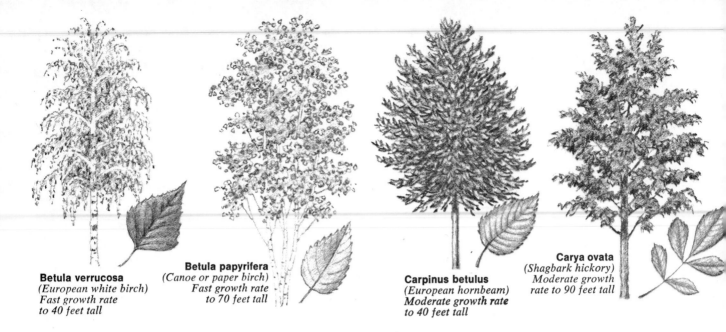

Betula verrucosa
(European white birch)
Fast growth rate
to 40 feet tall

Betula papyrifera
(Canoe or paper birch)
Fast growth rate
to 70 feet tall

Carpinus betulus
(European hornbeam)
Moderate growth rate
to 40 feet tall

Carya ovata
(Shagbark hickory)
Moderate growth
rate to 90 feet tall

Beech (see Fagus, p. 40)

Betula (Birch)

"Graceful," "refined," "feminine"—these are just a few of the pleasant words that have been used to describe birch trees. Some species may reach 100 feet tall, but birches, lightweights of the forest, never appear massive. And they are sociable trees: it is unusual to see one growing alone unless it has been intentionally planted apart from others. Decorative thin bark that peels in layers (though not always the traditional white) is a feature of all birch species.

Even without conspicuous flowers, birches are trees of all-season beauty: when out of leaf, their delicate limb structure, striking bark, and hanging seed tassels are on display; during the growing season they provide clean green foliage; and in autumn their foliage changes to a glowing yellow.

On the debit side, birches are susceptible to certain pests and diseases (although not all species are equally susceptible and not all parts of the country are affected). Most damaging in regions east of the Cascade and Sierra Nevada mountains is the bronze birch borer, a small grub that tunnels into stems and feeds beneath the bark. Frequently, the grubs begin by girdling and killing the upper limbs. Heavy infestations can kill an entire tree, but even a few dead limbs may be enough to disfigure an otherwise beautiful specimen. The favorite species of this grub seems to be the most popular and widely planted white-barked European white birch *(B. verrucosa)*. Trees growing poorly and in poor soil usually are the first ones to be invaded by the grubs.

In the Northeast and Northwest, a problem is the birch leaf miner. Eating the tissue between leaf surfaces, this insect will disfigure leaves for the duration of the season and, in severe infestation, cause entire leaves to turn brown.

Aphids can be a nuisance insect anywhere on any birch; the honeydew they secrete (which drips from the trees in heavy infestations) is messy on whatever is beneath. (Refer to pages 24-25 for control suggestions.)

Don't prune birches when you would most other deciduous trees—just before spring leaf-out: they will "bleed" excessively when the sap begins to flow. Wait until late spring.

B. alba. *See B. verrucosa*

B. lenta. CHERRY or SWEET BIRCH. Zones 4-8. Cherrylike bark—smooth and lustrous red brown—accounts for one common name: "cherry" birch. The wintergreen flavor of young branches is responsible for its being called "sweet." Young trees are pyramid shaped but mature into rounded canopies as high as 75 feet in the wild (but usually smaller in the garden). Oblong, dark green leaves are up to 5 inches long, paler with silky hairs on the undersides. *B. lenta* is native to moist soils in the eastern states.

B. maximowicziana. MONARCH BIRCH. Zones 6-10. This is the largest-leafed birch (each leaf is heart shaped to 6 inches long) and a reliable producer of golden yellow fall color—even in the warmest zones. Flaky orange brown bark eventually becomes gray to almost white on old trees. Habit is more stiffly upright (to 80 feet) than most other birches but is graceful nevertheless. Growth is fast.

B. nigra. RIVER or RED BIRCH. Zones 5-10. For moist soils or for areas subject to flooding, this is a tree that will feel right at home. Growth in early years is fast, eventually reaching 50-90 feet tall and 40-60 feet wide with a pyramidal outline. Young bark is pinkish white, smooth and shining; but as trees age, the bark becomes shaggy, flaking and curling in cinnamon brown to blackish sheets. Diamond shaped leaves are 1-3 inches long,

glossy bright green with silvery undersides. River birch is best used in an informal or "wild" garden where its relatively short life and tendency to breakage (because of weak wood) will not cause a significant vacancy in the landscape. For areas with hot summers this is a more successful species than *B. verrucosa*.

B. papyrifera. CANOE or PAPER BIRCH. Zones 3-8. Aside from striking white bark, this birch is characterized by its see-through quality. Generations ago, this birch was prized by American Indians as a source of bark for their canoes.

Growth often is multiple trunked or branched close to the ground, creating an effect of several trunks. You can expect a height of 40-70 feet and a width of about half the height. Leaves are a strong green on upper surfaces and paler underneath, oval in shape, to 4 inches long, and irregularly toothed on the margins. This species appears to be bothered less by the bronze birch borer and by leaf miners than is *B. verrucosa*.

B. pendula. *See B. verrucosa*

B. populifolia. GRAY BIRCH. Zones 5-8. The common name is something of a misnomer, for the bark actually is quite white, appearing slightly gray only when compared side by side with the chalk white bark of *B. papyrifera*. Beneath the junction of each branch and the trunk (and even where missing branches were once connected) is a triangular black patch. Only about 30 feet tall, trees are also very slender (even though specimens usually have multiple trunks). They make good candidates for small gardens. Leaves have an almost triangular outline and are up to 3 inches long, ending in a long tapered point. With just the faintest stirring of air, the leaves flutter.

In nature, the gray birch grows in poor soils. In its native range, it often is the first tree to reappear after woods have been cleared or burned over. But plant

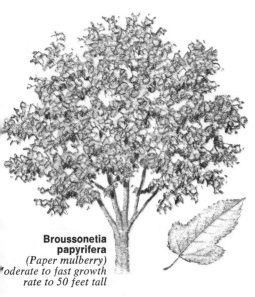

**Broussonetia
papyrifera**
(Paper mulberry)
*Moderate to fast growth
rate to 50 feet tall*

this birch only for your own enjoyment; it is short-lived and won't be around for your great-grandchildren to enjoy.

B. verrucosa. EUROPEAN WHITE BIRCH. Zones 3-10. Not good in the desert and not always successful in hot summer areas of Zones 9 and 10. In eastern states, performance is good through Zone 6 and fair in Zone 7. Though an undeniably beautiful tree and, nationwide, probably the most frequently planted birch, unfortunately this also is the species most favored by the bronze birch borer. Wherever the borer can be a troublesome pest, plant the European white birch only if you are prepared to attend to annual spraying or are willing to gamble with disappointment. Growth is upright and somewhat pyramidal, the branches angling upward but dropping at their ends to create a slightly weeping effect. Bark on twigs and young branches (and the trunks of young trees) is golden brown, but trunk and main branches develop white bark marked with black clefts. Eventually old bark on the trunk becomes dark gray. Diamond-shaped leaves are glossy green, about 2½ inches long, each with a slender, tapered point.

A number of different growth or color forms may be found in nurseries. 'Dalecarlica' (sometimes sold as 'Laciniata') is the cutleaf weeping birch, with drooping branches and deeply cut leaves. The cutleaf forms are more susceptible to aphids than are those with plain leaves. 'Fastigiata' is strongly upright and narrow, almost in a class with Lombardy poplar when young, although older trees spread somewhat wider. 'Purpurea' has purplish black twigs and maroon purple new foliage that matures to a maroon-tinted green. 'Youngii', or Young's weeping birch, has slender branches that hang straight down to form a very narrow weeping tree; its trunk must be staked upright to whatever height you want the tree to be. Keep staking as the tree grows. It starts hanging

at the point where you stop staking.

Birch (see Betula, p. 32)

Broussonetia papyrifera

PAPER MULBERRY. Zones 6-10 (6-9 in eastern regions). Poor and alkaline soils, strong winds, dry air, heat, drought, grimy city atmosphere—all these trying conditions the paper mulberry takes in stride. And a fairly big stride it is: mature trees may reach 50 feet with a nearly equal spread in fairly good soil with periodic watering. They become broadly rounded and cast dense shade (height and bulk will be less where environmental conditions are harsh). Growth is moderate to rapid.

The only sure things about the leaves are their rough texture (hairy beneath) and dull green color; size is variable and shape may be oval or variously lobed. The gray trunk tends to branch low, becoming fairly massive as it ages. Male and female flowers occur on separate plants, and where the two grow near one another, you'll get round, ¾-inch orange red summer fruits that are favored by the birds. If disturbed by cultivation, trees tend to send up numerous suckers from the roots. But suckering is only a slight problem in poor soils or "difficult" climates.

Carpinus

HORNBEAM. These trees are neat, well behaved, moderate sized, and unprepossessing—characteristics that add up to good, if undramatic, landscape specimens. Their fruits (which actually are nutlets) are carried in attractive, drooping clusters, each nutlet encased in a 3-winged structure.

C. betulus. EUROPEAN HORNBEAM. Zones 6-9. For many years this tree is a dense pyramid of dark green to 40 feet tall. With age, however, the form becomes broader, with drooping outer branches. Oval leaves are up to 5 inches long with toothed edges. They turn yellow in autumn and remain on the tree into winter. Excellent for screening or hedging of any height, habit is naturally dense (even denser when sheared). The variety 'Fastigiata' has many upright branches that form a narrow crown in early to middle age but become more spreading as trees mature. 'Columnaris' also is tall and narrow, but it has a single central trunk with short branches radiating out from it.

C. caroliniana. AMERICAN HORNBEAM (also known in its native eastern states as Blue Beech and Ironwood). Zones 3-9. American hornbeam often grows in the wild at forest edges or even as underplantings beneath taller trees. In the garden, you can use it in a shady spot that needs a filler. Its moderate growth rate leads to a rounded crown about 30-40 feet high and 20 feet wide. The bark is smooth and blue gray, often described as having the appearance of muscles flexing just under the surface. Dark green leaves are similar to those of the European hornbeam *(C. betulus)*, but are smaller, to 3

inches long. They turn red or a mottled yellow and red in autumn. A tendency toward several trunks is not unusual. Grows well only in acid or neutral soil.

Carya

PECAN and HICKORY. Unless you need really big trees—or feel that you simply must grow your own pecans—you might pass these by in favor of less imposing trees. But where they have room to show off without overpowering, pecan and hickory are undeniably attractive. They're not always easy to find in nurseries because they are difficult to transplant except when quite small—before their deep taproot has grown to great length.

C. illinoinensis. PECAN. Zones 6-9. Because of pecan's importance as a crop tree, a number of different varieties are available, the differences being in nut size or quality, hardiness, and ability to produce nuts where summers are short. In the colder parts of its climate adaptability, summers usually are not long enough or hot enough (or both) for a crop to mature or even for flowers to be pollinated. A reasonably rapid grower when young, but slowing down as it attains size, a pecan can ultimately reach 100 feet high with equal spread when planted in its favored conditions of deep, rich, and moist soil combined with hot summer weather. Foliage consists of large, oval 4-5-inch leaflets similar to English walnut but narrower and longer (to 7 inches) and with a greater number (11-17) of leaflets per leaf. Yellow is the fall color. For nut production, many if not most pecans need another seedling tree or different named variety (or wild trees) nearby as a pollinizer.

C. ovata. SHAGBARK HICKORY. Zones 5-9. Young trees that aren't yet producing nuts give no indication of the distinctive bark that lends this hickory its common name. Only after many years, when specimens reach fruiting age, does the smooth gray bark develop its shaggy look—producing shreds, ribbons, and plates of bark that partially peel away from the trunk.

Leaves consist of 5-7 leaflets, each shaped like a pointed teardrop, the three at the end being larger (to 6 inches long) than the rest. Shagbark hickory's outline is tall, somewhat irregular, and no wider than half its height; in good soil (and in time) the trees will reach 100 feet or more. Edible nuts are enclosed in nearly round, 2½-inch fruits that have a distinctive cross mark on the bottom and split into four sections when the nut is ripe. Fall leaf color is yellow to golden brown.

Cassia fistula

GOLDEN SHOWER TREE. Zone 10. For warm and frost-free territory, this is a tropical version of the goldenchain tree *(Laburnum,* see pages 44-45). Foot-long hanging clusters of yellow flowers decorate the tree in spring before the leaves appear. Later come the 1-2-foot flat seedpods that hang on branches like black

To find your climate zone, see page 96

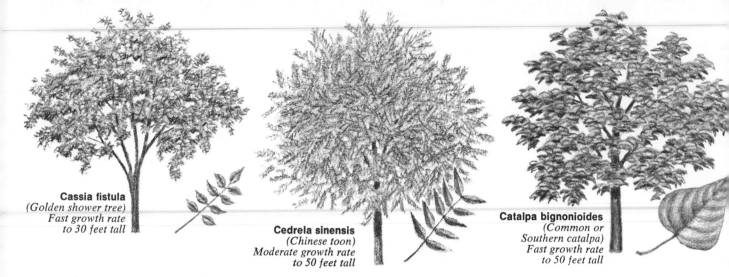

Cassia fistula
(Golden shower tree)
Fast growth rate
to 30 feet tall

Cedrela sinensis
(Chinese toon)
Moderate growth rate
to 50 feet tall

Catalpa bignonioides
(Common or
Southern catalpa)
Fast growth rate
to 50 feet tall

beans. Leaves are about 1 foot long, consisting of 8-16 oval, 2-inch leaflets that drop in late winter shortly before flowering begins. This is a fast-growing, light-textured tree to about 30 feet high and wide.

Castanea (Chestnut)

The stately American chestnut was an important timber, landscape, and food tree until destroyed in this century by a fungus disease accidentally imported from the Orient. Fortunately, the void is partially filled by chestnut species from other parts of the world; and the Oriental species (*C. mollissima*) appears to be resistant to the disease that killed our native. European chestnuts are not immune but can be planted in the western states where the fungus has never existed. All chestnuts must have a neutral or acid soil.

C. mollissima. CHINESE CHESTNUT. Zones 5-9. Dense shade is cast by the handsome, polished, dark green leaves. Each leaf is 3-7 inches long, narrow, and prominently veined from the midrib to leaf edge—where each vein ends in a hollylike tooth. In autumn the foliage becomes yellow to bronze, and in late spring fuzzy, yellow male tassels add decorative interest but have a somewhat unpleasant odor. Broad and rounded, the tree ultimately reaches a height of about 60 feet, usually with a short trunk.

For nut production you'll need two different trees; if you plant one of the named varieties, the second tree should be a different named sort or a seedling; very few, if any, nuts will form on a tree pollinated by itself or another tree of the same variety. A prickly green burr encases 2 or 3 shiny brown chestnuts, about an inch across, that ripen in fall. These are edible both raw and cooked. Fast growth brings trees to bearing age in about five years.

C. sativa. SPANISH CHESTNUT. Zones 5-9. This species is the source of most chestnuts now sold in markets but is safe to plant only where chestnut blight has never been active—primarily in the western states. It is a worthy rival of the American chestnut in size: 100 feet is

possible, but a rounded and spreading habit to 40-60 feet is a more usual garden size. Leaves are very similar to those of the Chinese chestnut (*C. mollissima*) but slightly longer. Flower display is showy but the odor is unpleasant, eliminating it from the list of trees for close-up planting. Nuts must be cooked to be palatable.

Catalpa

Usually these trees are described as "coarse" because of their tropically huge, fuzzy leaves. But unless you dislike large foliage, "dramatic" would be a much more charitable description. The drama is heightened in late spring and summer when large clusters of bell-shaped flowers appear. Long, dark, bean-shaped seedpods follow the flowers and are somewhat conspicuous. Where winds are strong, locate catalpas in the lee of taller trees or buildings to protect their large leaves from damage. Trees are unusually adaptable to extremes in climate and almost any kind of soil. Growth is rapid. In the East, they can be defoliated by larvae of the catalpa sphinx moth—a caterpillar that resembles the tomato horn-worm.

C. bignonioides. COMMON or SOUTHERN CATALPA, INDIAN BEAN. Zones 5-10. Smaller in most respects than the western catalpa (*C. speciosa*). Leaves are heart shaped, 4-8 inches long, on a tree that grows 25-50 feet high and nearly as wide. The 2-inch flowers, in upright spikes at ends of branches, are white, spotted yellow and purple in their throats.

C. speciosa. WESTERN CATALPA. Zones 5-10. In contrast to *C. bignonioides* this species is larger (to 70 feet high and somewhat narrower) with foot-long, heart-shaped leaves. Blossoms are the same shape as those on *C. bignonioides* and are carried in clusters at tips of branches. The differences are their slightly larger size and spots that are light purple.

Cedrela sinensis

CHINESE TOON. Zones 6-10. Cedrela has a strong resemblance to the tree of heaven (*Ailanthus altissima*), both in its appear-

ance and its willingness to grow in poor soils and in the air pollution of cities. Growth, however, is slower, shorter (to 50 feet), and more dense and rounded. Leaves to 2 feet long consist of as many as 20 separate leaflets each 4-7 inches long. New growth is especially attractive, tinted in shades of cream, rose, and soft pink, or even maroon. Hanging, foot-long clusters of yellowish flowers appear in spring, followed by woody, star-shaped capsules that contain winged seeds.

Celtis

HACKBERRY. In general appearance, these trees may remind you of their near relatives, the elms, but in all details the hackberries are smaller. They also have the virtue of deep roots that won't crack nearby pavement and won't prevent you from growing lawn beneath them. Another distinguishing feature is the small, berrylike fruit of hackberries (which birds seek out), compared to the dry, winged seeds of elms. Bark on mature hackberries has corky warts and ridges. Leaves turn yellow in autumn. When established, hackberries will perform admirably in desert heat, strong winds, and dry, alkaline soils.

C. australis. EUROPEAN HACKBERRY. Zones 7-9. Early growth is fairly rapid, later settling down to a slower rate. Final size is in the 40-70-foot range, round-topped and narrower than tall. Lance-shaped, dark green leaves are 2-5 inches long with coarsely toothed margins and distinctly pointed tips. Small fruits are dark purple.

C. laevigata. MISSISSIPPI HACKBERRY, SUGARBERRY. Zones 6-9. As wild trees in the eastern United States, they can reach 100 feet high, but when grown in gardens, they are only about half as tall. The somewhat open crown is broad and rounded, the branches somewhat drooping. Thin, 4-inch oval leaves usually have smooth edges. Where the common hackberry (*C. occidentalis*) is native, Mississippi hackberry is a better tree to plant because, of the two species, it resists the unsightly witches' broom disease. Fruits furnish winter food for birds.

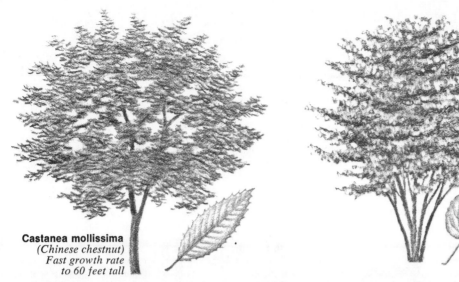

Castanea mollissima
(Chinese chestnut)
Fast growth rate
to 60 feet tall

Cercidiphyllum japonicum
(Katsura tree)
Moderate growth rate
to 70 feet tall

Celtis laevigata
(Mississippi hackberry)
Slow growth rate
to 50 feet tall

Cercidium floridum
(Blue palo verde)
Fast growth rate
to 25 feet tall

C. occidentalis. COMMON HACKBERRY. Zones 3-10 (3-8 in eastern regions). Like the Mississippi hackberry *(C. laevigata),* this is a 100-foot-plus tree in the wild but grows not much more than 50 feet tall in gardens. Its form is rather irregular to rounded, with the crown about as wide as the tree is tall. The 4-5-inch leaves broaden quickly from the base and then taper more gradually to a distinct pointed tip; edges are smooth or only lightly toothed. The berries are black. Throughout much of its native region (a wide area extending from the Rocky Mountains to the Atlantic), it may be subject to infection by a witches' broom disease which, though not fatal or even debilitating, is unattractive, producing thick clusters of small twigs where only one shoot should grow.

C. sinensis. CHINESE HACKBERRY. Zones 8-9. This Oriental hackberry species is similar to the common hackberry *(C. occidentalis)* only smaller. Up close, you'll see that the leaves are smooth and glossier than those of other hackberries and that edges are scalloped rather than toothed. Small fruits are red or yellow. Its great virtue is its resistance to witches' broom infection.

Cercidiphyllum japonicum

KATSURA TREE. Zones 4-9 (4-8 in eastern regions). The Katsura tree will be an elegant and pest-free asset to the landscape as long as you can protect it from scorching sun and drying winds and give it ample water. Early growth rate is moderate but slows down as the tree matures. Eventually, trees become 50-70 feet tall and almost as wide. Trained to a single trunk, a specimen will grow upright and narrow for many years before spreading out to any notable degree. But if its low branches and multiple trunks are permitted to develop naturally, you'll get a broadly spreading tree whose branches angle upward and outward, holding foliage in almost horizontal layers.

The nearly round leaves have heart-shaped bases and are 2-4 inches across. They present an attractive bronze color when they emerge in spring. Leaf surfaces are a dark blue green above and, when mature, may take on a grayish color on the underside. They often show red tints throughout the growing season. Before leaves appear in spring, the tree flowers; individually, the blossoms aren't showy, but they give a red purple "haze" to the bare branches. In autumn, leaves turn to a beautifully brilliant yellow or red. At all times the trees appear fine textured, neat, and graceful.

Cercidium

PALO VERDE. For the desert dwellers, these are trouble-free, hard-as-nails trees that will provide light shade with any amount of care—or neglect. But even though they will survive much drought, they grow faster and denser with periodic watering and some fertilizing.

C. floridum. BLUE PALO VERDE. Zones 8-9. With irrigation, this is a rapid grower, building quickly to 25 feet high and wide in an intricate mass of spiny blue green branches, twigs, and leafstalks. Leaves—consisting of 1-3 pairs of smooth, tiny leaflets—do not cling to the tree very long, so the lightly filtered shade results from branches and leafstalks (which persist after leaves drop). The intricate branch form is nearly hidden in spring by short clusters of bright yellow flowers.

C. microphyllum. LITTLELEAF PALO VERDE. Zones 8-9. This species has the same general appearance as *C. floridum,* but its leaves have more leaflets and are yellowish green, while the blossoms, appearing in 1-inch-long clusters, are a paler yellow. It also is a smaller specimen. For dry locations, this is a better choice because it requires less water.

Cercis (Redbud)

A lavish, preleaf spring display of purplish pink flowers emphatically announces redbud's presence. Small, sweet-pea-shaped blossoms literally cover the tree, appearing on twigs, branches, main limbs—even on the trunk. These blossoms later develop into flat seedpods that become red to red brown when mature. Seedpods are somewhat conspicuous during summer

To find your climate zone, see page 96

and fall and decorative during winter after leaves have fallen. All species have broad, rounded leaves with distinctly heart-shaped bases and a strong yellow color in autumn. They need well drained soil.

C. canadensis. EASTERN REDBUD. Zones 5-9 (4-8 in eastern regions). Fairly rapid growth gives you a slightly irregular but round-topped tree in the 25-35-foot range. Older specimens tend to carry branches in horizontal tiers, the bark and trunk being very dark brown.

Eastern redbuds' 3-6-inch leaves are distinguished from those of other redbuds by their pointed tips. Nurseries sometimes stock selected varieties of this species. 'Alba' (or 'White Texas') has white blossoms, flowers of 'Oklahoma' are wine red, 'Plena' (or 'Flame') has double blooms and a more upright branch habit, and 'Forest Pansy' has the usual purplish pink flowers but then comes out with purple foliage on reddish branches.

C. siliquastrum. JUDAS TREE. Zones 6-9. The Judas tree will develop into multiple trunks or can be trained to a single trunk, but in either case its growth tends to be smaller than that of the eastern redbud (*C. canadensis*). Thirty feet is about the greatest height you can expect. The 3-5-inch leaves have the typical heart-shaped bases and may be either rounded or notched at the tips. In windy locations the brittle limbs may be snapped off. One variety features white flowers.

Cherry (see Prunus, pp. 53-55)

Chestnut (see Castanea, p. 34)

Chionanthus (Fringe tree)

These trees are botanical counterparts to the White Rabbit in *Alice in Wonderland,* always very late for an important flowering date. Most other flowering trees have already leafed out and blossomed by the time fringe trees decide to do both—almost simultaneously. Individually the flowers are unimpressive: only about 1 inch long and composed of four threadlike petals. It is the masses of blooms, carried in lacy clusters, that give a really first-rate show. The equally showy male and female flowers usually occur on separate trees, the female flowers forming ½-inch, dark oval berries. In autumn the foliage turns yellow before falling. Both species are slow growers. Plant them in full sun to part shade in moist, good garden soil.

C. retusus. CHINESE FRINGE TREE. Zones 6-10. Except for the flowers, this species is smaller in every way than the American species (*C. virginicus*). Oval, smooth-edged, glossy green leaves are 2-4 inches long; ultimate height is around 20 feet. Flowers are produced on new growth.

C. virginicus. FRINGE TREE. Zones 5-9. This species grows to 30 feet in its native eastern United States, but in the West it may be shorter. The oblong, 6-8-inch leaves are pale green on their undersides. Flowers come from the previous year's growth, not the growth just emerging.

Cladrastis lutea

YELLOW WOOD. Zones 4-9. Even if it didn't bear conspicuous, foot-long clusters of wisterialike white blossoms, the yellow wood still would be an asset to the garden. The tree roots deeply so that you can grow other plants beneath it. Foliage is attractively light textured, and the smooth gray bark completes the neat, refined appearance. Growth rate is moderate, eventually to around 50 feet, although 30-35 feet high by 20-25 feet wide is about what you should anticipate. Leaves are up to a foot long, consisting of 7-11 oval leaflets; in fall they turn bright golden yellow. Flowering is erratic—usually a heavy crop occurring only every two or three years—and a tree may wait until it is as much as 10 years old before producing its first blossoms. Young trees tend to develop narrow, weak branch crotches that should be removed while still small. If any pruning is necessary, do it in summer or early fall; in other seasons, the tree "bleeds" profusely if cut.

Cornus (Dogwood)

Throughout the year, dogwoods are superlatively good looking. The spring bloom of the eastern native flowering dogwood (*C. florida*) equals that of the various *Prunus* species in its overwhelming abundance and even goes them one better by lasting almost twice as long. What appear to be flowers in many dogwoods actually are petal-like, modified leaves called bracts; these bracts surround the inconspicuous true flowers, which come into their own later in the season when they develop into decorative fruits. Dogwood leaves are easily recognized by their vein pattern: secondary veins branch from the midvein out towards the leaf edges, but just before reaching the edge, they bend and extend down to the leaf tip. Give dogwoods a well-drained, slightly acid soil and regular watering. These are forest-edge plants that appreciate similar garden locations where they will get some high shade. Planted in a lawn, they are very susceptible to "lawn mower disease"; when a lawn mower bumps into a trunk, it causes a bruise that easily can become fatally infected.

C. controversa. GIANT DOGWOOD. Zones 6-9. A height of 40-60 feet doesn't make this species a giant among trees in general but does qualify it for near giant status among its kin: only *C. nuttallii* is taller. Beautiful, regular, and rapid growth habit builds layer upon layer of horizontally arranged branches to form a wide-spreading pyramid. In spring, before foliage emerges, branches are laden with fluffy, flat clusters of creamy white flowers. Each flower is small, but the clusters are up to 7 inches wide and so profuse that the tree is literally covered with a floral snowfall. In late summer, the ½-inch, blue black fruits ripen, to the delight of many birds. After flowers finish, the tree becomes dark

green, covered with oval leaves to 6 inches long and 3 inches wide with silvery green undersides. In autumn, the leaves change to a glowing red before falling.

C. florida. FLOWERING DOGWOOD. Zones 5-9. To this species goes the honor of having been most often nominated the most beautiful native American flowering tree. Spring finds it covered with 4-petaled "flowers" (actually rounded flower bracts), each up to 4 inches across with a characteristic notch at the end. The most common color in the wild is white, but shades of pink to almost red have been found and propagated.

Branch pattern is fairly horizontal with upturned branch tips resulting in a rather flat-topped crown. Bark on older trees is ridged and broken into a checked pattern. Trees may reach 40 feet high with equal spread, although smaller sizes are more common. Oval, bright green leaves are lighter on their undersides, each up to 6 inches long and 2½ inches across. In autumn, they turn flaming red, coinciding with ripening of the small, berrylike fruits that are a brilliant red in small clusters.

Horticulturists have named a number of varieties that differ in various ways from the basic species. 'Cherokee Chief', which has a consistently better color than *C. f. rubra* is noted for its "red" bracts (actually a deep, rosy red). Among the pink-flowering types are 'Apple Blossom' and 'Spring Song'; in Zones 8 and 9 in the East, look for 'Junior Miss'. For heavy production of white blossoms, choose 'Cherokee Princess', 'Cloud 9', or 'White Cloud'; 'Fragrant White Cloud' is a fragrant variety. The tricolor dogwood 'Welchii' offers a foliage color variation: leaves are variegated creamy white, pink, deep rose, and green; in autumn they turn to deep rose verging on red. ("Flowers" of this variety, though, are not as profuse or conspicuous.) For variegated yellow and green leaves and a quantity of white flowers, choose 'Rainbow'. For a different growth form, there's 'Pendula' with its stiffly drooping branches.

The native range of the flowering dogwood extends from New England to central Florida. Since trees raised from seed of plants in the northern part of that range are more cold tolerant than those raised from southern seed specimens, northern gardeners should make sure that nursery trees they buy come from cold-winter stock.

C. kousa. KOUSA OR JAPANESE DOGWOOD. Zones 6-9. Without encouragement, this dogwood usually is content to grow as a bulky, many-stemmed shrub. But with only a little guidance it can become a 20-foot tree with delicate limb structure and spreading, dense, horizontal growth habit. It blossoms several weeks after the flowering dogwood (*C. florida*) finishes, so there is reason to have both trees in the same garden. Flowering that also comes after the tree has leafed out is showy because blossoms are carried along the tops of branches with the leaves hanging below them. Bracts are creamy white, up to 2

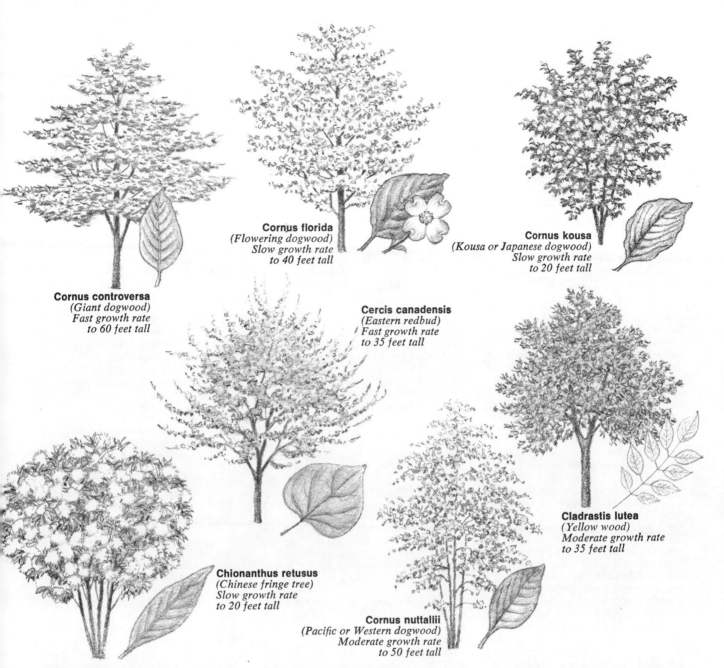

Cornus controversa
(Giant dogwood)
Fast growth rate
to 60 feet tall

Cornus florida
(Flowering dogwood)
Slow growth rate
to 40 feet tall

Cornus kousa
(Kousa or Japanese dogwood)
Slow growth rate
to 20 feet tall

Cercis canadensis
(Eastern redbud)
Fast growth rate
to 35 feet tall

Cladrastis lutea
(Yellow wood)
Moderate growth rate
to 35 feet tall

Chionanthus retusus
(Chinese fringe tree)
Slow growth rate
to 20 feet tall

Cornus nuttallii
(Pacific or Western dogwood)
Moderate growth rate
to 50 feet tall

inches long, and narrower than those of *C. florida,* coming to a distinct sharp point at the tip. In autumn, rounded red fruits that resemble large, rounded strawberries hang below the branches. Lustrous, oval, medium green leaves are up to 4 inches long, turning red (sometimes yellow) in the fall. The Chinese dogwood, *C. k. chinensis,* has slightly larger flower bracts but loses a bit in hardiness.

C. nuttallii. PACIFIC or WESTERN DOGWOOD. Zones 7-9. Zone indications for this species apply only within its native range from British Columbia to southern California mountains. Elsewhere, especially where summers are hot and humid, it has failed. And unfortunately so, as this is a majestic tree, growing taller—and with larger flower bracts—than any of the other dogwoods. Gleaming white flower bracts appear on bare branches in early to midspring, each "flower" being up to

6 inches across and containing 4-6 bracts. Often there will be a second blooming period in August and September while the tree still is in leaf. Trunks (single or multiple) ascend to 50 feet or more, the branches spreading horizontally only to about 20 feet. Form usually is narrowly pyramidal. Oval, 3-5-inch-long leaves—a rich green on their upper surfaces, grayish green beneath—turn to beautiful shades of yellow and red in autumn. Fruits, which become tinted red to orange red in late summer or fall, are grouped together on short stems in dense, buttonlike clusters.

In addition to preferring a fairly cool atmosphere, the Pacific dogwood does not tolerate regular garden watering once it is established. For best chance of success locate your specimen where it won't require regular watering, in well-drained soil, and under the influence of high-branching trees (either beneath them or

where shaded by them during the hottest part of the day). Shade or protection is necessary to keep the plant cool and to prevent sunburn on its trunk. The variety 'Goldspot' has leaves splashed with creamy yellow and flower bracts that are somewhat larger than the species. It also has shown better adaptability to normal garden conditions, and blooms more heavily in fall than does the species.

Cottonwood (see Populus, p. 52)

Crabapple (see Malus, pp. 48-49)

Crataegus (Hawthorn)

Despite differences in details that exist among the many hawthorn species and varieties, a reassuring overall similarity usually makes for easy recognition. Most hawthorns are small, dense, and thorny to about 25 feet high with angular branching

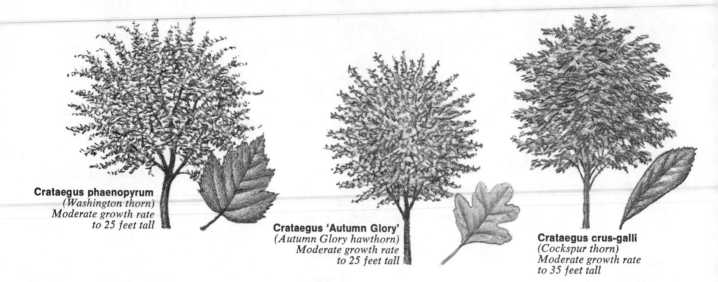

Crataegus phaenopyrum
(Washington thorn)
Moderate growth rate
to 25 feet tall

Crataegus 'Autumn Glory'
(Autumn Glory hawthorn)
Moderate growth rate
to 25 feet tall

Crataegus crus-galli
(Cockspur thorn)
Moderate growth rate
to 35 feet tall

(shorter species are large shrubs) and have a tendency to grow multiple trunks covered with rough bark divided into ridges and furrows. The most usual flower color is white, and single blossoms carried in branched and flattened clusters come in great profusion after leaves have formed for the year. (This characteristic causes them to be later blooming than most other widely planted flowering trees.) Usually red in color, fruits that follow the blossoms also are clustered, each looking more or less like a tiny apple (under an inch in diameter). They ripen from summer to fall. Some birds are partial to them. Those fruits that aren't eaten by birds persist through winter, adding a touch of color to the most colorless season. Leaves run the gamut from simple to lobed. (Sometimes strong new growth will have lobed leaves even though the rest of the tree doesn't.) Red fall color is typical of most American species.

As far as pest and disease problems are concerned, hawthorns could be known as the trees that invite everything: aphids, scale, various caterpillars or worms, spider mites, lace bug, leaf miners, Japanese beetles, borers, rust, fireblight. Of course, not all potential problems will strike at once or in the same year; and some may never occur (Japanese beetles, for example, are not present in the western states). So you shouldn't be discouraged from planting a hawthorn. The problems do suggest, however, that hawthorns perhaps are not the best trees for planting in quantity. Countless species are native to the United States, so if you find wild ones flourishing in your area, these might be among the most successful you could plant.

Regular thinning out is a good idea if your area experiences heavy storms while these trees are in leaf. The dense foliage canopy offers so much resistance to wind that trees can blow over in a storm.

On the positive side, hawthorns will grow well in good or poor, acid to alkaline soil so long as it is reasonably well drained. In fact, good soil may not be advisable because it promotes succulent new growth that is the most subject to fireblight.

Hawthorns are best used as small patio trees (but may tend to drip sap) or for accent specimens in the landscape foreground. With their thorns, they have few equals as barrier hedge plants (trimmed or left alone) and can be used any time you need a large shrub-tree that branches all the way to the ground. Soil adaptability, combined with tolerance of polluted atmosphere, makes them good city trees.

C. arnoldiana. ARNOLD HAWTHORN. Zones 5-9. A dense, rounded crown to about 35 feet high is covered with small white blossoms earlier in spring than most other hawthorns. The bright red fruit that follows blossoming ripens in mid to late summer and falls soon after, even before leaves drop. Oval leaves are up to 3 inches long.

C. 'Autumn Glory'. Zones 6-9. A vigorous hybrid to 25 feet high and about 15 feet wide with a dense, twiggy habit. White spring flowers lead to bright red fruits in early autumn that last into winter. Leathery leaves are 2 inches long with 3-5 toothed lobes.

C. crus-galli. COCKSPUR THORN. Zones 5-9. Density, combined with horizontal branching (and the ever-present thorns), makes this species a first-rate hedge candidate. As a tree, it grows to 35 feet with a distinctive flat top, spreading to about 25 feet. Glossy, oval, 3-inch leaves change in autumn to orange or red orange. White ½-inch blossoms form tiny bright red fruits that remain long into winter. This is the most successful hawthorn for Oklahoma and the adjacent Southwest climates, even though it often can be defoliated by rust in summer.

C. lavallei. (Sometimes sold as *C. carrierei*.) LAVALLE or CARRIERE HAWTHORN. Zones 5-9. Open-branching growth of this species is more erect and less twiggy than that of some other hawthorns. Ultimate height is about 25 feet with nearly equal spread. The root system sometimes may

not provide a secure anchor for the tree. Leathery, dark green oval leaves turn bronze red in autumn. Spring white flowers form ½-inch (or larger) fruits in loose clusters that change to flamboyant orange red in fall and persist on leafless branches during winter.

C. mollis. DOWNY HAWTHORN. Zones 5-9. This is an eastern United States native notable for its 1-inch red fruits and up to 4-inch lobed leaves. Fruits ripen in late summer to contrast with the green foliage. Flowers are white and larger (to 1 inch across) than those of most other species.

C. monogyna. SINGLE SEED HAWTHORN. Zones 5-9. A round-headed tree to about 30 feet tall, the single-seed hawthorn is used widely in Europe for hedging. The species is not as interesting a tree as many other hawthorns (it has no fall color), but its variety 'Stricta' has a narrow, upright growth habit that, in a closely planted line, will form a high and narrow screen. Singly, it will make a vertical accent about 30 feet tall and no more than 10 feet wide.

C. nitida. GLOSSY HAWTHORN. Zones 5-9. Dark, glossy leaves become brilliant orange red in fall. Red or orange fruit persists on the tree through winter. This hawthorn is native to the lower Midwest. Blossoms are white.

C. oxyacantha. ENGLISH HAWTHORN. Zones 5-9. A round-headed tree to 25 feet high and 15 feet wide, the white-flowered species usually is not planted because several of its varieties have more striking blossoms. Paul's scarlet hawthorn ('Paulii') is the best known of these, with deep rose to bright red double flowers. Double flowers nearly always result in little or no fruit production, the fertile flower parts having been converted into petals. With 'Paulii', as well as with 'Double Pink' and the double white forms ('Plena' and 'Double White'), only a few fruits will form. On all forms, the leaves are about 2 inches long with 3-5 deep lobes and no autumn color. In the East, Zones 7-9, foliage will burn during prolonged hot spells; in the

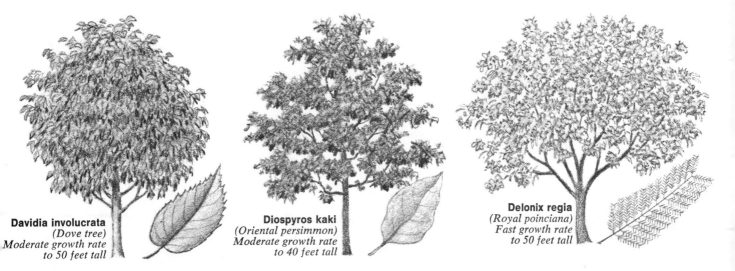

Davidia involucrata
(Dove tree)
Moderate growth rate
to 50 feet tall

Diospyros kaki
(Oriental persimmon)
Moderate growth rate
to 40 feet tall

Delonix regia
(Royal poinciana)
Fast growth rate
to 50 feet tall

Northwest, trees are subject to early defoliation from leaf spot. In the hot-summer areas of the Midwest, the trees are not long-lived.

C. phaenopyrum. WASHINGTON THORN. Zones 5-9. This species has several points to recommend it, not the least of which is its greater resistance to fireblight. Its habit is more graceful and delicate than that of other hawthorns, partly because of a more open structure. Trees will reach about 25 feet high and 20 feet wide, clothed in 2-3-inch leaves that have up to 5 pointed lobes and a maplelike appearance. In autumn, the foliage turns orange and red. Masses of small white flowers in late spring are transformed into clusters of ¼-inch fruits that turn brilliant orangy red in fall and hang on through winter. The hot summers of the lower Midwest are not favorable to this species.

C. pinnatifida major. Zones 6-9. An Oriental species, this tree is noted for deeply lobed leaves and large (for a hawthorn), pear-shaped fruits that are dark red and edible. Height is to about 20 feet with a spread slightly more than half that. Thorns are short or sometimes absent.

C. 'Toba'. Zones 4-9. This hybrid hawthorn from Canada resembles the English hawthorn (*C. oxyacantha*) but will withstand colder winters. Double flowers begin white but age to pink, later producing only a few fruits.

Davidia involucrata

DOVE TREE. Zones 7-9 (6-8 in eastern regions). Another common name for this tree—"handkerchief tree"—gives an idea of its spring flower display. The actual flowers are tiny and grouped together in 1-inch-wide balls, but surrounding each cluster are two white petal-like modified leaves (one about 6 inches long, the other 4 inches) that hang downward like pieces of cloth draped on the branches. Fruits that follow hang on the tree like green golf balls, lasting into winter (when tree is leafless) and turning brown. Trees take their time about flowering—you may have

to wait 10 years before the "doves," or "handkerchiefs," appear.

The tree grows 30-50 feet high with a round top that spreads about as wide as the tree is tall. Its vivid green, elongated, heart-shaped leaves are especially attractive when contrasted against a background of darker green plants. Dove trees have no fall color.

Give dove trees a location sheltered from strong winds. Where summers are hot and dry, the dove tree is not a good risk: there it will need partial or afternoon shade and regular watering.

Delonix regia

ROYAL POINCIANA, FLAME TREE. Zone 10 (Southeast and Hawaii). Deliberately designing a more spectacular flowering tree than this one would be difficult. Another common name, "Flamboyant," accurately describes its effect in the landscape. For a month or more in summer, royal poinciana is aflame with clusters of yellow-tinged scarlet flowers. Bloom begins just as leaves start to emerge; they make the tree look almost totally red. Following the flowers come narrow, 1½-2-foot, flat and woody pods that remain on the tree for a year. Foliage resembles that of *Albizia* and *Jacaranda,* two other members of the pea family: leaves are up to 2 feet long, light, and ferny because of the many tiny leaflets. The trees are tall—to about 50 feet—and spreading wider than tall, inclined toward an umbrella shape. Growth is fast; roots will lift pavement if planted close to it.

Diospyros (Persimmon)

All-season good looks is a claim the persimmons can make—from their neat, tailored spring and summer appearance to their autumn color and showy, edible fruits and finally to a picturesque bare-branch pattern in winter.

D. kaki. ORIENTAL, JAPANESE, or KAKI PERSIMMON. Zones 7 (warmer parts)-9. In spring the new leaves are at first

light green, later developing into leathery, dark green ovals to 7 inches long and 3½ inches wide. Even in warm winter regions the leaves turn yellow, orange, or scarlet in autumn. By fall, the large, orange red fruits are already conspicuous, but after leaf drop they hang on the tree like Christmas ornaments for a number of weeks. Growth rate is moderate, eventually to 30-40 feet high with a rounded crown as wide as the tree is high. Nurseries offer a number of named varieties that differ in fruit size, shape, and character. If you desire fruit, it's safest to buy two different named varieties to pollinate one another. (Most Oriental persimmons will not set fruit with their own pollen.)

D. virginiana. AMERICAN PERSIMMON. Zones 5-9. This differs markedly in growth habit from the Oriental persimmon. In the wild it reaches as much as 75 feet tall, although garden height usually is lower—30-50 feet with a broadly oval head spreading about half as wide as the height. The deep root system adapts to a wide range of soils. Its gray brown bark is characteristically fissured, both vertically and horizontally, to form a checkerboard pattern. The 3-6-inch, broadly oval leaves have bronzy or reddish color when new and turn yellow, pink, and red in autumn. Yellow to orange fruits are smaller (to 2 inches across) than Oriental persimmons and must be "ripened" by a hard frost (which removes their astringency) before they are palatable. Male and female flowers often appear on separate trees, so you'll need one of each for fruits to form. Some nurseries carry named varieties that have been selected for their superior fruit.

Dogwood (see Cornus, pp. 36-37)

Elaeagnus angustifolia

RUSSIAN OLIVE. Zones 3-9, but not satisfactory in humid eastern regions. A special virtue of the Russian olive is its ability to perform well in harsh climates where other trees wouldn't withstand the stress imposed by hot summers, cold winters, drought, or poor soil. Fortunately, it's a good-looking tree with plenty of individuality. The single or multiple trunks are covered with dark brown, shredding bark, against which the silver gray foliage contrasts nicely. Individual leaves are about 2 inches long and narrow, like those of willows or olives. Growth is upright but angular to a height of 20-25 feet with an equal spread. Sometimes the trunk and branches are thorny. (Some nurseries do sell thornless varieties.) Fragrant but inconspicuous, silvery yellow summer flowers are followed by berrylike fruits that resemble miniature olives. This tough tree also gives admirable service as a windbreak hedge.

Elm (see Ulmus, p. 61)

Erythrina

CORAL TREE. Many tropical and sub-tropical deciduous trees lose their leaves not in autumn but in winter or spring (sometimes only for a very brief period), often just before flowers appear. Most coral trees conform to this pattern.

Coral trees are thorny, with brilliant blossoms. Their strong trunk and branch structure give them a considerable "garden sculpture" value throughout the year. Leaves of all species consist of 3 oval leaflets. Flowers produce seedpods that contain colorful beanlike (and poisonous) seeds. Give all coral tree species well-drained soil and regular watering.

E. caffra. KAFFIRBOOM CORAL TREE. Zones 9-10. This species needs plenty of elbow room: height is 25-40 feet but spread is 40-60 feet, with conspicuous surface roots. Leaves shed in January; soon after, the angular, bare branches decorate themselves with large clusters of deep red orange, tubular flowers that drip honey. These flowers last for 4-6 weeks and then give way to a new crop of fresh, light green foliage. Because the leaf canopy often is dense, this species is a good summer shade tree. Vicious thorns on young wood disappear as the wood matures. This is the best species for seashore planting.

E. coralloides. NAKED CORAL TREE. Zones 9-10. A bit of late fall color is provided when the 8-10-inch leaves turn yellow before dropping. During winter you can appreciate the irregular, twisted branch pattern decked out in black thorns. Then from early to midspring, fiery red flowers in pine-conelike clusters are produced at the branch tips. When these finish, new leaves appear in time to provide summer shade. Tree size is about 30 feet high and wide, although you can control its spread by selectively cutting branches that reach too far.

E. crista-galli. COCKSPUR CORAL TREE. Zones 9-10. Cockspur coral will grow in colder regions (to Zone 8) but only as a shrubby perennial because frosts will kill it to the ground every year. Within the milder zones listed it will be a many-stemmed, rough-barked tree 15-20 feet tall and broad. Leaves are to 6 inches long, each leaflet a 2-3-inch oval. Blossoms appear in large, loose spikes at the tip of each branch after the tree has leafed out in spring. Because they are grown from seed, not all trees bear the same flower colors; the range of possibilities is from warm pink to wine red. In favorable locations you may get as many as three distinctive flowering periods from spring through fall.

E. humeana. NATAL CORAL TREE. Zones 8-10. Bright orange flowers, which shine like candles above the dark green foliage, appear in elongated clusters at branch tips almost continuously from late summer through most of autumn. Even small, young plants bear flowers. Trees reach about 30 feet high.

E. lysistemon. Zones 9-10. Heavy, angular branch structure develops into a tree to 40 feet tall and as much as 60 feet wide, broadly oval to nearly flat-topped. Black thorns are a decorative asset. Light orange to shrimp pink flowers appear off and on any time from October to May, occasionally with a few scattered in the summer months. Trees are very sensitive to water-logged soil.

E. sandwicensis. WILIWILI. Zones 9-10. This is a small Hawaiian native that hails from the drier parts of the islands. Growth is 15-30 feet high and widespreading; bloom season is spring. Not all trees have the same bloom color: colors include light red, bright orange to yellow, yellow green, and nearly white.

Fagus (Beech)

"Majestic" and "imposing" are appropriate adjectives for the beeches. They are not trees to work into the landscape but rather to work a landscape around. Their heavy shade and mass of surface roots rule out growth of other plants beneath. Since the natural growth form includes lower branches starting almost at the ground, the simplest way to use beeches is as specimen trees set on a lawn or at the background of a garden.

F. grandifolia. AMERICAN BEECH. Zones 4-10 (but not the desert), 4-9 in eastern regions. Our native beech is not as easy to find in nurseries as the European species (*F. sylvatica*), but that doesn't mean it is a poorer tree. It simply is a little more difficult to transplant, slow to establish, and doesn't have all the fancy-leafed varieties that the European species has. Slow growing, but eventually a magnificent tree to 100 feet, the American beech is narrower than the European species, forming a broad pyramid to oval shape. Bark is typical beech: thin, smooth, pale gray with irregular darker bands running horizontally. Leaves are prominently veined, pointed ovals in shape, and 3-5 inches long with distinct serration on the edges; new spring foliage is a lovely soft green color. Autumn frosts change them to golden brown, after which they remain on the tree into winter. Flowers are inconspicuous but later produce bristly burrs, each of which contains 2 or 3 edible nuts that are favored by various birds.

Trees tend to produce many suckers from the roots.

F. sylvatica. EUROPEAN BEECH. Zones 5-10 (but not good in hot, dry areas such as the Great Plains to southwest regions), 5-8 in eastern regions. These trees are similar in height (to 100 feet) to the American beech (*F. grandifolia*) but attain much greater spread (to 60 feet) and thicker trunks. Glossy dark green leaves, about 4 inches long, lack the definite serrated edges of the American species' leaves, and the bark, although of similar character, is darker gray. Shallow roots are sensitive to heavy foot traffic.

The many varieties with colored or differently shaped leaves have contributed greatly to the popularity of this species; the best known are those with bronze purple to purple foliage. The variety 'Atropunicea' (also sold as 'Riversii', 'Purpurea', 'Spaethiana', and probably other names) retains deep red purple to purple foliage throughout the season. When grown from seed, some color variation occurs, so that an unnamed purple-leafed plant may not compare in all respects with this variety; usually the seedlings become bronzy green in summer instead of retaining a purple color. The copper beach, sometimes offered as 'Cuprea', is a selected form of 'Atropunicea' and has lighter, bronzier young foliage. Variety 'Rohanii' has purple leaves with rounded lobes that resemble foliage of some oaks. Green-leafed forms with interesting leaf shapes include 'Asplenifolia', with narrow, finely divided (almost ferny) foliage, and 'Laciniata', the cutleaf European beech, with deeply cut but wider leaves. The variety 'Pendula', the weeping beech, has long branches that sweep to the ground in irregular, spreading form; unless the main trunk is staked upright it will grow wider than high. There's also a weeping purple beech: 'Purpureo-pendula'. Aphid infestations sometimes are a problem with European beeches.

Ficus carica

FIG. Zones 7-10; in the East, a shrub in Zone 7, and may be killed to the ground there and in eastern Zone 8. Although edible fig is not a tropical native, its bold leaves can lend an exotic touch to colder gardens. Fairly rapid growth gives you a spreading tree 15-30 feet tall. You can train it to a single trunk or let it branch low for a multiple-trunked or shrub-tree effect. Winter branch pattern is especially attractive because of the smooth, light gray bark and relative simplicity of branching (the trees are not particularly twiggy); older trees become more gnarled with the picturesque appearance of great age. Rough-textured bright green leaves may reach 9 inches long and nearly as wide, with 3-5 large lobes; they cast a dense shade.

Roots are close to the surface, so plant your fig where you won't need to cultivate underneath it; fruit drop can be messy on pavement. Other than a need for good

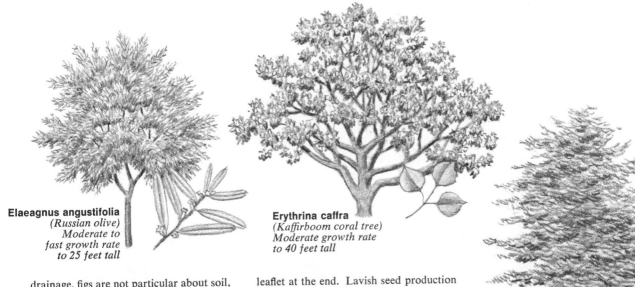

Elaeagnus angustifolia
(Russian olive)
Moderate to
fast growth rate
to 25 feet tall

Erythrina caffra
(Kaffirboom coral tree)
Moderate growth rate
to 40 feet tall

Fagus grandifolia
(American beech)
Slow growth rate
to 100 feet tall

drainage, figs are not particular about soil, and established trees are quite drought tolerant. In the colder zones of the tree's adaptability, shelter it from winter winds. If you're interested in heavy fruit production, avoid using high-nitrogen fertilizers, for they stimulate growth at the expense of fruit. There are many named fig varieties, differing in fruit color and flavor, tree size, and, most important, in climate adaptability. Check with a good local nursery operator or agricultural extension agent for varieties that are most suited to your particular region.

Franklinia alatamaha

FRANKLINIA. Zones 6-9 (but not desert regions), 6-8 in the East. Apparently this tree was on the verge of extinction when it was discovered in Georgia in the late 18th century, for no wild plants have been seen since around 1800. It is a camellia relative with white flowers that resemble 3-inch, single camellia blossoms. One of its characteristics is unusual for a flowering tree: its blossoms appear in late summer and early fall—sometimes coinciding with the tree's red to orange fall foliage color. Autumn color is better if soil moisture is reduced toward the end of summer. Oblong or spoon-shaped leaves are 4-6 inches long and a glossy bright green during spring and summer; spring leaf-out is late. Upright, slender growth reaches 20-30 feet high and 10 feet wide at a slow to moderate rate, often branching low. Bark on the trunk and branches is reddish brown. Franklinia prefers the same growing conditions as camellias and rhododendrons: well-drained, acid to neutral soil, regular water, and partial shade. Where summers are hot and dry, it is not a good risk. If you choose this tree, plant it where it will be protected from winter winds.

Fraxinus (Ash)

Fast, tough, and undemanding, ashes have widespread use, particularly in regions where climate extremes pose hardships to many other plants. All ashes have oval, pointed leaflets growing opposite one another along the leafstalk, with a single leaflet at the end. Lavish seed production (each seed is contained in a narrow, flattened "wing") results in excessive germination of seeds. Many ash species have male and female flowers on separate trees, with the female trees producing the seeds. To get around excessive seed germination, nurseries have looked for and named some seedless male varieties which are the best to plant if available.

F. americana. WHITE ASH. Zones 4-9. A broadly oval form and a height of 80 feet or more make this species a good shade tree on a large piece of property. Where it has room, it's quite handsome. Leaves are 8-15 inches long, consisting of 5-9 dark green leaflets with pale undersides. Autumn color is purplish yellow, more purple in colder climates. Dark gray brown bark on the tall, straight trunk is fissured into a narrow diamond pattern. Two selected male (and therefore seedless) varieties are 'Autumn Purple' (its name describes the fall foliage) and 'Rosehill', which has red fall foliage.

F. excelsior. EUROPEAN ASH. Zones 4-10. (4-9 in eastern regions). Lack of any fall color is this species' shortcoming when compared to the white ash (*F. americana*). Otherwise, it is a round-headed specimen of similarly majestic proportions—to 80 feet or more in the garden and much over 100 in its native haunts. Leaves are up to a foot long, containing 7-11 dark green (but paler beneath), oval, toothed leaflets. But the most distinctive feature is the winter color of its growth buds: black. A selected male variety, 'Kimberly', is a good shade tree, especially in the coldest zones of adaptability. The weeping European ash ('Pendula'), forms a stiffly drooping, irregular umbrella. (Not a tree on its own, the variety must be grafted at any height onto an upright trunk of the regular European ash.)

F. holotricha. Zones 6-10. This species is known chiefly by its variety 'Moraine', a nearly seedless form. Considerably smaller than most ashes, the trees are upright and rather narrow, growing in the 35-40-foot range. The dull green leaves consist of 9-13 toothed leaflets (each about 3 inches long) that turn yellow in autumn.

Ficus carica
(Fig)
Fast growth rate
to 30 feet tall

Franklinia alatamaha
Slow to moderate growth rate
to 30 feet tall

To find your climate zone, see page 96

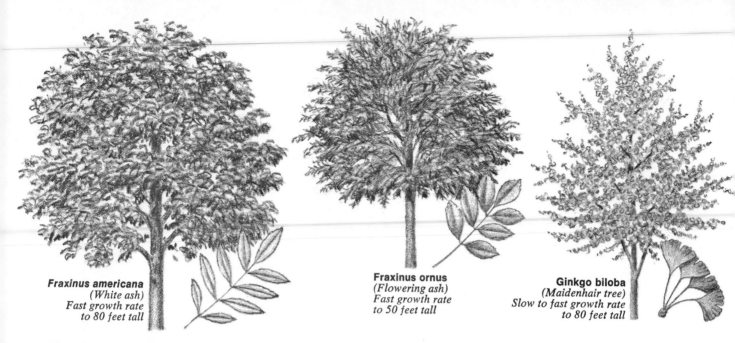

Fraxinus americana
(White ash)
Fast growth rate
to 80 feet tall

Fraxinus ornus
(Flowering ash)
Fast growth rate
to 50 feet tall

Ginkgo biloba
(Maidenhair tree)
Slow to fast growth rate
to 80 feet tall

Then they obligingly fall, dry up, and sift down into lawn, ground cover, or earth beneath. Growth is rapid; shade is light and filtered.

F. latifolia. OREGON ASH. Zones 7-10. Though 40-80 feet high may seem large, a fairly narrow habit puts Oregon ash more within the scope of most medium-sized gardens than either the white *(F. americana)* or European *(F. excelsior)* ashes. Its typical ash leaves are up to a foot long with 5-7 light green, oval leaflets. They depart from the usual ash leaf form in that the end leaflet is distinctly longer and wider than those on the sides. Male and female flowers form on separate trees, but female trees may have to be as much as 30 years old before they produce a crop. And even after that, they produce heavy crops only once in every several years. They will also tolerate water standing around roots in winter. In parts of its native Oregon, the tree is subject to a variety of insect and disease problems that make it a poor candidate for gardens there.

F. ornus. FLOWERING ASH. Zones 6-8. The common name points out this species' most striking difference from other ashes: flowers with petals. Actually, all ashes do have flowers, but this one has clusters of them that put on a really fine show of fluffy white in spring. Individual blossoms are small but come in 3-5-inch-long clusters—and they're fragrant, too. The seed clusters that follow on all trees of this species hang on well into winter after foliage has dropped.

Although its leaves follow the usual ash pattern—7-11 oval leaflets on a leaf to 10 inches long—they are a bright, shiny green and appear in copious quantities that cast quite a dense shade. In autumn they change to shades of soft yellow and lavender. The tree's height is 40-60 feet, its broadly rounded form extending to about 30 feet wide.

F. pennsylvanica. RED ASH; and *F. p. lanceolata,* GREEN ASH. Zones 3-8. Dif-ferences between the red and green ashes are very slight: green ash has smooth leaflets and twigs; those of red ash are covered with short hairs. Red ash also has slightly wider and longer leaflets of a duller green color. Growth of both ashes is a dense, compact oval, to 60 feet tall and about half as wide. Bark on older trees has distinct ridges that intersect to form elongated diamond patterns. Heavy seed crops are the rule whenever male and female trees grow near one another, and the seedlings that develop from them can be a particular nuisance. To circumvent the problem, look for the variety 'Marshall's Seedless', which has no seeds but still maintains all the good qualities of the green ash from which it was selected. It has dark, glossy green leaves and a uniform shape. All have yellow fall foliage.

F. velutina. ARIZONA or VELVET ASH. Zones 8-10. The "velvet" is a gray fuzz that covers the young twigs and leaves. Young trees are pyramidal, but the shape becomes more rounded and open as mature height of 40-50 feet is reached. Leaves consist of 3-5 narrowly oval leaflets, each about 3 inches long. This is an especially useful shade tree where summers are long, hot, and dry, and where soils are alkaline. It is the species (with its varieties) used most in desert areas.

The Montebello ash (subspecies *F. v. corlacea*) has broader, more leathery leaves. Probably the most widely planted form is the Modesto ash, 'Modesto'. It forms a broad, rounded, and spreading crown to 50 feet high and wide. Leaves are bright green (but without the characteristic fuzz of the species), turning bright yellow in autumn. Following a wet spring, the foliage may appear scorched, a problem caused by the anthracnose fungus. (See page 25 for suggested treatment.) Because branches tend to form narrow, V-shaped crotches, the Modesto ash may be damaged in storms or high winds more easily than other ashes. The variety 'Rio Grande', the Fantex ash, is a good choice for the hot, dry climate and alkaline soils of much of the Southwest. Its leaves are larger and darker green than the Modesto ash and appear earlier in the spring. Fall color is yellow.

Ginkgo biloba

GINKGO, MAIDENHAIR TREE. Zones 5-10 (but can have marginal leaf burn during summer in the desert), 5-9 in eastern regions. Fossil records indicate that many millions of years ago, a number of ginkgo species flourished around the world. Yet only this single species has persisted to be enjoyed by modern man. Perhaps part of the secret to its survival through the ages is adaptability: it thrives in a great variety of climates and soils, wanting only good drainage, and it is virtually pest free, presumably having simply outlived any former enemies. The leaves are unmistakable, shaped like an open paper fan on a stick—just like the "leaflets" of a maidenhair fern (or, as the Chinese say, shaped like a duck's foot). The top of the "fan" is wavy edged and shallow to deep clefted in the center; size varies from 1-4 inches across the widest part. Autumn color is brief but dazzling: absolutely pure, brilliant yellow; then leaves fall all at once. Spring leaf-out is fairly late. Growth habit—unless you buy one of the named selections (below)—is irregular and rather unpredictable but more or less upright. In addition to planting a single ginkgo tree, you can grow ginkgos as low-branched or multi-trunked specimens—or even plant several in a clump. Young trees often go through an "awkward stage," during which growth is not particularly symmetrical. As trees age, however, the basic outline becomes more and more regular. In general, ginkgos grow upright to 60-80 feet and not more than half as wide; but some may end up distinctly narrower, more spreading, or even umbrella shaped.

**Gleditsia triacanthos
inermis 'Moraine'**
*(Thornless honey locust)
Fast growth rate
to 60 feet tall*

Gymnocladus dioica
*(Kentucky coffee tree)
Moderate growth rate
to 70 feet tall*

Halesia carolina
*(Carolina silver bell)
Moderate growth rate
to 30 feet tall*

Male and female reproductive parts (you can't really say "flowers") are on separate trees. When a male is nearby, female trees produce quantities of ½-inch, plum-shaped yellowish fruits that enclose an edible nut; but when fruits drop and the fleshy covering bursts, they emit a powerfully repulsive odor. Because of this, most people prefer to plant male trees (seedling trees are a gamble, since they don't reach reproductive age for many years). Nurseries sell several named varieties that are male and of a more certain growth pattern. 'Autumn Gold' is eventually a broad spreading tree; 'Fairmount' grows rapidly and is shaped like a pyramid. The sentry ginkgo, *G. b. fastigiata,* forms a narrow, very upright column. Rate of growth varies. With casual care they are rather slow; but if treated to regular watering and fertilizing, they may put on as much as 3 feet per year. The bark of young trees may sunburn where exposed to hot summer sun. If that is a possibility in your area, keep the trunk wrapped (see page 17) until bark has thickened for a few years.

Gleditsia triacanthos inermis

THORNLESS HONEY LOCUST. Zones 5-9. The word *inermis* means "unarmed"—in this case, without thorns—which is one good reason to avoid the "armed" species and plant only one of the thornless selections. Another reason is that the thornless forms have few (or none) of the 1-1½-foot-long seed pods that form in quantities on the species and create a messy litter. Many outstanding qualities favor planting of thornless honey locusts. They grow quickly, root deeply, and cast only filtered shade (allowing growth of other plants beneath). They are not bothered by hot summers or cold winters, growing best where these extremes prevail. They tolerate both acid and alkaline soils and (when

established) drought. Leaves dry up and disintegrate after falling, so you have little or no litter problem. Late to leaf out in spring, the thornless honey locust also is one of the first to shed in fall, turning a light yellow before it does. Each fernlike leaf is up to 10 inches long and consists of opposite pairs of oval leaflets to 1½ inches long. In the South the trees may be bothered by mimosa web worm and borers.

Named selections are the best buy because you can be more sure of their growth habits and sizes; seedling trees are likely to be irregular. 'Imperial' is upright and spreading to about 35 feet, with denser foliage than other named varieties. 'Moraine' grows to 60 feet or so, with upward and outward-angled branches that form a somewhat spreading, vase-shaped tree. Deep red new growth that darkens to a bronzed green is a feature of 'Rubylace', a smaller and slower-growing tree than the two previous varieties. 'Shademaster' grows faster than 'Moraine' and is more definitely vase shaped. 'Shademaster' has even been recommended as a substitute for disease-prone American elm (*Ulmus americana*). Its dark green leaves hang on longer in autumn than those of other varieties. 'Skyline' forms a 50-foot, narrow pyramid. Golden yellow new foliage is the hallmark of 'Sunburst'. Its leaves gradually turn green, but new growth is produced into midsummer so there is a long period of gold-on-green contrast (some people think it looks chlorotic). Bark on young trees sunburns easily; keep trunks wrapped (see page 11) until branches grow long enough to shade the trunk.

Gymnocladus dioica

KENTUCKY COFFEE TREE. Zones 5-9 (5-8 in eastern regions). Related to the thornless honey locust (*Gleditsia*), Kentucky coffee tree is best used as a structural specimen—a piece of garden sculpture—rather

than for shade. Branches are few and inclined to be somewhat contorted on mature trees; winter silhouette looks like the basic skeleton of a tree without twigs. Growth is rapid in early years but then slows down, eventually producing a 50-70-foot tree that spreads only about half as wide. Although leaf size sounds impressive—to 3 feet long and 2 feet wide—leaves don't look at all imposing because they are subdivided into so many 1-3-inch leaflets. New spring foliage is pinkish, becoming deep green in summer and turning yellow early in autumn. It sheds in two stages: first the leaflets drop, leaving the leafstalks behind; later, the leafstalks fall to the ground like a multitude of sticks. Female trees, when pollinated by a nearby male, form flat pods to 10 inches long that remain on the branches into winter; male flowers are fragrant, but neither male nor female flowers are showy. Established trees withstand some drought, much heat and cold, and poor soil.

Halesia (Silver bell)

Size is the basic difference between the two silver bell species. The first, *H. carolina,* is a small tree that may be shrubby unless trained; the second, *H. monticola,* is a much taller tree. Both grow best in cool, good soil containing plenty of organic matter and with ample water.

H. carolina. CAROLINA SILVER BELL, SNOWDROP TREE. Zones 5-9 (but not desert), 5-8 in eastern regions. This is a 30-foot, arching tree with a spread perhaps as wide as the height. Its big show comes just as leaves are emerging: clusters of white, bell-shaped, ½-inch flowers hang all along the branches. After fading, the flowers form attractive 4-winged pods that remain on the tree into the following winter. Oval, 4-inch leaves change to an attractive yellow in autumn. Young trees may need some guidance (staking and perhaps pruning) to keep from growing lopsided toward the source of light, and pruning to a single stem if you don't want multiple trunks.

H. monticola. MOUNTAIN SILVER BELL. Zones 5-9 (but not desert). General characteristics are about the same as those of the Carolina silver bell (*H. carolina*), but because this species is larger in all ways, it stands out in the landscape. Height is about 60 feet, leaves reach about 6½ inches long, and flower bells are 1 inch long. The drooping flower clusters are reminiscent of cherry blossoms. Some specimens, offered as *H. m. rosea*, have pale pink flowers (at least when they first open).

Hawthorn (see Crataegus, pp. 37-39)

Jacaranda acutifolia

JACARANDA. Zones 9-10. It's not always easy to pin down jacaranda's characteristics. Usually an open, rather irregular tree to 40 feet tall and as much as 30 feet wide, it can have several trunks or even be shrubby. Guide growth of young plants to the form you want. Leaves usually drop in late winter, and the branches remain bare until flowering time. But new foliage may sprout again right after old leaves fall. Although blossoms usually appear in late spring, they may appear earlier or decide to open any time throughout the summer. Leaves are finely divided and fernlike because they consist of so many tiny leaflets. Flowers are lavender blue, each 2 inches long and tubular, appearing in thick, 8-inch-long clusters; nurseries sometimes carry a white-flowered variety. Attractive seedpods that follow blooms are nearly round, flattened, and woody. This is not a tree for the cool or foggy semitropical areas, for it needs warmth in order to produce its spectacular flower display. Though not really particular about soils, it grows best in sandy soil with deep (but infrequent) watering. Young trees suffer damage at 25° or below but may sprout back to grow as many-stemmed, shrubby specimens. Don't set out new plants in spring until after the last frost.

Juglans (Walnut)

You can count on walnuts to leaf out late in spring and drop their foliage before too much of autumn elapses. Trees are large and cast dense shade. And although growth is upright and spreading, there is a tendency for some branches to grow downward and then arch back up; keep these pruned off if they would make the crown too low. Branch structure is heavy limbed with relatively few, but thick, twigs. Male flower tassels are noticeable in spring when leaves emerge, but they can't be considered showy; they also cause a highly allergic reaction in some people. Aphids may be a problem.

J. hindsii. CALIFORNIA BLACK WALNUT. Zones 7-9. Generally a single, straight trunk grows 30-50 feet high, the branches spreading to about half the height. It is a finer-textured tree than *J. regia* because of its much narrower leaflets. Each leaf is

composed of an odd number of leaflets (usually 15-19), each 3-5 inches long but less than 1 inch wide. This is a good-looking tree, drought tolerant when established, with fine yellow fall color. Because it is resistant to oak root fungus (*Armillaria*), it is often used as rootstock for English walnut varieties that are susceptible to the disease in the West. The nut crop is unimportant.

J. nigra. BLACK WALNUT. Zones 5-8. Though common in the eastern United States, black walnut isn't a good candidate for garden planting, since its roots (and decomposing leaves) exude a toxic substance that inhibits or prevents the growth of many nearby ornamental plants. Ultimate height is 100-150 feet, rounded, with 2-foot-long leaves composed of 15-23 narrow leaflets that are downy on their undersides. Nuts have excellent flavor but are hard to crack; occasionally you will find named varieties that have been selected for thinner-shelled nuts.

J. regia. ENGLISH (or Persian) WALNUT. Zones 7 (warmest parts)-9. This is the tree that produces commercial walnuts. It's smaller (to about 60 feet high) but bulkier looking than the previous species (*J. nigra*). Leaves have about 7 leaflets, the largest up to 8 inches long and 4 inches across. Branching tends to be low and spreading to horizontal, forming a broadly rounded crown without a well-defined central leader (see sketch, page 21). To produce the best nuts, trees should have periodic deep watering, best accomplished by irrigating in a broad basin surrounding the tree. Homeowners who have old orchard-grown walnut trees in their garden need to take some precautions to keep the trees healthy: trees need deep soil moisture (best accomplished by irrigating in a broad basin) but must have bases of trunks dry to avoid disease. If a lawn grows beneath your tree, remove soil around the trunk down to the level of the first roots and replace with coarse gravel or rock. Or pave the area near the trunk with bricks or stone *set in sand* (not mortar). Don't grow plants beneath this tree's branches. Nuts (somewhere between golf and tennis ball size) are encased in round, green husks that split open in fall and drop the ripe nuts to the ground. Many named varieties exist, their performance varying according to climate. A good local nursery or agricultural extension agent will be able to suggest those best adapted to your area. For the coldest regions of this walnut's adaptability, a good bet is the Carpathian walnut, which is simply a strain of this species grown from seeds originally collected in Central European mountains. A few named varieties of this strain are selected for their superior nut quality. Late spring frosts are a hazard to new growth on walnut trees.

Koelreuteria

Yellow flowers in summer, seedpods that resemble Oriental paper lanterns, and gen-

Jacaranda acutifolia
Moderate growth rate to 40 feet tall

eral good garden manners are the outstanding attributes of the following two species.

K. henryi. CHINESE FLAME TREE. Zones 9-10. "Chinese flame" refers to the clusters of 2-inch orange, red, or salmon lanternlike seed capsules that light up the tree in late summer and fall. Growth is upright but spreading (20-40 feet or more), becoming flat topped after many years. Leaves are 1-2 feet long but divided into many small, oval leaflets that turn yellow late in autumn. You can grow other plants beneath this tree because it has deep, uninvasive roots. Chinese flame tree is not particular about soils and requires only moderate watering.

K. paniculata. GOLDENRAIN TREE. Zones 5-9 (5-8 in eastern regions). As if to compensate for its lack of autumn color, goldenrain's emerging spring leaves are salmon red. Each leaf is up to 15 inches long with 7-15 oval but lobed or toothed leaflets to 3 inches long. The tree's principal period of glory is in summer when the 15-25-foot tree billows with large clusters of yellow blossoms. The fruits that follow bloom are lanternlike and red when young but mature to buff to brown shades. Young trees need regular watering, but older ones are quite drought tolerant. In addition, the tree thrives in a wide range of soils (including alkaline) and in heat, cold, and wind.

Laburnum watereri

GOLDENCHAIN TREE. Zones 5-9 (5-7 in eastern regions). This tree is a hybrid of two other *Laburnum* species: *L. alpinum* and *L. anagyroides*. It is more graceful than its parents, with longer flower clusters, and has largely replaced them in garden plantings. But if it were not for the spectacular display of yellow, wisterialike blossom clusters to 20 inches long, even this might not be a first-rate ornamental. For one thing, all parts of the plant are poisonous. The brown pods that follow the blossoms hang on until winter unless picked off; removal is a good idea because

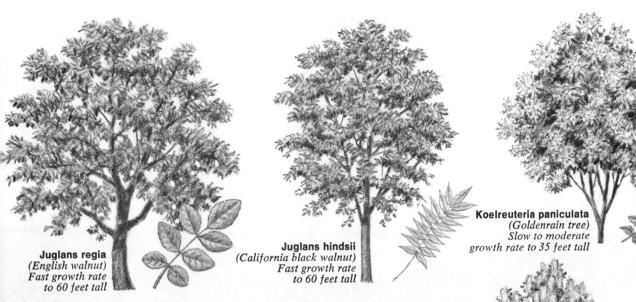

Juglans regia
(English walnut)
Fast growth rate
to 60 feet tall

Juglans hindsii
(California black walnut)
Fast growth rate
to 60 feet tall

Koelreuteria paniculata
(Goldenrain tree)
Slow to moderate
growth rate to 35 feet tall

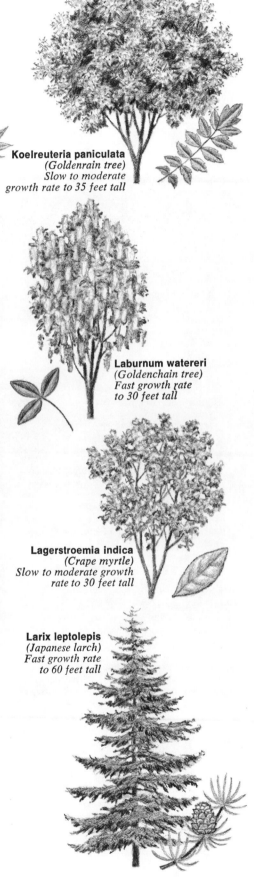

Laburnum watereri
(Goldenchain tree)
Fast growth rate
to 30 feet tall

Lagerstroemia indica
(Crape myrtle)
Slow to moderate growth
rate to 30 feet tall

Larix leptolepis
(Japanese larch)
Fast growth rate
to 60 feet tall

a heavy seed crop is a strain on the tree. The root system does not always provide good anchorage. Green, 3-leaflet leaves resemble clover but have no autumn color.

When the tree is trained to a single trunk, growth form is vase shaped to about 25 feet high and about half as wide. When allowed to develop several trunks, the tree will be broader. The variety 'Vossii' is a more graceful selection of this hybrid. Where summers are hot and humid, foliage may be troubled by leaf spot fungi. Mature trees sometimes die suddenly for no apparent reason. In hot and dry summer regions of the lower Midwest, the tree's chances of survival are poor.

Lagerstroemia indica

CRAPE MYRTLE. Zones 7-9. Showy to almost gaudy flower clusters are crape myrtle's claim to attention during the summer months. Individually, the blossoms are small and crapelike, but they're carried in dense clusters to 1 foot long at branch tips, with smaller clusters appearing lower on the stems. Color range includes shades of red, rose, pink, orchid to lavender, purple and white. Nurseries offer some named varieties, but more often you'll find plants just labeled according to flower color. Flowers aren't crape myrtle's only asset. In autumn the 1-2-inch oval leaves turn yellow, orange, or red, the colors more pronounced when trees are grown on the dry side. And at all times of the year the bark is attractive—smooth gray to light brown in color and flaking off to reveal patches of pinkish inner bark. Trained to a single trunk, crape myrtle becomes a 30-foot, round-topped, and rather vase-shaped tree; in the colder limits of its range it often is shrubby. Warm to hot summers are necessary for the best flower production. More flower-producing wood is encouraged if branches are cut back lightly during the dormant season. Cool climates encourage mildew on the leaves. Foliage also is likely to become chlorotic where soils are alkaline.

Larix

LARCH. The larch stands among the elite—being one of the few cone-bearing, needle-leafed trees that is deciduous. Most other needle-leafed trees are evergreen; you'll find them described on pages 82-93. (Other deciduous conifers are *Metasequoia*, page 50; *Taxodium*, page 60.)

The larches are mostly high altitude and/or high latitude trees, growing best where summers are cool and winters cool to cold. They have much the same pyramidal shape as the other needle-leafed evergreens with which they frequently grow. In nature they form a striking fall picture when they change color, suddenly lighting up the dark conifer forests with brilliant yellow to orange.

Soft needles are carried in clusters on all but vigorous new shoots, where they appear singly. Cones resemble small rose flowers and persist on the tree during winter to create a polka dot pattern among the bare branches. Larches are not particular about soil and will get along with regular lawn watering. Larch canker can be a serious problem, especially where a number of the trees grow together. The canker is recognized by swollen blisters on the bark that ooze pitch. About the only control is to cut out infected branches and burn them.

L. decidua. EUROPEAN LARCH. Zones 3-8. Of the larches, this species has the lightest green foliage—a fresh grass green. Moderate to fast growth gives you a 30-60-foot tree in the garden (higher in the wild). The shape of young specimens is pyramidal, but older trees develop wide spreading branches.

L. laricina. ALPINE or AMERICAN LARCH: TAMARACK. Zones 3-6. In mountains and in the northern states where it is native, this species will grow satisfactorily, reaching about 60 feet tall. In warmer regions, the Japanese larch (*L. leptolepis*) would be a better choice.

L. leptolepis. JAPANESE LARCH. Zones 5-8. Fast growth gives you a bluish green,

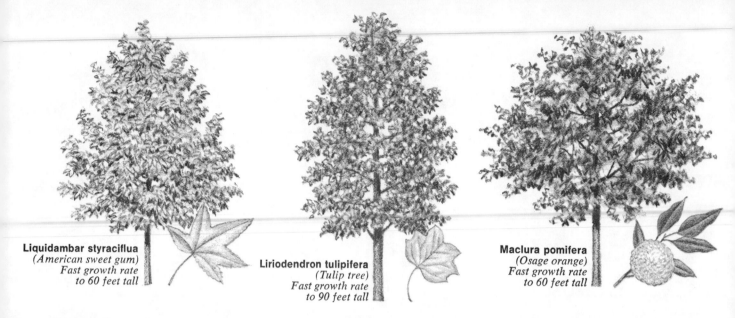

Liquidambar styraciflua
(American sweet gum)
Fast growth rate
to 60 feet tall

Liriodendron tulipifera
(Tulip tree)
Fast growth rate
to 90 feet tall

Maclura pomifera
(Osage orange)
Fast growth rate
to 60 feet tall

wide-spreading tree to 60 feet high or even more. This species has the most resistance to larch canker.

L. occidentalis. WESTERN LARCH. Zones 6-7. Native to mountains of the Pacific Coast and eastward into the Rocky Mountains, western larch forms a rather narrow pyramid of sharp, stiff, bright green needles. Although much taller in the wild, it grows at a moderate rate to 30-50 feet high in the garden.

Linden (see Tilia, pp. 60-61)

Liquidambar styraciflua

AMERICAN SWEET GUM. Zones 6-10 (but foliage burns in desert heat), 6-9 in eastern regions. At first glance you might mistake this tree for a maple: its foliage is 5-lobed like some "typical" maples, and the fall color includes shades of brilliant red, orange, or yellow. But quite unmaplelike are the seeds (carried in hanging, 1-1½-inch balls covered with points like a medieval mace) and corky ridges that are present on young twigs and branches. In its native southeastern United States, the sweet gum grows fairly rapidly to great height when in deep, moist soils. Garden trees will grow fastest with ample water (the amount you give a lawn) but usually to no more than about 60 feet high and 40 feet wide. Even in rather poorly drained soils they will grow well. Trees are pyramid shaped and fairly narrow, maintaining a tall, straight trunk for many years. Grove plantings are especially attractive. Only in maturity do the trees become more round topped and filled out, the branches then thickening and becoming more pronounced. The leaves tend to wilt quickly in areas subject to drying winds. In alkaline soils trees may develop chlorosis (see page 25).

Fall color varies in seedling trees (the ones usually offered in nurseries), but several named selections guarantee a particular color. 'Burgundy' becomes deep purple red in autumn, and the leaves hang on into winter unless storms knock them off. A more nearly columnar tree is 'Festival', whose foliage turns to shades of yellow, pink, and orange. 'Palo Alto' exhibits the flaming maple tints of orange and red. Fall color is less brilliant in mild autumns and in mild-winter areas. In the Northwest, the branches may be easily broken in ice storms.

Liriodendron tulipifera

Zones 5-9 (but not the desert). For the large garden where its ultimate great size won't look uncomfortably giant, the tulip tree will become a good shademaker as well as conversation piece. Its leaves—variously described as lyre shaped, saddle shaped, and truncated—are outstanding. They're like broadly lobed maple leaves with one too many (or one too few) lobes, so that their ends are nearly straight across except for a dip in the middle. The blossoms ("tulips") that appear on trees that are 10 or more years old are cup shaped like 2-inch tulips in green and orange. But since they bloom among the leaves, they are not really showy, especially since trees grow rather rapidly and a 10-year-old will have its leaves well in the air.

Although much taller in the wild, garden trees reach 60-90 feet, spreading about half as wide, with a straight, columnar trunk. Autumn color is a clear, soft yellow, even in mildest climates. They prefer a deep, rich, neutral to acid soil and plenty of summer water. But they will succeed in soils that are rather poorly drained. There is a variety, 'Fastigiata', that is densely columnar in growth.

Locust (see Robinia, p. 57)

Maclura pomifera

OSAGE ORANGE. Zones 5-9. If you live where climate runs to extremes of heat, cold strong winds, and drought and where the soil is poor, perhaps even alkaline, then this is the tree for you. It will thrive with no coddling. A feature that helps it survive harsh environments is an expansive, greedy root system. Of course, growth is also good in areas that have much better growing conditions; but the tree really shines where the "bad" elements conspire to rule out many other plants.

Fast growth will reach 50-60 feet high with equal spread and a fairly dense and somewhat irregular habit, typically branching low to the ground and often suckering from the roots. With trimming, an osage orange hedge can be maintained as an impenetrable barrier of any height from 6 feet up. Sharp, 1-inch-long thorns on young branches account for its popularity as a farm or range hedge in place of barbed wire. If you want a thornless variety, try *M. p.* 'Inermis'. Glossy, medium green leaves are 6-inch, pointed ovals that turn yellow before dropping in autumn. If you break a leaf stem or leaf, it will exude a milky juice that irritates the skin of some people. In warm to hot summer regions when both male and female plants are in the same garden, the females will produce 3-4-inch round, inedible fruits that resemble bumpy, greenish oranges.

Magnolia

MAGNOLIA. (Sometimes incorrectly called "tulip tree"; for the real tulip tree, see *Liriodendron*, p. 46.) The delicate beauty of magnolia blossoms is perhaps the most elegant offering to spring that any flowering tree provides. Thick, waxy petals and pleasant fragrance are typical in blossoms of most species. Seed structures that follow flowers are elongated and cylindrical, shaped something like a cucumber, and studded with orange red seeds when ripe. Some magnolias grow rapidly into very large trees (a few of the evergreen sorts have even been used for timber). But several of the most popular species are shrubby for a number of years.

Deciduous magnolias fall into two groups: those that flower on bare branches

Magnolia cordata
(Yellow cucumber tree)
Fast growth rate
to 30 feet tall

Magnolia loebneri 'Merrill'
Fast growth rate to 50 feet tall

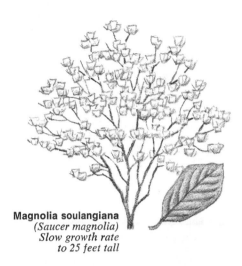

Magnolia soulangiana
(Saucer magnolia)
Slow growth rate
to 25 feet tall

before leaves come out in spring and those that blossom later when trees are in full leaf. Where late frosts are not unusual, the first group occasionally may have flowers damaged, especially if planted in a sheltered location that warms up early in spring and encourages earliest bloom. A more exposed or cooler garden location will avoid this problem as much as possible. None of these magnolias that blossom when branches are bare of leaves will be happy in the desert or in any other hot, dry, windy area (a possible exception is *M. soulangiana*). Best soil for magnolias is fairly rich, neutral to slightly acid, and well drained so that you can supply plenty of water without suffocating roots; if possible, add generous amounts of organic matter when you plant.

You can grow magnolias where soil is on the alkaline side, but you may have to contend with chlorosis because of unavailability of iron. To correct this, periodically treat soil with iron chelates. Where salts are present in the soil—because of the soil's chemistry or because of watering or fertilizer—regular deep watering will flush them from the root zone as long as drainage is good.

Best locations are in a lawn (with a good-sized, grass-free area around the tree) or in a shrub border that won't be subject to digging; magnolia roots are shallow, often fleshy, and easily damaged. Magnolias always will appreciate a cooling mulch over the root area. If new trees are big enough to offer much wind resistance, stake them to prevent rocking and subsequent tearing of the fleshy roots. Prune magnolias as little as possible; cuts heal slowly.

M. acuminata. CUCUMBER TREE. Zones 5-10, 6-8 in eastern regions. This species is the exception to the typical magnolia rule of showy blossoms: tulip-shaped, 3-inch flowers are present, but their greenish yellow color in late spring is not conspicuous among the fully grown foliage. The species' value is as a fast-growing, pyra-

midal shade tree. Mature specimens reach 60-80 feet and about 30 feet wide, becoming round headed with age. Shade is dense, cast by handsome leaves that are pointed ovals 5-11 inches long and 6 inches across. Before falling in autumn, the leaves turn pale yellow. Bark on old trees is ridged and deeply furrowed.

M. cordata. YELLOW CUCUMBER TREE. Zones 6-9. As the common name implies, this species resembles *M. acuminata* except that its yellower blossoms are showier. For garden purposes, it can be looked upon as a nearly half-size version of *M. acuminata*: leaves are only half as large (to 6 inches long), and height is only to about 30 feet. Fast growth makes it a good shade tree for the small to moderate-sized garden.

M. denudata. YULAN MAGNOLIA. Zones 6-10. After this tree is about 7 years old, it begins to produce creamy white, fragrant cupped blossoms, 6-7 inches across, before leaves unfold each spring. A moderate rate of growth leads to a 40-foot tree of rounded to irregular habit. Medium green, oval leaves, downy on their undersides, are up to 7 inches long.

M. loebneri 'Merrill'. Zones 5-10, 5-9 in eastern regions. This is a hybrid magnolia in which the blossoms of one parent (the shrubby and slow-growing star magnolia) have been retained on a fast-growing tree guaranteed to flower at an early age (about 5 years old). Before leaves emerge, this tree blossoms into 4-inch white flowers, each having 12-18 fairly slender petals. Habit is openly pyramidal to an eventual 50 feet high and about half as wide. Leaves are rich green ovals, about 4 inches long and widest toward the tip.

M. macrophylla. BIGLEAF MAGNOLIA. Zones 6-9. Considering the tropically gigantic leaves and flowers it's hard to believe that this magnolia is native to the United States. The leaves really are big: from 1-3 feet long and up to 1 foot across. The equally impressive, creamy white, 12-inch (or larger) blossoms (some with pur-

ple blotches at the base of petals) appear in late spring or early summer as leaves are maturing. Because of its leaf size, plant the tree only where it will be sheltered from wind. Otherwise, much of the magnificence will be lost to a wind-tattered appearance. Plants are 12-15 years old before they flower.

M. salicifolia. ANISE MAGNOLIA. Zones 6-9. Graceful, slender, upright to pyramidal growth builds fairly slowly to an eventual 30 feet, making this species a good candidate for planting in the foreground of other taller trees. Narrow-petaled, white flowers to 4 inches across appear before the leaves come out; larger blooms are produced by its variety 'Else Frye'. The species may need up to 10 years to begin flowering, but another variety, 'W. B. Clarke', produces heavy crops of blossoms at an early age. Smooth, lance-shaped leaves smell like anise when crushed.

M. sargentiana robusta. Zones 8-10. This tree differs from the basic species, *M. sargentiana,* because it is a smaller tree with larger flowers and leaves and a better ornamental for most gardens. It also blooms at an earlier age, when plants are about 10 years old. It grows to a rounded tree to 35 feet high and wide. Before the 5-8-inch leaves emerge in spring, it produces breathtaking bluish pink, bowl-shaped blossoms up to 1 foot across. Flowers face upward at first but later bend down to a horizontal position.

M. soulangiana. SAUCER MAGNOLIA. Zones 5 (warmer parts)-10. For many years, this hybrid magnolia will function as a rather open, many-stemmed shrub. But where most shrubs would stop growing, the saucer magnolia grows on to 25 feet or more high with an equal or greater spread. Raising a saucer magnolia requires patience and advance planning—advance planning because you'll want it to have enough room when it becomes tree size yet not look out of place during the years it is small.

To find your climate zone, see page 96

Cup-shaped blossoms about 6 inches across are produced each spring (before leaves come out) after trees are only 3-5 years old. Because it is a hybrid plant, flower color varies from white through pink to purplish red in seedling plants. For guarantee of particular colors, buy one of the many named sorts offered by nurseries. Late spring frosts can ruin the blossoms. If late frosts do occur in your area, plant one of the late flowering varieties such as 'Lennei'. Foliage is light to medium green, oval, and to 6 inches long, turning brown before dropping in autumn. The structure of the gray branches forms attractive patterns in the winter garden. Some desert gardeners have succeeded with this magnolia but only with special attention to soil, water, and a sheltered location.

M. sprengeri diva. Zones 7-10. Young plants usually are broad and twiggy but in time will build into a pyramidal tree to 40 feet high and up to 30 feet across. The rose pink and white flowers, carried upright on the branches, seem especially bright because the pink is on the outside of petals, the white on the inside. Their form is cup shaped to about 8 inches wide. Plants may begin to bloom when they reach 7 years old.

M. veitchii. VEITCH MAGNOLIA. Zones 7-10. Where you can protect this hybrid magnolia from strong winds, it will be a fine tree, valuable for both good flowers and foliage. Growth is fast (and rather brittle) to as much as 40 feet high and 30 feet across. Trees begin to flower when about 5 years old: 10-inch blossoms appear before spring leaves emerge. They are rose red at petal bases, shading to white at the tips. The variety 'Rubra' has smaller, purplish red flowers. Oblong leaves to 12 inches in length are dark green.

Malus (Apple and Crabapple)

The dividing line between apples and crabapples is arbitrary, based on fruit size: apples are *Malus* species and varieties with fruits over 2 inches in diameter. The common eating apples are varieties or hybrids of *Malus pumila*, while crabapples comprise many other *Malus* species and hybrids between those species. In fact, you have an almost bewildering choice of crabapples, new ones being introduced yearly.

Despite the diversity in *Malus* types, some generalizations do apply. All trees are more tolerant of wet soils and more adaptable to varying climates than are most other flowering fruit trees (only the pear tree exceeds the apple's tolerance for wet soil).

Trees prefer good, well-drained, and deep soil, but they will grow in soils that range from acid to slightly alkaline and don't mind rocky or gravelly soils. Generally they are not happy in the low desert. Flowers may be white or shades of pink to nearly red. Flower forms are single, semidouble, or double, from 1-2 inches across. The double forms almost never produce fruit. From midsummer into fall, the fruits ripen, becoming red, yellow, or green, depending on the species or hybrid. On some trees they will hang on well into winter or even through winter and into spring. Some of the smaller-fruited crabapples are favorites of birds. Autumn leaf color is not a feature of most *Malus* types, but there are exceptions.

Where fruit production is not greatly important, a number of crabapples and apples can be considered fairly pest free. Fireblight sometimes occurs. Other possible problems are aphids, tent caterpillars, spider mites, and, in the Northwest, scab, powdery mildew, and rust. Apple scab can be so serious that trees may lose over half their leaves by late summer. Susceptibility varies according to species and variety, and this is mentioned in the descriptions. If quality fruit is your goal, check with your county agricultural agent or farm advisor for specific advice about scab free and scab resistant varieties as well as any other problems to watch for and what controls to use.

Although they share many physical characteristics and cultural preferences, crabapples and apples are dissimilar enough to cause them to be used differently in the landscape. Crabapples derive their ornamental value from masses of spring flowers (usually before leaves appear or as they emerge) and later on, in some sorts, from decorative fruits. Because most are small to medium-sized trees (on the average about 25 feet high and wide), they function well as lawn specimens, foreground trees in flower borders, high screens when planted side by side in a row, or in a semiformal procession along a path or drive. Spring-flowering bulbs and later semishade plants grow well beneath them.

In contrast to the crabapples, apples (*Malus pumila*) attain heights to about 40 feet unless grown on a dwarfing rootstock (see page 24), putting them out of the small-tree category. Gnarled old trees have a picturesque quality that most crabapples lack unless they are pruned to create that effect. Apples don't flower with the overabundance that crabapples do, but they still are famous for their springtime display of single white flowers.

M. arnoldiana. ARNOLD CRABAPPLE. Zones 5-9, 5-8 in eastern regions. Rapid growth reaches 20 feet high, but habit is broad and spreading to about 30 feet wide with long, arching branches. Red flower buds open to 2-inch pink flowers that fade to white. Yellow and red ½-inch fruits ripen in early fall. Trees are susceptible to scab.

M. atrosanguinea. CARMINE CRABAPPLE. Zones 5-9, 5-8 in eastern regions. Masses of 1-inch crimson to deep rose pink blossoms are followed by notably glossy, purplish green leaves. Its relatively small size (to 18 feet high and wide) and moderate growth rate suit it to small gardens or foreground plantings. Habit is rather open and irregular (even markedly contorted in older plants) with branches that tend to grow upright but droop at the tips. The dark red fruits are not especially ornamental. Trees are scab resistant.

M. baccata. SIBERIAN CRABAPPLE. Zones 3-9; 3-8 in eastern regions. Its height, early flowers, and hardiness set this species apart from most other crabapples. For a tree to be 50 feet tall—upright but rounded—is

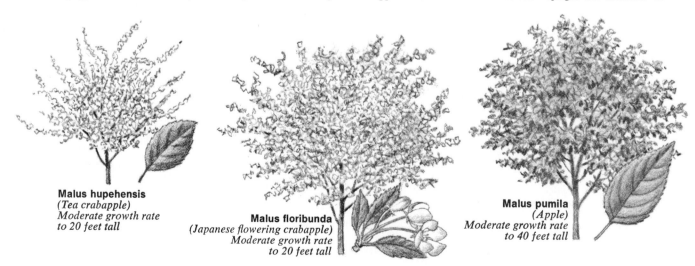

Malus hupehensis
(Tea crabapple)
Moderate growth rate to 20 feet tall

Malus floribunda
(Japanese flowering crabapple)
Moderate growth rate to 20 feet tall

Malus pumila
(Apple)
Moderate growth rate to 40 feet tall

not unusual. Flowers are pure white, opening from pink buds, followed by many small red and yellow fruits from late summer into fall. Many birds find the fruit appealing. A narrow, upright, almost columnar variety is *M. b.* 'Columnaris'; height is to 30 feet, but it grows only 5-8 feet wide (older trees sometimes spreading a bit wider). Both this variety and the basic species are susceptible to scab. A vase-shaped, smaller form (to 40 feet high by 20 feet across) is *M. b. mandschurica,* and it is very resistant to scab.

M. coronaria. Zones 5-9. This native American species is best known for its variety 'Charlotte' (or 'Charlottae'), which has 2-inch, double and very fragrant pink blossoms in mid to late spring and which produces sparse crops of 1-inch, greenish fruits. Trees grow dense and rounded to about 30 feet high and wide. The tree is susceptible to scab and rust.

M. 'Dolgo'. Zones 4-9, 4-8 in eastern regions, but is poor in the South. Although this hybrid does not bear heavy crops of flowers each year, its other attributes compensate. Bright red decorative fruits over an inch in diameter ripen in summer (earlier than most other species) and are edible. The trees, which grow to 40 feet high and wide with willowy, spreading branches, are more cold tolerant than many other crabapples. Early spring flowers are white and single, followed by a dense canopy of reddish green leaves. This variety is very resistant to scab.

M. 'Dorothea'. Zones 5-9, 5-8 in eastern regions. Every year this hybrid produces heavy crops of double pink flowers (to 2 inches across) and ½-inch yellow fruits. Flowers appear in early to midspring and even young trees bloom profusely. Growth is dense to 25 feet high and equal width. The tree is susceptible to scab.

M. 'Flame'. Zones 3-9, 3-8 in eastern regions. Unusual hardiness and an annual crop of small, bright red fruits are two outstanding assets of this hybrid. Rounded, 25-foot trees bear pink-budded white flowers in midspring. Susceptible to scab.

M. floribunda. JAPANESE FLOWERING CRABAPPLE. Zones 5-9. Delicate white blossoms smother the tree every spring. The buds are rose red and blossoms open pink, so the tree provides a multicolored spectacle. Small yellow and red fruits ripen in late summer, eagerly awaited by numerous birds. Habit is wide and spreading (to 20 feet high, with greater spread), generally dense with irregularly angled or twisted branches. This tree is very resistant to scab.

M. halliana parkmanii. PARKMAN CRABAPPLE. Zones 6-9, 6-8 in eastern regions but poor in the South. Branches grow upright and angle outward to produce a vase-shaped structure different from most other crabapples. Growth is slow and only to about 12 feet high with a lesser spread. Clusters of double pink flowers over an inch across appear in profusion in mid-spring, each blossom on a wine red stalk. Leaves are a leathery, glossy dark green. Tiny dark red fruits are less ornamental than fruits of most other crabapples. The tree is very scab resistant.

M. 'Hopa.' Zones 5-9, 5-8 in eastern regions but poor in the South. Rapid growth consists of upright branches that form a rounded crown, spreading from the weight of early-summer fruit. Trees reach 25 feet high and about 20 feet wide. Single, 1½-inch, rose red blossoms appear in early to midspring and produce orange red, early-ripening (summer) fruits that are edible and good for jellymaking. Foliage is dense and dark green with a brownish cast. This tree is very susceptible to scab.

M. hupehensis. TEA CRABAPPLE. Zones 5-9, 5-8 in eastern regions. Its Y-shaped, open growth form sets tea crabapple apart from other crabapples. Rigid main branches grow upward at about a 45° angle from the trunk, bearing only short lateral stems; this habit produces an open rather than dense tree, 15 feet tall by 20 feet wide. Deep pink flower buds open to become 1½-inch lighter pink flowers that later fade to white. Their season is midspring, but heavy bloom is not reliable every year. The small yellow and red fruits in autumn are not especially decorative but are favored by birds. The tea crabapple is very resistant to scab.

M. 'Katherine'. Zones 5-9, 5-8 in eastern regions. A loose, open growth habit and a foliage cover that is not impenetrably dense make this hybrid one of the more graceful crabapples when not in flower. Size is about 20 feet high and wide. Double blossoms are over 2 inches wide, opening pink but fading to pure white. The dull red, pea-sized fruits are good bird food but are not especially decorative. *M.* 'Katherine' is moderately resistant to scab.

M. pumila. APPLE. Zones 4-9 (some varieties even into Zone 10). The familiar apple tree, cultivated for its large and tasty fruit, is supposed to be derived at least in part from this species. During the apple's long history of cultivation, countless varieties have been named and grown. Even now you have a vast and often confusing selection of names from which to choose. All will grow into good-looking shade trees to 40 feet high, rounded and spreading. But not all varieties will fruit well in all regions. If you want a tree that also will give you good apples, you'd be wise to consult your county agricultural agent, farm advisor, or a knowledgeable local nursery owner for the names of varieties best suited to your particular part of the country. In order to produce fruits, some varieties need another variety nearby as a pollinizer, so if you want only one tree, be sure to buy one that is self-fruitful. Pink-tinted white blossoms open in late spring; fruit ripens any time from summer into late fall, depending on the variety. Broadly oval leaves (to 3 inches long) are a soft green, slightly dulled by the downy hairs on the leaf surfaces.

M. purpurea 'Lemoinei'. Zones 5-9, 5-8 in eastern regions. Purple color infuses all parts of this crabapple. The single and semidouble dark red flowers have a purple tinge; foliage emerges purplish (on purple-tinted branches) and retains a purple overcast even after turning green in summer. Even the ½-inch fruits are purplish red. Trees are up to 25 feet high, rounded and spreading in form. The tree is susceptible to scab.

M. 'Red Jade'. Zones 5-9, 5-8 in eastern regions. Long, slender, weeping branches are the hallmark of this hybrid crabapple. Moderate growth reaches about 20 feet high and as much as 15 feet wide. Flowers are small, white, and single, appearing in midspring. But the real show comes with the heavy crop of bright red, ½-inch fruits that hang on the pendulous branches throughout fall and into winter. *M.* 'Red Jade' is resistant to scab but more susceptible to fireblight than many others.

M. scheideckeri. SCHEIDECKER CRABAPPLE. Zones 5-9, 5-8 in eastern regions. Upright growth reaches a rather modest 20 feet high by 15 feet wide, making this hybrid particularly suited to patios and foreground plantings. Semidouble rose pink blossoms appear in midspring, later forming small orange yellow fruits that last into autumn. Foliage is dense and dark green. The tree is scab-susceptible.

M. zumi calocarpa. REDBUD CRABAPPLE. Zones 6-9, 6-8 in eastern regions. Midspring flowers open soft pink and then fade to white. But fruits are the chief decorative feature of this crabapple. Glossy, bright red, ½-inch fruits ripen in late summer while leaves are still green, and they remain on the tree well into winter until seized upon by hungry birds. Growth is at a moderate rate to 25 feet high and about 15 feet wide—dense and upright to pyramidal. The 'Bob White' crabapple is similar but with yellow fruits instead of red. The redbud crabapple is highly resistant to scab.

Maple (see Acer, pp. 27-29)

Melia azedarach

CHINA-BERRY. Zones 7 (warmest part)-10. This is another trouble-free tree for areas

Melia azedarach
(China-berry)
Fast growth rate
to 50 feet tall

To find your climate zone, see page 96

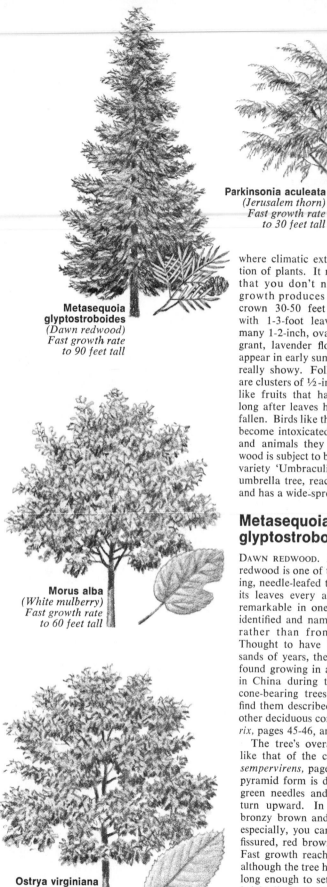

Metasequoia glyptostroboides
(Dawn redwood)
Fast growth rate
to 90 feet tall

Morus alba
(White mulberry)
Fast growth rate
to 60 feet tall

Ostrya virginiana
(Hop hornbeam)
Slow growth rate
to 50 feet tall

Parkinsonia aculeata
(Jerusalem thorn)
Fast growth rate
to 30 feet tall

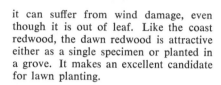

Parrotia persica
(Persian parrotia)
Slow growth rate
to 30 feet tall

where climatic extremes limit your selection of plants. It makes a fine shade tree that you don't need to pamper. Fast growth produces a rounded, spreading crown 30-50 feet high densely covered with 1-3-foot leaves, each divided into many 1-2-inch, oval, toothed leaflets. Fragrant, lavender flowers in loose clusters appear in early summer but can't be called really showy. Following these, however, are clusters of ½-inch, hard, yellow, berry-like fruits that hang on through winter long after leaves have turned yellow and fallen. Birds like the fruits (and sometimes become intoxicated by them), but to man and animals they are poisonous. Weak wood is subject to breakage by storms. The variety 'Umbraculifera', called the Texas umbrella tree, reaches only about 30 feet and has a wide-spreading, flattened crown.

Metasequoia glyptostroboides

DAWN REDWOOD. Zones 6-10. The dawn redwood is one of the very few cone-bearing, needle-leafed trees that entirely sheds its leaves every autumn. But it is also remarkable in one other respect: it was identified and named from fossil remains rather than from a living specimen. Thought to have been extinct for thousands of years, the tree was unexpectedly found growing in a few isolated locations in China during the 1940s. Most other cone-bearing trees are evergreen; you'll find them described on pages 82-93. (For other deciduous cone-bearing trees see *Larix,* pages 45-46, and *Taxodium,* page 60.)

The tree's overall appearance is quite like that of the coast redwood *(Sequoia sempervirens,* pages 92-93) except that its pyramid form is decked out in soft, light green needles and its branchlets tend to turn upward. In fall, the needles turn bronzy brown and then drop. In winter, especially, you can appreciate the deeply fissured, red brown trunks of older trees. Fast growth reaches up to 90 feet or so, although the tree hasn't been in cultivation long enough to set a completely accurate height limit. Best growth is in moist but well-drained soil with plenty of organic matter. Where winters are cold and dry,

it can suffer from wind damage, even though it is out of leaf. Like the coast redwood, the dawn redwood is attractive either as a single specimen or planted in a grove. It makes an excellent candidate for lawn planting.

Morus (Mulberry)

Few people grow mulberries for their tasty fruit. For one thing, the birds usually get to them first. For another, they stain pavement and clothing. As a result, the mulberries most favored for ornamental use are the fruitless varieties of *M. alba.*

M. alba. WHITE MULBERRY. Zones 5-10. In the Orient, this tree plays host to the silkworm. In the United States, it is an extremely fast-growing shade tree that performs especially well where many other trees falter—in hot summer areas and alkaline soils. Given ample water in early years, it will withstand considerable drought once established. The fruit-bearing form may reach 60 feet, but the fruitless varieties top out at around 35 feet high with a somewhat greater spread. 'Fruitless', 'Stribling', and 'Kingan' (sometimes called 'Mapleleaf') are the fruitless sorts you'll find in nurseries. Leaves reach 6 inches long and 4 inches wide and are sometimes oval shaped but just as likely to have one or more lobes. Autumn color is bright yellow. Stake new plantings securely for the first few years because the crowns grow so rapidly that they can snap from slender young trunks in high winds. Limbs, particularly those on young trees, may grow long and drooping; when this happens, shorten them back during the dormant season to an upward-facing bud. The weeping mulberry, 'Pendula', is always grafted onto an upright trunk of the species; from its graft point it sends down a cascade of branches to the ground.

Mulberry (see Morus, above)

Nectarine (see Prunus, pp. 53-55)

Nyssa sylvatica

BLACK or SOUR GUM, PEPPERIDGE, TUPELO or BLACK TUPELO. Zones 5-9 (but not the desert). Like some maples and *Liquidambar,* this is a large tree with blazing early

Paulownia tomentosa
(Empress tree)
Fast growth rate
to 50 feet tall

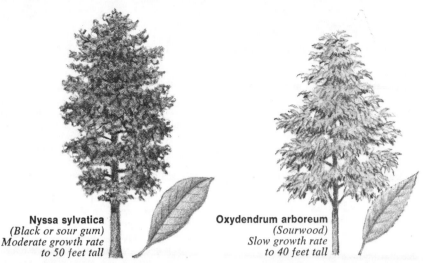

Nyssa sylvatica
(Black or sour gum)
Moderate growth rate
to 50 feet tall

Oxydendrum arboreum
(Sourwood)
Slow growth rate
to 40 feet tall

autumn color, even in mild-winter regions. Although tolerant of some drought when established, its native location usually is in moist soil—often near water—and best (and fastest) growth will come if you give it ample water. Young trees are pyramid shaped and develop at a moderate rate into 30-50-foot specimens in the garden (taller in the wild) with characteristic short, horizontal branches and flat tops. Spread is 15-25 feet. In winter, the crooked branches, twigs, and dark, red-tinged bark create a rugged silhouette. Leaves are dark green and lustrous, oblong, to 2-5 inches long; they emerge rather late in spring and turn a hot, coppery red in autumn. The species has no particular soil preference and will tolerate poor drainage. If male and female trees are close to each other, the female tree may produce small blue black fruits that aren't showy but are relished by birds.

Oak (see Quercus, pp. 56-57)

Ostrya virginiana

HOP HORNBEAM. Zones 4-9. Slow growth and difficulty of transplanting limit the availability of this otherwise fine tree. Rather pyramid shaped, it will reach 40-50 feet high and about 25 feet wide after many years. Limbs are slender and spreading but so strong that they rarely break. Elmlike leaves (oval with toothed edges) reach 5 inches long and turn yellow in autumn. The drooping seed clusters have overlapping scales that make their structure resemble hops; they appear in summer.

Oxydendrum arboreum

SOURWOOD, SORREL TREE. Zones 5-9 (but not the desert). Although the sourwood is a tree growing to as high as 50 feet or more in the wild, its small, bell-shaped flowers reveal its kinship to rhododendrons, azaleas, and heathers. And like those plants, the sourwood requires an acid soil, ample water, and—because of its shallow roots—no cultivation underneath. Plant it in full sun or partial shade. In gardens it grows slowly to 25-40 feet tall in a slender pyramid shape to about 20 feet across. New spring leaves emerge bronzy red, soon become a rich, glossy

green, and finish up the year in an autumn burst of brilliant scarlet. Leaves are 5-8 inches long, slender and curving upward from the central vein. New foliage is highly susceptible to frost damage. Midsummer flowers come in clusters shaped somewhat like an outspread hand with fingers pointing downward and outward. Along each 10-inch "finger" hang creamy white bell-shaped flowers. These form small seed capsules that are green during fall leaf color but later turn silver gray and hang on into winter. Best performance is in regions having definite winter chill and cool summers.

Parkinsonia aculeata

JERUSALEM THORN, MEXICAN PALO VERDE. Zones 8-10. In desert regions this tree finds its best home. It has almost no pest or disease problems, tolerates alkaline soil, and requires practically no attention when established. It also provides welcome shade in hot desert climates. This tree grows fast: ultimate height is 15-30 feet high and wide. The Jerusalem thorn doesn't cast dense shade but rather filters the sun through its sparse foliage and many branches. Leaves are 6-9 inches long and composed of many tiny leaflets that quickly fall in periods of drought or cold, leaving the leafstalks and bare branches. Without leaves, the tree still appears presentable because of its yellow green bark and many spiny twigs and leafstalks. Beginning in spring, loose, 7-inch clusters of yellow flowers decorate the tree for over a month; intermittent blooms appear throughout spring and summer (year-round in warmer zones). Stake a young tree and trim off its lower branches if you want a tree to walk under; otherwise it will branch low. If trimmed as a hedge the tree makes a formidable barrier because of the thorns. It does not do well with watering necessary to maintain a lawn beneath. Best use is as a patio tree (though it produces a pine needle-like litter), background planting, or in a desert landscape.

Parrotia persica

PERSIAN PARROTIA. Zones 6-9 (but not a good candidate in Zones 6 and 7 in the

Midwest and West). Strongly horizontal, wide-spreading branches build up into one of the most graceful of "fat" trees. It has a strong tendency to grow with several trunks, but you can train it to one trunk by shortening side branches and removing growth from ground level. When the tree reaches the height where you want lowest branches to be, let those limbs extend; later, cut off lower, shortened branches. Growth is fairly slow, to about 30 feet.

Before leaf-out come the flowers—not with showy petals but rather with red stamens. Clustered along the limbs, they give the tree a hazy red appearance. Then the new foliage emerges to become a dense canopy of oval, dark green leaves to 4 inches long. In autumn these turn from golden yellow to orange, rosy pink, and finally bright red. In winter you get a good look at the attractive, smooth gray bark that flakes off here and there to show patches of white. Persian parrotia performs best in well-drained soil and in a location sheltered from strong winds.

Paulownia tomentosa

EMPRESS TREE. Zones 6-10. People continually confuse this tree with the *Catalpa* (page 34). Both have tropically big, heart-shaped leaves, grow rapidly to an ultimate 50 feet high and 30-40 feet across, and have 2-inch, trumpet-shaped flowers. It's the flowers that can point out the difference. With the empress tree, buds—brown and olive-sized—form in autumn and persist over the winter. Then in early spring, as the tree leafs out, flowers open in clusters to 1 foot long. Their color is lilac blue with yellow stripes in the throat; they have a permeating pleasant fragrance. After bloom, the top-shaped seed capsules form, staying on the tree into the following winter and early spring. Because flower buds form in autumn, they may be damaged (even though the tree survives) where winters are very cold or where late frosts follow early warm spells. Where winters are mild, buds may drop off. Success is doubtful in dry, windy regions of the lower Midwest and Southwest. Best use is as a background tree where the litter of falling flowers and leaves, surface roots, and dense shade won't interfere with other elements of the landscape. Sometimes it can multiply like a weed because of many seeds that germinate, along with its tendency to sprout from the roots.

Peach (see Prunus, pp. 53-55)

Pear (see Pyrus, pp. 55-56)

Persimmon (see Diospyros, p. 39)

Phellodendron amurense

AMUR CORK TREE. Zones 4-9. With no showy flowers or fruits, dramatic foliage, or fiery autumn color to offer, the Amur cork tree has capitalized on *form*. Trunk and branches are thick and massive, with deeply furrowed, corky bark. Leaves consist of oval, pointed leaflets to 4½ inches long, each leaf up to 15 inches long with an odd number (to 13) of glossy green leaflets. Foliage turns yellow in fall. Despite its heavy limb structure, it is not a huge tree (to about 35 feet high and wide) and the shade cast is not dense but filtered so that a good lawn can be maintained beneath. Pest and disease free, established trees also tolerate drought, as well as hot, dry summers and frozen winters, and the harsh atmospheric conditions in some cities. Small dark fruits on female trees appeal to birds but aren't decorative.

Pistacia chinensis

CHINESE PISTACHE. Zones 6-10. Anyone familiar with the deciduous sumacs (*Rhus* species) might guess this tree's kinship. Not only is the foliage similar—1-foot-long leaves comprised of 4-inch, narrow, paired leaflets—also they have the same luminous orange red autumn color. Although young trees may not grow symmetrically, in time they become regular and rounded, to 60 feet tall and nearly as wide. With a male tree nearby, female trees will bear small red fruits; these turn dark blue when they ripen but are not especially showy. The pistache tolerates a wide range of soils (including alkaline), and either regular lawn watering or no summer water (after the tree is established), as long as the soil is not shallow. This is the only tree adapted to desert conditions that will provide bright red autumn color.

Plane tree (see Platanus, below)

Platanus (Sycamore, Plane tree)

The sizes and growth habits vary among the plane tree species and hybrids, but in other characteristics they reveal many similarities. Leaves are large and lobed like a "typical" maple leaf; seed clusters are small, hanging balls; and bark sheds in patches to disclose paler (often white) new bark. All are subject, more or less, to a foliage fungus called anthracnose that attacks new spring growth. (See page 25 for suggested treatment.)

P. acerifolia. LONDON PLANE TREE. Zones 5-10 (subject to chlorosis and leaf burn in the desert). Noted for being one of the urban warhorses, this tree often is planted along city streets because it will put up with the worst city atmospheres and tolerates most soils. Rapid but brittle growth with good care will send it up to as much as 80 feet with a spread about half that. Trunk and limbs are cream colored, flaking off here and there to show yellowish inner bark. The rather coarse leaves may reach 10 inches across with 3-5 lobes; in fall they simply turn a dusty brown before dropping off. Seed clusters usually are paired on the end of a stem.

P. occidentalis. AMERICAN SYCAMORE or PLANE TREE, BUTTONWOOD. Zones 5-10. This is one parent of the preceding hybrid and is similar to it in many ways. The differences are that the new bark is whiter, the tree is out of leaf longer, and seed clusters usually are one to a stem. Nor is this species at all happy in urban atmospheres. This latter trait, combined with its greater size (to 120 feet in the wild), makes American sycamore a tree better suited to country places. Sometimes it grows with multiple trunks or with a leaning trunk.

P. racemosa. CALIFORNIA SYCAMORE. Zones 7-10 (only in the West). Without a doubt, this is the most unusual of the sycamores. More often than not, the trunk grows at an angle rather than straight up. It can also branch low to form secondary trunks that lean or form two or more trunks that grow in a clump, each taking whatever direction it pleases. Height is 50-100 feet, depending on how old and how vertical the tree is. Similarly, spread varies according to the angle at which the trunk leans. Basically, the tree is considerably taller than wide. This tree's bark is a patchy combination of buff and white. The deeply lobed leaves may reach 9 inches long; they turn dusty brown early in autumn. During winter in particular, you will notice the seed balls hanging in clusters of 3-7. Unfortunately, this species is the one most susceptible to anthracnose (see page 25) in a wet year.

Plum (see Prunus, pp. 53-55)

Poplar (see Populus, below)

Populus (Poplar, Cottonwood, Aspen)

All *Populus* species are fast-growing, tough trees with a network of aggressive surface roots. The latter trait accounts for their reputation for raising pavement and clogging sewer and drainage lines. Brittle wood and disease susceptibility are drawbacks of some species. Yet if their limitations are realized so that they are not planted where they could cause problems, the various poplars can be extremely valuable landscape additions. They are especially suited to country planting where rapid growth, toughness, and low maintenance are required. And much landscape on arid desert or semi-arid plains would be almost totally devoid of trees were it not for poplars or cottonwoods.

P. alba. WHITE POPLAR. Zones 4-10. The slightest stirring of air will cause the leaves to flutter, revealing the white undersides in contrast to the dark green upper leaf surfaces. Individual leaves are up to 5 inches long, usually with 3-5 lobes. Autumn color is yellow or reddish. A wide-spreading 60-80-foot tree would be a typical mature specimen. A narrow, columnar form of this species is the variety 'Pyramidalis', the Bolleana poplar. Both the species and its variety tend to sucker profusely from the base.

P. nigra 'Italica'. LOMBARDY POPLAR. Zones 3-10. Because it has been so widely planted, this probably is the most familiar poplar—a 40-100-foot exclamation point in the landscape. Its columnar form with upward-reaching branches lines many a country lane, as much for windbreak as for beauty alone. Leaves are 4 inches wide, triangular, and coarsely toothed, their summertime bright green giving way to brilliant golden yellow in fall. Unfortunately, the Lombardy poplar falls victim to a canker disease in many parts of the country. The canker will kill the top branches first and eventually the entire tree. The Lombardy poplar is best used as a fast-growing, temporary screen; one that will give quick effect while slower growing but more permanent trees have a chance to become established.

P. tremuloides. QUAKING ASPEN. Zones 3-7 (but only where summers are not hot). Fluttering leaves, even when there seems to be no breeze at all, are this poplar's trademark. Native to mountains and northern latitudes across the country, it usually requires sharply cold winters to grow with any enthusiasm. Round, 1-3-inch leaves are a fresh light green during spring and summer but are most renowned for their spectacular golden yellow display in autumn. Trunks and limbs are a smooth, light gray green to nearly white. Although in favorable sites it is capable of reaching 60 feet or more, this is usually much smaller and not a massive tree. Like many birches, it looks most natural in grove plantings. Often it grows in clumps of several trunks arising from a single base.

Prosopis glandulosa torreyana

MESQUITE. Zones 7-9 (only in the Southwest). This native of the Southwest is one of the wide-spreading shade trees that make comfortable outdoor living possible in the desert. Much of its success is due to far-reaching roots that will grow great distances to tap water. Consequently an established tree is quite drought tolerant. It also tolerates alkaline soil, regular watering that a lawn beneath it would need, and even shallow, rocky soil if you're content to have it just as a shrub. With good growing conditions, the mesquite tree tends to branch out at ground level into several trunks, forming a tree to

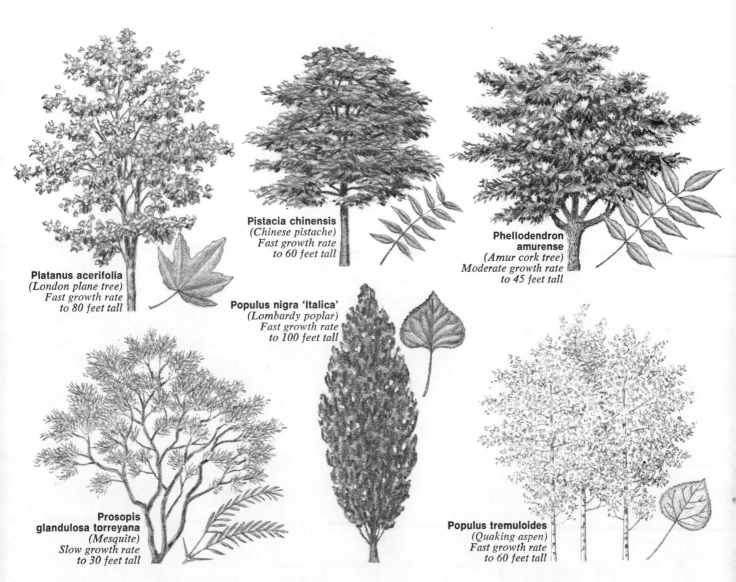

Platanus acerifolia
(London plane tree)
Fast growth rate
to 80 feet tall

Pistacia chinensis
(Chinese pistache)
Fast growth rate
to 60 feet tall

Phellodendron amurense
(Amur cork tree)
Moderate growth rate
to 45 feet tall

Populus nigra 'Italica'
(Lombardy poplar)
Fast growth rate
to 100 feet tall

Prosopis glandulosa torreyana
(Mesquite)
Slow growth rate
to 30 feet tall

Populus tremuloides
(Quaking aspen)
Fast growth rate
to 60 feet tall

30 feet high and 40 or more feet in spread. The tiny green leaflets and the thicket of branches and thorns in the crown create an airy rather than a dense shade. Throughout spring and summer, it produces small spikes of tiny, greenish yellow blossoms that bees find very enticing. Besides providing shade, mesquite also serves well as a screen or windbreak.

Prune (see Prunus, below)

Prunus

ALMOND, APRICOT, CHERRY, NECTARINE, PEACH, PLUM, and PRUNE. Just a glance at the common names included here gives an idea of the bewildering array of related trees available to the gardener. Although all are fruiting trees and contain varieties of commercial importance, the most ornamental garden types are those which have been selected for their blossoms rather than their fruit. And among these flowering trees, the cherries form the largest and generally the best group, followed by almonds, plums and prunes, apricots, nectarines, and peaches.

P. amygdalus. ALMOND. Zones 7-9. Extremely early bloom limits the planting of almonds more than does any lack of hardiness. Late frosts often will catch trees in bloom, and this will ruin the nut crop as well as the blooms for the year. But if the crop is not important or if late frosts present little or no threat, an almond serves as a useful herald of spring. Blossoms are palest pink or white and 1-2 inches across. Trees grow upright when young but in age become spreading and dome shaped to 20-30 feet high. Fruit is like a small green peach without flesh; the hull splits open to disclose the pit that is the familiar almond. Soil must be at least 6 feet deep and well drained. Growth is poor in shallow soils; root rot takes over in wet ones. Otherwise, almonds accept a variety of soils and will get along with just moderate amounts of water. Infrequent but deep watering is best.

A number of varieties are sold, and for fruit production you need two different ones. 'Mission' (also sold as 'Texas') is late blooming and so is best for late-frost areas. 'Nonpareil' is the most widely adapted.

P. armeniaca. APRICOT. Zones 6-9. Like almonds, apricots flower early, and fruit production will be limited or destroyed in regions where late frosts can be expected. In addition, fruit rot can be a problem in cool, humid coastal areas. Regions with little winter chill are restricted to just a few varieties that can get along without a strong cold season.

Single blossoms, which blanket the branches in earliest spring, are white to palest pink. Trees will reach 30 feet tall with equal spread. Fall color of the roundish, leathery leaves is yellow to red. For best growth in your area, you should select those types that are most likely to fruit well. Consult with your county agricultural agent or farm advisor for the best varieties and for information on what pest or disease problems you may have to watch for.

P. avium. MAZZARD CHERRY, SWEET CHERRY. Zones 4-9 (but not desert), 4-7 in eastern regions. The flowers are small and short-lived and the tree is not an exciting ornamental. In fact, the only reason this species would be cultivated rather than one of the more ornamental types is for its tasty fruit. And if it's fruit you want, you'll have to find a good way to foil birds, for they are extraordinarily fond of cherries.

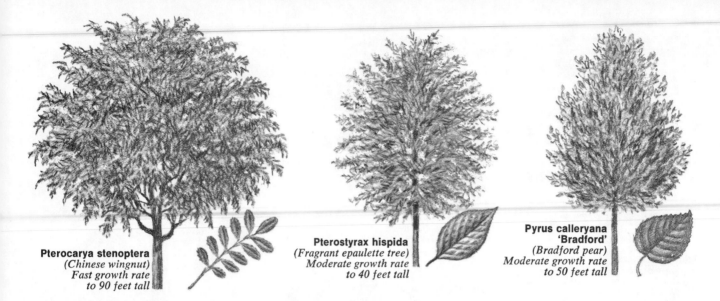

Pterocarya stenoptera
(Chinese wingnut)
Fast growth rate
to 90 feet tall

Pterostyrax hispida
(Fragrant epaulette tree)
Moderate growth rate
to 40 feet tall

**Pyrus calleryana
'Bradford'**
(Bradford pear)
Moderate growth rate
to 50 feet tall

Trees are 30-35 feet tall and sometimes as broad (depending on variety). Best growth is in deep, well-drained soils and in regions with definite winter cold. To produce fruit, many varieties need a different variety as a pollinizer; and not just any combination of varieties will do the job. Consult your county agricultural agent or farm advisor to see if sweet cherries will grow and produce well in your area, and, if so, which ones should be planted.

P. avium 'Plena'. Double-flowered mazzard cherry. Zones 4-9. Flowers, resembling 1½-inch white roses in drooping clusters, adorn this 30-50-foot tree in early spring before most other double cherries put in an appearance. And *P. avium* 'Plena' will succeed in regions too cold for the famous Oriental sorts such as *P. campanulata* and *P. serrulata*. Oval, pointed leaves turn red in autumn.

P. blireiana. BLIREIANA PLUM. Zones 5-9 (but not desert). Several plums and prunes have purple leaves, but this hybrid combines them with some of the loveliest (and most rain and wind resistant) pink flowers among that group. Semidouble to double blossoms 1 inch across cover branches in late winter or early spring, after which the red purple leaves emerge. By summer, foliage is greenish bronze. Graceful, long, and slender branches form a rounded tree to 25 feet high and about 20 feet wide. Stake young trees (see page 11) to prevent them from leaning in the wind. The willowy limbs will need some pruning back and thinning to maintain a well-formed tree. The shallow root system doesn't always provide enough anchorage for trees exposed to heavy storms while trees are in leaf.

P. campanulata. TAIWAN FLOWERING CHERRY. Zones 8-9 (but not in the desert) and coldest parts of 10. This species has the ability to perform well in regions where winters are too warm for other flowering cherries. Habit is graceful, densely branched, but slender and upright to 20-25 feet. Single bell-shaped flowers

hang in clusters of 2-5, their shocking blush pink color a beacon in the garden. Bloom begins in late winter or early spring.

P. cerasifera 'Atropurpurea'. PURPLE-LEAF PLUM. Zones 4-9. This variety was the forerunner of purple-leafed types, the foliage beginning copper red, deepening to dark purple, but turning to greenish bronze by late summer. Ephemeral white flowers are followed by a usually heavy crop of small, edible red plums. A rounded tree, it is fast growing to 25-30 feet, and may need some pruning back of its vigorous growth to maintain a good shape. Newer varieties present variations on the same theme. 'Hollywood' is a larger, more upright tree, 30-40 feet tall and to 25 feet wide with leaves that are dark green above and red on the underside. Pale pink to white flowers come early in the season, later producing tasty, 2-inch red plums. 'Newport' is similar to 'Atropurpurea' but slightly smaller, with purplish red leaves and pink flowers. 'Thundercloud' is a rounded tree 20 feet high and wide with dark purplish copper leaves and light pink to white flowers. Although it produces few, if any, pink flowers (and no fruits), 'Vesuvius' (or 'Krauter Vesuvius') still is valuable for its darkest of purple black foliage. These trees are small, to 18 feet high and 12 feet wide.

P. cerasus. SOUR CHERRY. Zones 4-9 (but not desert), 4-8 in eastern regions. Here is another commercial cherry that should be planted only after considering the advice presented under *P. avium*. In contrast, this is a spreading, irregular tree to about 20 feet high. You can selectively prune to increase the irregularity or to encourage a more regular, upright pattern by cutting out drooping side branches. A number of varieties exist, none of which need a separate pollinizer. These all have single white flowers; for double blossoms (but not fruit) look for 'Rhexii'. Your county agricultural agent or farm advisor can give best advice on which ones are good in your region.

P. mume. JAPANESE FLOWERING APRICOT, JAPANESE FLOWERING PLUM. Zones 7-9. Its two common names highlight the fence-straddling position of this species: it is neither a real apricot nor a true plum. Considered the longest-lived flowering fruit tree, it eventually forms an aged-looking, picturesque, 20-foot specimen. Small, fragrant flowers appear very early in spring, later developing into yellow and unspectacular small fruits. Nurseries offer a number of varieties that differ in flower color and doubleness. 'Rosemary Clarke' is double white; 'Dawn' and 'Peggy Clarke' are double pink and deep rose, respectively. 'Bonita' has double, rosy crimson blossoms earlier than any of the others.

P. persica. PEACH. Zones 6-9. A variety of pest problems combined with a short life (about 15 years) make the planting of a peach tree worth careful consideration. Many peaches that are selected and named because of their flamboyant spring flower display (vivid pinks and reds) produce edible, if not top-quality, fruit. But because they need the same attention as varieties with superior fruit, you might think of planting peaches that will produce a quality crop, even though their flowering is somewhat less spectacular. If you really want peaches and have an out-of-the-way spot in the garden for them (or won't mind seeing them fade from the landscape after about 15 years), then consult your county agricultural agent or farm advisor for recommended varieties for your area. Fruiting peach varieties vary in their need for winter chill.

Nectarines, *P. persica nectarina,* are just peaches without fuzz on the fruit. Otherwise, they have the peach's spreading, rounded form to 25 feet high and wide. Leaves are narrow and downward curving.

P. sargentii. SARGENT CHERRY. Zones 4-9 (but not desert). The upright, spreading branches of this cherry form a rounded crown 40-50 feet tall but not as wide. Spring finds the tree laden with single, blush pink blossoms in clusters of 2-4. And in autumn, the leaves turn orange red.

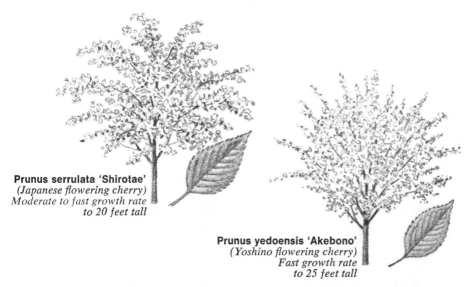

Prunus serrulata 'Shirotae'
(Japanese flowering cherry)
Moderate to fast growth rate
to 20 feet tall

Prunus yedoensis 'Akebono'
(Yoshino flowering cherry)
Fast growth rate
to 25 feet tall

Small, cherrylike black fruits aren't especially ornamental because they are largely hidden by the leaves.

P. serrula. BIRCH BARK CHERRY. Zones 5-9 (but not desert), 5-8 in eastern regions. Here is a cherry that is unusual because it is valued not for its flowers or fruit but for its decorative bark. Trunk and limbs are a glossy mahogany red with some of the peeling associated with birch trees. Habit is broadly rounded, to 30 feet high and as wide. Small white flowers are partly obscured by foliage; the red fruits that follow are tiny but edible.

P. serrulata. JAPANESE FLOWERING CHERRY, ORIENTAL CHERRY. Zones 5-9 (but not desert), 5-8 in eastern regions. This is the basic species from which the Japanese for centuries have selected improved varieties and hybrids to enrich their gardens and sacred places. Most are small trees no more than 25 feet tall, with long, slender leaves. 'Amanogawa' is columnar to 25 feet tall but only 8 feet wide. Its flowers are light pink and semidouble. 'Beni Hoshi' (or 'Pink Star') grows rapidly, with arching, spreading branches to form an umbrella-shaped crown· 20-25 feet high and wide. Vivid pink single flowers hang below branches. Blooming late, 'Fugenzo' (also sold as 'Kofugen' and 'James H. Veitch') has double soft pink flowers coming out with bronzy new leaves. Its habit is broad, spreading, and flat topped to 25 feet high and wide.

'Sekiyama' (more often sold as 'Kwanzan') branches stiffly upright to form an inverted cone 30 feet high, 20 feet wide; deep rose pink double blossoms appear in hanging clusters with red new leaves. 'Shirofugen' has a horizontal branch pattern, to 25 feet wide and high; pink, double blooms fade to white and open later than most varieties. 'Shirotae' (or 'Mt. Fuji') also is horizontal branching but only to about 20 feet high and wider spreading. Single to semidouble blossoms open white from pink buds and then fade to purplish pink. 'Tai-Haku' presents single white flowers clustered 2-3 in striking contrast

with copper red new leaves; habit is vigorous and upright, spreading to 25 feet high and wide with 7-inch foliage. 'Ukon' offers a color departure with semidouble greenish yellow flowers just as bronzy new growth begins. Its habit is open, rather sparse to 30 feet tall and broad with orange-red autumn foliage.

P. subhirtella. HIGAN CHERRY. Zones 5-9; in eastern regions best in Zones 6-7. Only a few of this species' varieties are planted as ornamentals. Warm autumns or winters will bring out a crop of double white or pink-tinted blossoms on *P. s. autumnalis.* But if such weather doesn't materialize, the tree will wait until early spring. Growth is loose and bushy with a rounded to flattened crown, 25-30 feet high and wide. In wet spring seasons it is susceptible to a blight that causes much twig dieback.

The single weeping cherry, *P. s. pendula,* will droop its branches to the ground when grafted onto an upright understock, displaying in spring a cascade of small pale pink, single blossoms. The tree grows slowly only 10-12 feet tall and about as wide. Similar to *P. s. pendula,* but with double rose pink blossoms, is *P. s.* 'Yae-shidare-higan'—the double weeping cherry.

P. yedoensis. YOSHINO FLOWERING CHERRY. Zones 5-9 (but not desert), 6-8 in eastern regions. Rapid growth to 40 feet high and 30 feet across creates a graceful, open pattern of curving branches that are fairly flat topped at maturity. Early-blooming, fragrant flowers are single and light pink to white. Its variety 'Akebono' (sometimes sold as 'Daybreak') is a smaller tree (to 25 feet high and wide) with more definitely pink flowers.

Pterocarya stenoptera

CHINESE WINGNUT. Zones 8-10. Aggressive surface roots rule this tree out of many cultivated gardens and lawns. But its special feature, an ability to grow well in compacted, poorly aerated soils, puts it high among choices for heavy-traffic places such as play yards and parking

areas. Rapid growth reaches 40-90 feet with heavy, wide-spreading limbs. Leaves resemble those of walnuts (a close relative). They are 8-16 inches long and divided into 11-23 oval, finely toothed leaflets, each up to 4 inches long. Small, one-seeded, winged nuts form in 1-foot-long hanging clusters to become noticeable decorative feature in late summer. These may germinate freely where they fall or are distributed.

Pterostyrax hispida

FRAGRANT EPAULETTE TREE. Zones 7-9. Visualize the fringed, golden epaulettes on a military uniform done instead in creamy white, and you have an idea of this tree's blossoms. They're carried in drooping clusters to 9 inches long in early summer. Small, furry gray fruits form after flowers fade and then hang on to decorate the tree in winter after leaves have fallen. A moderate growth rate results in a mature tree to 40 feet high. The crown is rather open and spreading toward the top; ultimate width is about half the height. Light green leaves are pointed ovals to 8 inches long, coarse textured and grayish on their undersides. Well-drained soil is preferred.

Pyrus (Pear)

Something attractive in every season is offered by the pears. Creating a sturdy silhouette in winter, dark, muscular-looking branches wear masses of white flower clusters in spring. During the rest of spring and summer you have a canopy of glossy green foliage that, in fall, turns brilliant shades of red or, in some varieties, orange or yellow. Trees are long-lived and will thrive better than most other fruit trees in damp heavy soil.

P. calleryana 'Bradford'. BRADFORD PEAR. Zones 5-9. The basic species (*P. calleryana*) is a small, thorny, horizontally branching tree with a high degree of resistance to fire-blight. The variety 'Bradford' is a thornless selection of the species that also possesses a few other· significant ornamental differences. Most noticeable is its upward-sweeping (rather than horizontal) branching pattern that results in a taller tree—to 50 feet high and somewhat pyramid shaped with a 30-foot spread. Blossoms appear very early in spring. They're followed by small, round, inedible pears that are inconspicuous but sought out by some birds. Broadly oval, scallop-edged leaves are up to 3 inches long, dark green, and leathery; in autumn they turn to glossy carmine red in Zones 6 and 7.

P. communis COMMON PEAR. Zones 5-9 (but not too successful in southern California and low deserts). To produce quality fruit and/or resist fireblight, the many named pear varieties differ in their climate preferences within the zones of adaptability. Trees are generally pyramidal and 30-40 feet tall when mature with a strongly vertical branching pattern. As the trees age, branches become more gnarled and heavy. White, early spring flowers ap-

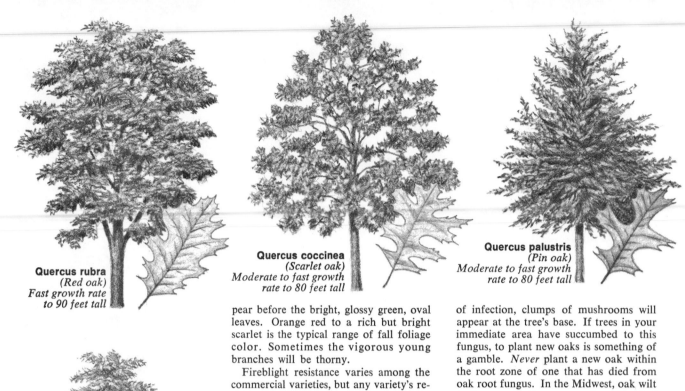

Quercus rubra
(Red oak)
*Fast growth rate
to 90 feet tall*

Quercus coccinea
(Scarlet oak)
*Moderate to fast growth
rate to 80 feet tall*

Quercus palustris
(Pin oak)
*Moderate to fast growth
rate to 80 feet tall*

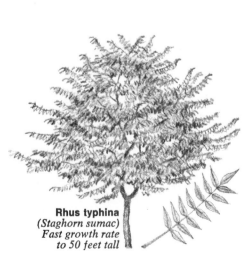

Robinia 'Idaho'
*Fast growth rate
to 40 feet tall*

Rhus typhina
(Staghorn sumac)
*Fast growth rate
to 50 feet tall*

pear before the bright, glossy green, oval leaves. Orange red to a rich but bright scarlet is the typical range of fall foliage color. Sometimes the vigorous young branches will be thorny.

Fireblight resistance varies among the commercial varieties, but any variety's resistance is greater in regions where summers are warm and dry. To determine the best pear varieties for your particular area, check with your county or state agricultural agent or a reliable nurseryman. Some varieties are self-fruitful; some need pollinators in certain regions to produce fruit; some always need another pear variety for crop productions. If fruit production is your goal, be sure to ask which of the preferred varieties for your area need a pollinator.

Quercus (Oak)

Many but not all oaks are big. Neither do all oaks have lobed leaves, nor are they all deciduous (read about evergreen oaks on pages 79-80). Some grow faster than others; some are deeper rooted. Many have excellent autumn color, often red but sometimes yellow. Yet some just turn brown. What, then, makes an oak an oak? They all have acorns!

Pest and disease problems are few in number but should be noted. Oak leaves may be attacked by various caterpillars and worms—the larvae of various moths. Most common in the western states is the oak moth larva; in the East the gypsy moth larva is a problem. Only a few of either larva won't be serious (unless the tree is very small), but heavy infestations can defoliate a tree, forcing it to replace the leaves later in the season. Serious, unchecked infestations two or more years in succession will seriously weaken or even kill a tree. Two diseases are almost invariably fatal. In the West, oak root fungus (*Armillaria*) spreads from oak to oak (and from oak to numerous other plants) through infected roots. Black, shoestringlike threads will be found in the dead roots of infected trees; in late stages

of infection, clumps of mushrooms will appear at the tree's base. If trees in your immediate area have succumbed to this fungus, to plant new oaks is something of a gamble. *Never* plant a new oak within the root zone of one that has died from oak root fungus. In the Midwest, oak wilt is the enemy of some species. The first symptom of this root disease is curling, blackening leaves. As with oak root fungus, new oaks should not be planted anywhere near the spot where one has died from oak wilt.

Although many oaks are not really slow growers, pruning can speed the growth of some kinds. A number of young oaks naturally have very twiggy growth. Because the trees' energies are divided among so many twigs, none develops rapidly. To promote more rapid vertical growth, pinch off the tips of small branches that will have nothing to do with the framework of the tree when it is mature. Leave as much foliage as possible to help sustain maximum growth in the leader and in whatever branches you don't pinch back. In desert regions the deciduous oaks don't perform as well as do the evergreen species (see pages 79-80).

Q. alba. WHITE OAK. Zones 4-9. Slow growth eventually builds into a 70-90-foot, open-branching specimen with a broad, spreading crown. Bright green, deeply lobed leaves are 4-9 inches long and turn purplish red in autumn. Winter reveals its rugged framework and gray bark.

Q. bicolor. SWAMP WHITE OAK. Zones 4-9. This species is quite similar to *Q. alba* but of shorter stature (to about 60 feet). In moist soil within its preferred zones, it might be substituted for *Q. alba*.

Q. cerris. TURKEY OAK. Zones 7-9. Fairly rapid growth forms a broad pyramid to 90 feet. But for all that size, its 2-4-inch oval leaves give it a fine texture.

Q. coccinea. SCARLET OAK. Zones 5-9. Its deep rooting system, combined with a light and open branching habit, make this a splendid oak to grow a lawn or other plants beneath. But the root system presents difficulty in transplanting, so that the tree's availability is limited. Small trees are the best to plant. Height may reach 60-80 feet with rounded crown. Shiny, bright green leaves are deeply lobed and toothed, to 6 inches long, coloring bright scarlet in crisp autumn weather.

Q. imbricaria. SHINGLE OAK. Zones 6-9. From its youthful pyramid shape to its round-topped maturity, this is an always attractive species. Height is to 75 feet (spreading about half as wide), clothed in dark green narrowly oval leaves that turn rusty yellow in fall. Aside from use as a specimen shade tree, it makes a good windbreak or even a clipped hedge because the lower branches remain attached and healthy.

Q. nigra. WATER OAK. Zones 7-10. As the name implies, this is a good tree for moist or even wet soils. Growth is broadly conical to about 75 feet high and somewhat more than half as wide. Narrow, 6-inch leaves may be simple ovals or shallowly 3-lobed. Yellow autumn color comes late.

Q. palustris. PIN OAK. Zones 5-9. This might as well be called the "stubborn oak" because it always tries to resume its natural branching habit even after pruning. Upper limbs grow upward, middle limbs spread roughly horizontal, and lower branches point downward. If you remove the downward-pointing lowest limbs, the limbs just above gradually bend down to spoil the work you've done.

The species is a fine, fast-growing lawn tree, 50-80 feet high and 30-40 feet wide, but not good for planting where you must walk or drive under it. For those locations, look for the variety 'Sovereign', which has an upright branching habit. Young trees are slender and pyramidal; mature specimens are more open and round headed. Glossy dark green leaves are deeply cut into bristly-pointed lobes. Fall weather turns leaves yellow, red, and finally rusty brown; many leaves will hang onto the tree all winter. Trees must have ample water and prefer good drainage although they will tolerate fairly wet soils. Avoid planting this tree in alkaline soils because it will develop chlorosis and need periodic treatment with iron chelates.

Q. phellos. WILLOW OAK. Zones 6-9 but sometimes experiences winter injury in Zone 6. Very slender, willowlike leaves are responsible for the common name of this most delicate-leafed oak, and like the willow tree, it is at home in moist soils. Fall color is yellow, or sometimes orange to red. Growth rate is moderately rapid, otherwise its habit and landscape limitations are similar to those of *Q. palustris*.

Q. rubra. RED OAK. Zones 4-10. Deep roots, high branching, and a fairly open crown make this a good species for growing a lawn or other plants beneath. Only its fast growth to 90 feet limits its use in smaller gardens. Young trees are pyramidal, maturing to a broad, spreading, round-topped form. Leaves are up to 8 inches long by 5 inches wide, with 3-7 pairs of pointed lobes. New spring leaves

and leafstalks are red. In autumn these become dark red, ruddy brown, or orange. Best growth is in moist, fertile soil.

Q. shumardii. SHUMARD OAK. Zones 6-9. In its native Midwest to southern United States, this tree is a more easily transplanted substitute for the Scarlet Oak, *Q. coccinea*. It will grow in heavy alkaline soils without developing chlorosis. Autumn color is red to yellow.

Redbud (see Cercis, pp. 35-36)

Rhus typhina

STAGHORN SUMAC. Zones 3-9. Growing in poor soils and cleared land along roadways, this tree is often looked upon as a weed tree or shrub-tree in its native eastern states. Its liabilities are brittle wood that breaks easily under winter snow and ice and a shallow root system that suckers profusely where it is disturbed by cultivation. The root system also provides poor anchorage against strong winds. But in a "wild" garden, in a low-maintenance landscape, or in the background, you can use the staghorn sumac to advantage. It's a lightly-structured tree with comparatively few branches and essentially no twigs; new growth is covered with a fuzz that resembles the down on emerging deer antlers in spring. Fruits (on female plants) are an attractive feature on winter trees. Size varies (depending on soil quality and amount of water) from about 15 feet to as much as 50 feet. Growth is single trunked, low branched, or in the form of a clump of several trunks. Leaves are divided into 11-31 toothed leaflets, each narrow and up to 5 inches long with a grayish underside. Fall color display is early and a blazing to rich red. Overall leaf effect is rather tropical. The variety 'Laciniata' has finely divided leaflets that produce a lacier effect on a somewhat smaller growing tree. In Zones 8 and 9 in eastern regions, the very similar *R. glabra* is a better choice. Main differences are a somewhat shorter plant and smooth (not fuzzy) new growth. It even has a cutleaf variety 'Laciniata'.

Robinia (Locust)

Two locusts are commonly available — one a hybrid of uncertain lineage and the other a native of the eastern states. Both have hanging clusters of sweet pealike blossoms and lightly-textured leaves that consist of many small, rounded leaflets. Spring leafout is late, autumn drop early, and summer shade is lightly filtered.

Both locusts are fairly rapid growers, performing well in hot, dry regions and in poor soil; established trees are quite drought resistant. Brittle wood and aggressive roots limit their usefulness in smaller, highly cultivated gardens.

R. 'Idaho'. Zones 5-10. Eight-inch clusters of red purple or magenta blossoms decorate this shapely, 40-foot tree soon after leaves unfold.

R. pseudoacacia. BLACK LOCUST. Zones 4-9 (in western states only). In its native

regions in the eastern states, the black locust has enough insect problems to rule it out as a desirable landscape specimen. But in the West, it is worth considering as a picturesque tree on country property or where a lawn would be its only competition. Growth is fast, from 40-75 feet high, with an open, rather sparse, and frequently zigzagging branching pattern. Branches and deeply furrowed bark are brownish black, making both a striking winter silhouette and a good contrast to the fresh green feathery leaves. Paired thorns arm the branches. White and fragrant flowers (each to ¾ inch) come in dense, hanging clusters up to 8 inches long. Following the bloom come 4-inch, beanlike pods that turn brown and hang on the tree throughout winter. Several named varieties may be available. 'Decaisneana' is a smaller tree, to 50 feet high and 20 feet wide, with pale pink blossoms. Narrow, columnar growth is offered by 'Fastigiata'. A striking plant against a dark background is the variety 'Frisia', with yellow leaves all season; new wood and thorns are red. The variety 'Umbraculifera' forms a dense, rounded crown, usually grafted onto a 6-8-foot trunk of another locust.

Salix (Willow)

It seems that wherever there's water there are willows. In farm country and on semi-arid plains, these trees trace the courses of streams and rivers. But they are not "high-quality" trees: their wood is brittle and breaks easily; most are subject to a variety of foliage, twig, and branch pests; all have shallow, invasive roots that will invade water pipes and septic tanks if planted near them; leaf drop is continuous; and nothing grows well beneath them. Nevertheless, several species are popular because they offer a striking weeping habit.

The weeping types all need assistance in order to become trees you can walk under. Stake the main stem up to a good height (15 feet or so) and shorten side branches by pruning. This will force out high branches and direct growth into a tall main stem. Remove shortened branches when they lose their vigor.

S. alba 'Tristis'. Zones 3-10. Golden weeping willow. Mature trees may be 70 feet high with a greater spread. The notable feature of this willow is the bright yellow color of 1-year-old twigs. Its narrow, 4-inch leaves are bright green or yellow green with paler undersides.

S. babylonica. WEEPING WILLOW. Zones 7-10. This is the smallest, the most weeping, and the most famous of the various weeping species and varieties. Long, gracefully drooping greenish or brown branches form a 30-50-foot tree with equal or greater spread. Lettucy green leaves are a slender 6 inches long. Normal life span is short — about 30 years.

S. blanda. WISCONSIN WEEPING WILLOW. Zones 5-10. One parent of this hybrid is the weeping willow (*S. babylonica*). Unlike its parent, the Wisconsin weeping willow is hardier, somewhat larger (40-50

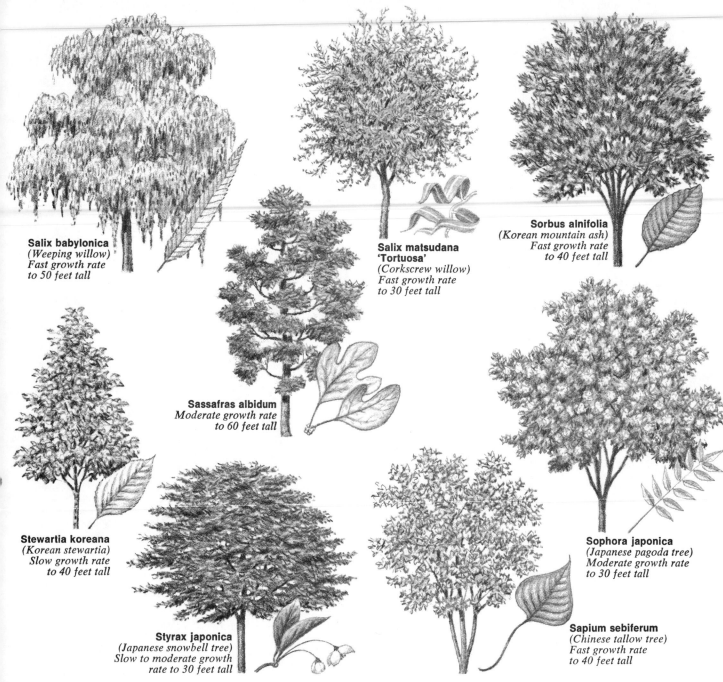

Salix babylonica
(Weeping willow)
Fast growth rate
to 50 feet tall

Salix matsudana
'Tortuosa'
(Corkscrew willow)
Fast growth rate
to 30 feet tall

Sorbus alnifolia
(Korean mountain ash)
Fast growth rate
to 40 feet tall

Sassafras albidum
Moderate growth rate
to 60 feet tall

Stewartia koreana
(Korean stewartia)
Slow growth rate
to 40 feet tall

Styrax japonica
(Japanese snowbell tree)
Slow to moderate growth
rate to 30 feet tall

Sophora japonica
(Japanese pagoda tree)
Moderate growth rate
to 30 feet tall

Sapium sebiferum
(Chinese tallow tree)
Fast growth rate
to 40 feet tall

feet or more, with a greater spread), and produces broader and more bluish green foliage on shorter weeping branches.

S. elegantissima. THURLOW WEEPING WILLOW. Zones 5-10. Presumed to be from the same parentage as the Wisconsin weeping willow (*S. blanda*), this willow more nearly approximates the grace of its weeping willow parent (*S. babylonica*). It is the same size as Wisconsin weeping willow, but has much longer pendent branches.

S. matsudana 'Tortuosa'. CORKSCREW WILLOW. Zones 5-9. The species *S. matsudana* will grow well with less water than most other willows, but most of its fame lies in the distinctive growth form of its variety 'Tortuosa'. A tree to 30 feet high by 20 feet wide, the branches and twigs of

this variety are twisted and contorted into spiraling, upright patterns. Its most dramatic landscape value is as a winter sculpture. It does need periodic thinning to keep from becoming a tangled thicket of branches. Leaves are narrow and bright green, to 4 inches long.

Sapium sebiferum

CHINESE TALLOW TREE. Zones 8-9. In the Orient, the Chinese tallow tree has been cultivated as a source of tallow (derived from the coating on its seeds) for soap and candles. But as an ornamental in this hemisphere, it serves as a pest and disease-free poplar replica with the added bonus of red autumn color. Like the leaves of many poplars, its leaves are roundish, to

3 inches long, and tapering to a slender point. They're light green in color and flutter in the slightest breeze. Growth is rapid to 35-40 feet high and wide, with either a rounded or tapered crown and with a tendency to grow several trunks instead of just one. The tree's milky sap is poisonous. In regions having only moderate autumn chill, trees in full sun will change to brilliant red or, with some individuals, plum purple, yellow, orange, or a mixture of colors. If you want a particular color, autumn is the best time to select a tree from a nursery. Trees prefer, but do not demand, a slightly acid soil. Fastest growth comes with ample water. This fact, combined with the light to moderate shade it casts, makes the Chinese tallow tree a good lawn specimen.

Sassafras albidum

SASSAFRAS. Zones 5-9. Just one leaf from a sassafras won't necessarily allow you to identify the tree, for leaf shape is unpredictable. Some leaves are simple, pointed ovals. Others have the addition of a mitten-shaped lobe on one side or the other. Still others have a total of 3 lobes — sometimes only shallow ones, at other times very deep ones. Size is anywhere from 3-5 inches long, and up to 3-4 inches wide. Autumn color is orange to scarlet, better in some years than in others. Individual flowers are inconspicuous, but they bloom in clusters that outline the branches in early spring. Male and female blossoms appear on separate trees. Fruits on female trees are noticeable (but not showy) ½-inch, dark blue berries on bright red stalks.

"Irregular" describes the tree's growth habit. A heavy trunk supports rather short branches that often form nearly right angles with the trunk; from these, smaller branches reach upward. Branching from the trunk tends to be randomly placed and fairly sparse, creating a rather open, patchwork crown. Mature trees are 30-60 feet tall. The best growth is in sandy, well-drained (even poor but never alkaline) soils. In dry-summer regions, the sassafras requires some watering. Avoid planting the tree where you'll have to cultivate in its root zone: it suckers profusely from roots when they are disturbed.

Sophora japonica

JAPANESE PAGODA TREE. CHINESE SCHOLAR TREE. Zones 5-10. Flowers in mid to late summer mark this tree as unusual among flowering types. The yellowish white, sweet-pea-shaped blooms are only ½-inch long, but they are produced in dense, foot-long clusters at the ends of the branches. Unfortunately, blossoming is not always reliable where summers are cool and damp, and trees usually must be five or more years old before they begin flowering. If blossoms fall on concrete paving they can stain it yellow. Leaves are locust-like: small, oval leaflets on opposite sides of a midvein give a soft, ferny effect. In autumn, without coloring, they drop and disintegrate, eliminating the need for raking. On young trees the foliage hangs on and remains green during winter. The young tree grows at a moderate rate to a rounded 20-30 feet. Then growth slows down to give you, eventually, a 50-70 foot tree with equal spread. Trees tend to grow faster in sandy loam soils (with regular water) and slower in more claylike soils. Young wood is smooth and dark gray green, but old bark develops a much more rugged character. Trees are not particular about soil or the amount of water; they have almost no pest or disease troubles and are undaunted by polluted city atmospheres. It's also a good tree for shading a lawn. The variety 'Regent' is more upright than the species. It also grows a bit faster and begins flowering at about half the age usually required.

Sorbus (Mountain ash)

Showy flowers and showier fruits account for part of the popularity of mountain ashes. Blooms don't appear in the smothering spectacle that most *Prunus* species present but instead are grouped in broad, flat clusters scattered in the foliage canopy. Later, they become hanging clusters of usually red, small, applelike fruits. Autumn foliage color often is a good orange to red. Other reasons for popularity are the tree's relatively small size, symmetrical habit, and nonmassive structure, which put them in scale for small gardens or close-up planting. Most species can be bothered enough by several insect and disease pests that you may want to weigh planting them very carefully. Borers, in particular, may go for trunks and branches, killing limbs or even the entire tree if not discovered and eliminated. Sawfly larvae can destroy large amounts of foliage in summer; fireblight and scale are other problems. (See pages 18-19 for pest control information.) All trees need well drained, good garden soil and must have some summer water. Hot summer weather often spoils the foliage. None are good trees for hot lower Midwest and Southwest gardens.

S. alnifolia. KOREAN MOUNTAIN ASH. Zones 6-7. Unlike most commonly grown mountain ashes, this species has simple, broadly oval, shiny green leaves to 4 inches long with toothed edges. Autumn color is a good orange to bright red. Young trees are fairly fast-growing pyramids that mature to broadly oval or rounded 40-foot trees with a lesser spread. Open clusters of small red fruits last on the tree for some time after leaves fall.

S. americana. AMERICAN MOUNTAIN ASH. Zones 3-6. Both in their preference for cooler climates and in their appearance, this native mountain ash and one other North American species (*S. decora*, showy mountain ash, Zones 3-7) are very similar to the better-known European mountain ash *(S. aucuparia)*. The American natives, though, both make smaller, shrubbier trees (to about 30 feet), round topped and slender with slender limbs. If not multiple trunked, they will tend to branch low. Autumn color is yellow, contrasting with clusters of dark red berries. The showy mountain ash has larger fruits, to ½ inch across.

S. aucuparia. EUROPEAN MOUNTAIN ASH. Zones 3-7. Smaller leaves, larger flowers, and greater size (40-50 feet tall) distinguish this mountain ash from *S. americana* and *S. decora*. Branches rise distinctly upward, forming a dense, oval to round crown. Leaves consist of 9-15 opposite leaflets, each a 1-2-inch oval with toothed edges. Upper surfaces are dull green; undersides are gray green. Autumn color usually is yellow to rusty yellow to red orange. Five-inch clusters of white flowers in spring are followed by orange red ¼-½-inch fruits in summer that will remain on the tree throughout fall and winter unless discovered by hungry birds. The trees

must have ample summer water and good soil to remain healthy.

Stewartia

These refined, slow-growing trees are related to camellias — a fact that is apparent in their flowers and their preference for moist but well drained and slightly acid soils and a partially shaded garden location. All seasons find them good looking: neat, healthy foliage in spring; single white blooms in summer; strong autumn foliage color; and good winter branch pattern with multicolored, flaking bark. Stewartias do not succeed in the lower Midwest and Southwest.

S. koreana. KOREAN STEWARTIA. Zones 6-9 (but not desert), 6-8 in eastern regions. You can distinguish this tree from *S. pseudo-camellia* by its larger (to 3 inches across), flatter flowers, zigzag branches, overall smaller size, and different fall color. Habit is a rather narrow pyramid 20-40 feet high, clothed in pointed oval leaves to 4 inches long. White midsummer flowers have 5 wavy petals and a cluster of yellow orange stamens in the center. Autumn finds the leaves turning to orange or red orange.

S. pseudo-camellia. JAPANESE STEWARTIA. Zones 6-9 (but not desert), 6-8 in eastern regions. After many years, mature specimens will be tall pyramids up to about 60 feet. Oval, 1-3-inch leaves put on a show of bronze to dark purple in autumn, soon after the late summer blossoms have faded. Flowers are to 2½ inches across, single and white with a cluster of orange stamens in the center. They are more definitely cup shaped than the blooms of the Korean stewartia (*S. koreana*). Bark is reddish, peeling off on older trees.

Styrax

SNOWBELL. Here are two neat, well-behaved, flowering trees of modest size that are excellent for planting in patios, lawns, or in the foreground of larger and darker-colored trees. Both require good soil and ample water and will grow in partial shade as well as full sun. You can garden beneath them since roots are not near the surface. Neither tree is good in the lower Midwest or Southwest.

S. japonica. JAPANESE SNOWBELL, JAPANESE SNOWDROP TREE. Zones 6-9. Slow to moderate growth produces a 30-foot tree with a strongly horizontal branching habit that results in a broad, flat-topped specimen. Leaves are dark green ovals to 3 inches long with lightly toothed edges. Fall color may be yellow or red. Flowers are wide, open bells with 5 petals, giving the appearance of small white stars. They are especially conspicuous because of the way they are carried on the branches: leaves angle upward from branches while small clusters of flowers hang down underneath. Combined with the horizontal branch pattern, the effect is of parallel tiers of green and white. Trees tend towards shrubbiness unless lower branches are removed as trees grow.

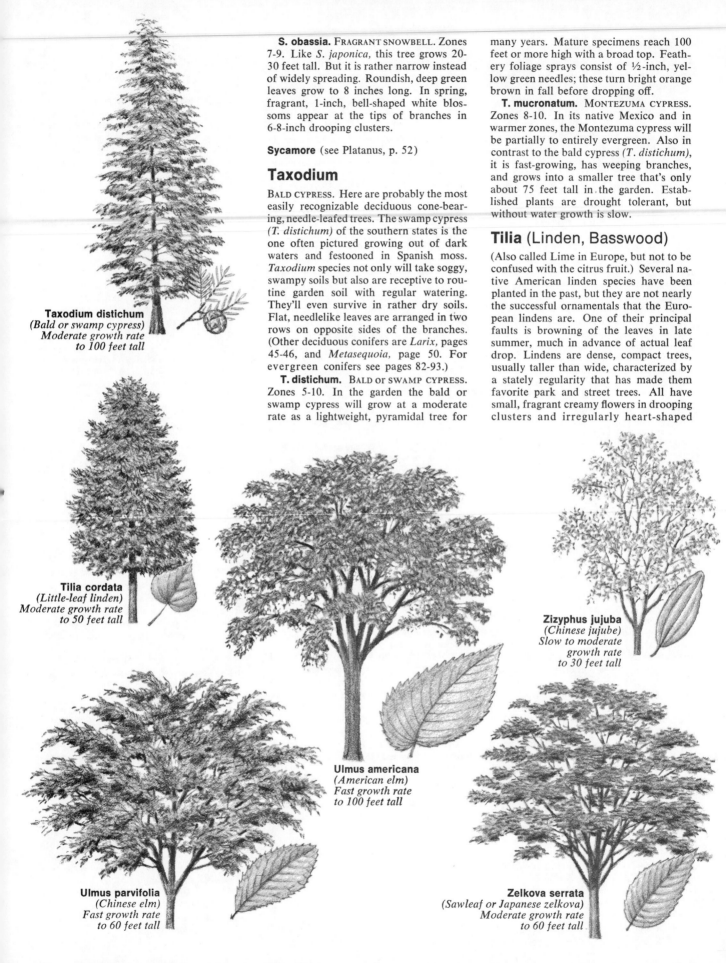

S. obassia. FRAGRANT SNOWBELL. Zones 7-9. Like *S. japonica,* this tree grows 20-30 feet tall. But it is rather narrow instead of widely spreading. Roundish, deep green leaves grow to 8 inches long. In spring, fragrant, 1-inch, bell-shaped white blossoms appear at the tips of branches in 6-8-inch drooping clusters.

Sycamore (see Platanus, p. 52)

Taxodium

BALD CYPRESS. Here are probably the most easily recognizable deciduous cone-bearing, needle-leafed trees. The swamp cypress (*T. distichum*) of the southern states is the one often pictured growing out of dark waters and festooned in Spanish moss. *Taxodium* species not only will take soggy, swampy soils but also are receptive to routine garden soil with regular watering. They'll even survive in rather dry soils. Flat, needlelike leaves are arranged in two rows on opposite sides of the branches. (Other deciduous conifers are *Larix,* pages 45-46, and *Metasequoia,* page 50. For evergreen conifers see pages 82-93.)

T. distichum. BALD OR SWAMP CYPRESS. Zones 5-10. In the garden the bald or swamp cypress will grow at a moderate rate as a lightweight, pyramidal tree for many years. Mature specimens reach 100 feet or more high with a broad top. Feathery foliage sprays consist of ½-inch, yellow green needles; these turn bright orange brown in fall before dropping off.

T. mucronatum. MONTEZUMA CYPRESS. Zones 8-10. In its native Mexico and in warmer zones, the Montezuma cypress will be partially to entirely evergreen. Also in contrast to the bald cypress (*T. distichum*), it is fast-growing, has weeping branches, and grows into a smaller tree that's only about 75 feet tall in the garden. Established plants are drought tolerant, but without water growth is slow.

Tilia (Linden, Basswood)

(Also called Lime in Europe, but not to be confused with the citrus fruit.) Several native American linden species have been planted in the past, but they are not nearly the successful ornamentals that the European lindens are. One of their principal faults is browning of the leaves in late summer, much in advance of actual leaf drop. Lindens are dense, compact trees, usually taller than wide, characterized by a stately regularity that has made them favorite park and street trees. All have small, fragrant creamy flowers in drooping clusters and irregularly heart-shaped

Taxodium distichum
(Bald or swamp cypress)
Moderate growth rate
to 100 feet tall

Tilia cordata
(Little-leaf linden)
Moderate growth rate
to 50 feet tall

Ulmus americana
(American elm)
Fast growth rate
to 100 feet tall

Zizyphus jujuba
(Chinese jujube)
Slow to moderate
growth rate
to 30 feet tall

Ulmus parvifolia
(Chinese elm)
Fast growth rate
to 60 feet tall

Zelkova serrata
(Sawleaf or Japanese zelkova)
Moderate growth rate
to 60 feet tall

leaves. Best growth (which is at a moderate rate) is in deep, rich soils with plenty of water. Where winters are mild, leaves will fall without changing color. But in colder regions, foliage will turn yellow. Aphids may be a problem requiring attention in order to prevent their honeydew from creating a sticky mess on the leaves and on anything beneath the tree.

T. cordata. LITTLE-LEAF LINDEN. Zones 4-9 (but not the Plains states). Small leaves, 1½-3 inches long and equally wide, give this species a finer texture than that found on other lindens. Their color is dark green with paler undersides. Densely pyramidal in shape, they make a fine shade tree to be used wherever you won't mind the bees that are attracted to its midsummer blossoms. The little-leaf linden also grows well in the trying atmospheric conditions present in many cities. Expect it to reach 30-50 feet with a spread half as wide in the West, to around 90 feet high (and correspondingly as wide) in eastern states. The variety 'Greenspire' has a particularly straight trunk and regular branching pattern, forming an oval or pyramidal crown. In the Northwest, foliage is susceptible to a mite that causes leaves to brown in midsummer.

T. euchlora. CRIMEAN LINDEN. Zones 5-9. This hybrid has as one parent the little-leaf linden (*T. cordata*) but in contrast to it, the leaves are larger (2-4 inches long) and glossy on slightly drooping branches. Crimean linden's shape is broader but its shade is not as dense. Its height is 35-50 feet with nearly equal spread. For a denser, pyramid form, shop for the variety 'Redmond'. In addition to tolerating city conditions, the Crimean linden will take more heat and drought than most other linden species.

T. tomentosa. SILVER LINDEN. Zones 6-9. The "silver" in this linden's common name comes from the grayish white fuzz on the undersides of leaves, noticeable because leaves flutter in even the slightest breeze and contrast with the dark green upper surfaces. Leaf size is 3-5 inches long and nearly as wide. Trees grow 60 feet tall (taller in eastern regions) and about half as broad. Established specimens are fairly drought tolerant.

Ulmus (Elm)

Not too long ago, the name "elm" automatically referred to the stately American elm (*U. americana*) whose graceful vase shape arched over countless city streets, adorned parks, and shaded many a country yard or pasture. Then along came the Dutch elm disease (spread by a bark beetle) and a phloem necrosis virus. Singly and together, these plagues have spread through the tree's native territory in the central and eastern United States, killing countless thousands of mature trees. Healthy American elms still exist within this area, but it is a definite danger zone within which no guarantee of the trees' safety can be made. Dutch elm disease

also has been found in some locations west of the Rocky Mountains. Because all elms are in some degree susceptible to Dutch elm disease, their use is something of a gamble in areas where the disease is known to have been active.

U. americana. AMERICAN ELM. Zones 3-9 (but develops leaf burn in the desert). As mentioned above, this species is the primary target of the Dutch elm disease and is not a good risk in many areas east of the Rocky Mountains. It will succeed in some western areas but should be used only with its liabilities clearly in mind. The pervasive roots can sucker profusely, totally dominating the area in which they extend. If crowded by pavement, they will easily lift it. Unfortunately, there is no real replacement for this elm's distinctive vase (or wineglass) shape, created by branches that grow upward and outward to great height and then droop back toward earth. (*Zelkova serrata*, though, does come close.) Fast growth takes the American elm up to 100 feet or more with equal or greater spread, but the wood is brittle. Leaves are rough, 3-6 inches long with toothed edges, and turn yellow in autumn. Pests are aphids, scale, and elm leaf beetle. Where winters are mild, trees leaf out very late in spring.

U. carpinifolia. SMOOTH-LEAFED ELM. Zones 5-9. This species is another big tree to 100 feet high with wide-spreading main branches and pendulous branchlets. Leaves, shiny deep green on the upper surface, are narrow ovals to 3½ inches long. Like the American elm (*U. americana*), it has aggressive, suckering roots. A more desirable form is the variety 'Christine Buisman', which was selected for its resistance (but not immunity) to Dutch elm disease. It is distinctly upright to 60-80 feet, mature trees spreading to little more than half the width. Fall color is yellow. Elm leaf beetle can be a serious pest to smooth-leafed elms.

U. parvifolia. CHINESE ELM. Zones 6-10. Some confusion exists in the nursery trade about forms of this species that approach evergreen status. Usually the so-called evergreen Chinese elms are offered as *U. p. sempervirens*, or as the variety 'Pendens'. Even these trees may lose leaves temporarily in an extremely cold spell. Growth habit is distinctly unlike that of the American elm (*U. americana*) and smooth-leafed elms (*U. carpinifolia*). Long, arching, semiweeping branches produce a tree of 40-60 feet in height, spreading to as much as 70 feet; the crown is very broadly rounded. Older trees have light-colored bark that sheds in patches to produce a beautiful mottled effect. Leaves are small, leathery, even-toothed ovals to 2½ inches long and a little more than half as wide. Autumn color is reddish where cold is pronounced but yellow in mild regions. Young trees need staking to establish a straight, strong trunk. For further strengthening, the low side branches may be shortened. Also shorten any branches that grow too long or are so weeping that

they distort the shape you're trying to establish. Typically, growth is very fast although it does vary with individual trees. This is one of the best-growing trees for the desert, but there it is especially prone to the fatal Texas root rot.

U. pumila. SIBERIAN ELM (but often called "Chinese elm", which really is *U. parvifolia*). Zones 5-9. This species is worthwhile only in such regions as parts of the Great Plains states, Rocky Mountain and Great Basin areas where any tree must cope with extremes of heat and cold, drought, high winds, and poor soil. It also succeeds in desert regions where it is less susceptible to Texas root rot than the Chinese elm (*U. parvifolia*). Its disadvantages are brittle wood and weak crotches that break easily in storms, a shallow and greedy root system, and susceptibility to canker and to elm leaf beetle. But it does make a good windbreak, shelter, and erosion-control tree, especially if clipped to increase its density. As a specimen tree, it reaches 50-75 feet with rounded, rather open crown. Smooth, dark green leaves may be 2 inches long and 1 inch wide, turning yellow in fall.

Walnut (see Juglans, p. 44)

Willow (see Salix, pp. 57-58)

Zelkova serrata

SAWLEAF or JAPANESE ZELKOVA. Zones 6-9 (6-8 in eastern regions). A close relative of the elms, this virtually pest-free tree has foliage that suggests the connection. Leaves are tooth-edged ovals to 5 inches long, turning yellow, rusty yellow, or (in some trees) orange red in autumn. Mature trees may be 60 feet tall and wide with a distinctive, bulky structure. The trunk is short and thick; from it sprout many ascending branches beginning at nearly the same point. Form ranges from urn shaped to quite spreading. It can send up suckers from roots if they are disturbed in cultivation. A selected variety, 'Village Green', comes close to duplicating the unique vase shape of the American elm (*U. americana*) and is resistant to Dutch elm disease.

Zizyphus jujuba

CHINESE JUJUBE. Zones 6-10. Attractive silhouette, edible fruit, toughness, and freedom from pests and diseases are the Chinese jujube's chief assets. Slow to moderate growth produces a 20-30-foot specimen with spiny, gnarled, and somewhat pendulous branches. Often it will send up much growth from the base to become multi-trunked or even thicketlike. Glossy, bright green leaves are 1-2 inches long with 3 prominent veins. In mid to late spring it bears clusters of small yellow flowers that produce the fall-ripening, datelike fruits. Deep roots enable the tree to tolerate drought. It also withstands saline and alkaline soils, although best growth comes in good soil with regular watering. 'Lang' and 'Li' are the most widely sold varieties.

To find your climate zone, see page 96

Eucalyptus sideroxylon, *a graceful member of broad-leafed group, flourishes in warmer zones.*

Broad-leafed evergreens

Here are trees clothed in broad, flattish leaves the year around. Every season they'll function dependably, giving consistent landscape beauty.

Unlike deciduous trees, which drop all of their leaves at some one time during the year and are often bare throughout the winter months, evergreen trees maintain a full dress of foliage all year long.

The "broad-leafed" evergreen trees described on these pages are distinguished from other evergreen trees, such as pines and firs, by their generally wide, flat leaves that are often similar to (but not necessarily larger than) the leaves of many deciduous trees. Their leaf shape differentiates them from the "needle-leafed" evergreens (see pages 82-93), which have slender, needlelike or scalelike leaves.

Native mostly to the warmer parts of the world, broad-leafed evergreens form a major part of the landscape in Zones 9 and 10 where winter temperatures are warmest. Although these trees won't survive in really cold-winter climates, gardeners in Zones 8 and 7 still can plant a limited variety of them.

The landscape roles of broad-leafed evergreen trees and deciduous trees are much the same. The major difference is that the broad-leafed evergreen offers relatively unchanging beauty year round whereas the deciduous tree is continually changing from bare branches in winter to flowers and foliage in spring or summer to autumn leaf color change followed directly by leaf drop. Some broad-leafed evergreens do have flowers; others have new growth that contrasts in color or form with mature foliage.

The trees in this section are listed alphabetically by their botanical name. Following each botanical name is the tree's common name (or names) and the climate zones in which the tree will grow well. These zones were prepared by the United States Department of Agriculture; a map of their locations can be found on page 96. Each tree's common name is listed in the index (page 94) with a cross-reference to the correct botanical name and the pages on which it is described.

In the descriptions of the trees, growth rates are often referred to: "fast" indicates that the tree will increase its height by 2 or more feet each year; "moderate" means 1 to 2 feet of growth per year; "slow" describes less than 1 foot of growth per year.

Acacia

Even in regions where they won't grow, acacias (also known as "wattles") may be familiar as the "mimosa" of florist shops. Among the many species, flower color ranges from white through cream to yellow, and all put on a display that ranges from noticeable to spectacular. The typical acacia blossom is a small, fluffy ball of stamens. The grouping together of these balls into clusters—and the numbers of clusters on a tree—create the show. Some acacias manage to be the first flowering trees of the new year in mild-winter areas.

Acacias have two types of leaves. In some species, the foliage is so finely divided that it appears feathery or fernlike. Others have flattened leaf stalks that give the impression of narrow leaves and fulfill all leaf functions. Some species are thorny.

No acacia has a long life expectancy (20-30 years represents a good average), but they grow so rapidly that you have a full-sized tree during most of their years of existence. Not too particular about soils, acacias also are quite drought tolerant when established. For the best start in life, plant a small tree (1-gallon-can size or even less) and stake it until roots are well anchored. To encourage good rooting, water deeply but infrequently; this also will help to discourage surface rooting, a tendency of all acacias. Large, older trees may need occasional thinning to open up the crown and lessen dieback of shaded branches and to offer less wind resistance. Whenever you trim an acacia, remove the twig, branch, or limb clear back to its point of origin at another branch or limb or at the trunk.

A. baileyana. BAILEY ACACIA, COOTA-MUNDRA WATTLE. Zones 9-10. This tree presents a January spectacle of brilliant yellow. For this reason, in part, it is the most popular acacia for planting as a specimen tree. But flowers aren't its only asset. A soft-looking crown of foliage 20-30 feet high and equally wide is made up of feathery, finely cut blue gray to gray green leaves. For a more informal effect, grow it as a multi-trunked specimen. Identical in all respects except one is the variety 'Purpurea', the purple-leaf acacia. All its new growth emerges lavender to purple, fading later to the usual acacia gray blue.

A. decurrens. GREEN WATTLE. Zones 9-10 and warmer parts of Zone 8. Visualize this as a taller, more upright, and greener version of the Bailey acacia (A. baileyana).

Leaves are slightly larger and dark green but still cut along feathery or fernlike lines. Expect this species to reach 50 feet high with perhaps an equal spread. If you can use the additional size, this species lives longer than the Bailey acacia and will tolerate more water and wind. Its peak flowering season is about a month later than that of the Bailey acacia. If you want silver foliage, this tree has it in the variety A. d. dealbata.

A. melanoxylon. BLACKWOOD or BLACK ACACIA. Zones 8-10. This species has an equal number of good and bad points. Only by understanding its potential faults can you possibly turn it into a rewarding tree. Roots are a primary problem: because they're aggressive and competitive, the tree should not be planted with any other plants that would suffer from the association. The roots also will lift nearby pavement. Above ground, you have a plant that suckers easily from the roots if they are disturbed, wood that splits fairly easily in storms, and a constant drop of leaves that don't decompose quickly. And because roots are close to the soil surface, the trees can be easily blown over when soil is saturated and top growth becomes heavy with rain water. On the positive side, this acacia is tough: It grows strongly anywhere, including in poor soil, drought, heat, or wind. And it is a good-looking tree. On rural properties or in uncultivated parts of the garden (where you might need a high screen or boundary planting), this tree really shines. Fast, upright growth reaches about 40 feet high by 20 feet wide with single or multiple trunks depending on how you train it. What look like dark green, narrow, 2-4-inch leaves really are flattened leaf stalks. You see the feathery true leaves only on young plants and on strong new growth. Straw yellow to cream colored flowers appear in early spring but don't put on a really splashy show.

A. pendula. WEEPING ACACIA. Zones 9-10. Plant this acacia not for flowers but for a weeping cascade of blue gray foliage. Narrow leaves (actually flattened leaf stalks) grow to 4 inches long, clothing the long, pendulous branches. Ultimate height is only about 25 feet, with a spread of about 15 feet. Yellow flowers appear erratically in spring.

A. pruinosa. FROSTY or BRONZE ACACIA. Zones 9-10. This has the same finely divided, feathery foliage of the Bailey acacia (A. baileyana), but individual leaflets are larger (to ¾-inch long). Mature leaves are light green, but copper tints color the new growth. One of the larger acacias, this species may reach 60 feet high, forming a dense crown that may spread as wide as 40 feet.

Arbutus

MADRONE and STRAWBERRY TREE. Botanists would find more in common between two arbutus species than would most gardeners. The madrone (A. menziesii) is potentially a large tree; the strawberry tree (A. unedo) is rather small. The madrone is very exacting in its requirements; the strawberry tree is quite adaptable. Both have attractive (but different) leaves, fruit, and bark. Only in the flowers do you see real similarity: whitish, urn-shaped small blossoms in showy clusters—but at different times of the year.

A. menziesii. MADRONE, MADRONA. Zones 6-9. Its cultural demands make the madrone something of a rarity in gardens outside its native Northwest and northern California range. Fast-draining acid soil (or at least not alkaline) and cool winters are musts for success. Height and aspect vary from a shrubby 20 feet to broad-crowned specimens sometimes as tall as 100 feet. Uncrowded locations and more water give you the larger trees. Where partly shaded by other trees, growth may be attractively irregular. The most noticeable feature is smooth red brown bark that peels off in thin flakes throughout the year. Thick and leathery leaves are broad ovals to 6 inches long, shiny dark green on the upper surfaces (with distinctly lighter midvein) but dull gray green below. These last on the tree for two years and then turn yellow, orange, or red before shedding in summer. New spring growth comes out a pinkish or bronzy light green. Also in spring appear large clusters of small, white, urn-shaped blossoms at the ends of branches. These are followed in fall by clusters of small, wrinkly, bright red and orange berries that are showy throughout winter if not discovered by birds. Since madrones are difficult to transplant, best results come from small plants (less than 2 feet high) that look as though they'd never grow up to tree size. Water regularly until established; then give deep but infrequent irrigation. Overwatering increases the danger of death from root rot.

A. unedo. STRAWBERRY TREE. Zones 7-10. Without early guidance, this is more

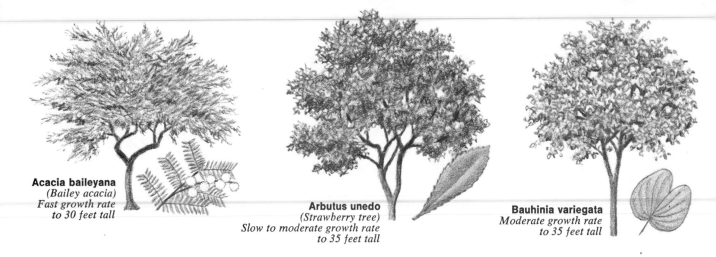

Acacia baileyana
(Bailey acacia)
Fast growth rate
to 30 feet tall

Arbutus unedo
(Strawberry tree)
Slow to moderate growth rate
to 35 feet tall

Bauhinia variegata
Moderate growth rate
to 35 feet tall

likely to grow as a bush for many years instead of as a tree. Its natural growth habit is multi-stemmed and shrubby. Select one or just a few stems to become a main trunk or trunks for a tree; keep any other basal sprouts pulled off. Slow to moderate growth builds up to a round-crowned tree to 35 feet tall and spreading as wide. Bark on the trunk and branches is a rich red brown color, cracking and shedding to show smooth reddish inner bark. Leaves are glossy dark green with red leaf-stalks, oval to about 3 inches long. The small, whitish, urn-shaped blossoms appear in clusters in fall and winter. Later these produce ¾-inch, round and rough-skinned fruits that turn from yellow to orange red. The fruits persist on the tree into the next flowering season, giving you a combined display of white blossoms and red fruits. Fruits are edible (though bland and mealy); they mainly serve as food for birds. The tree prefers a well-drained soil and only moderate amounts of water (to avoid root rot) but otherwise is not demanding. Trees have succeeded both in the desert (when shaded) and along the coast.

Bauhinia

ORCHID TREE. This tree's small stature and lightweight limb structure, combined with a season of showy flowers, recommend it for patios and small gardens wherever it will grow. On the borderline between evergreen and deciduous, one species loses part of its leaves at flowering time whereas the other sheds them all at once but blooms at the same time so the tree is never really bare. Distinctive foliage has 2 lobes, as though a single, roundish leaf were cleft down the middle. The flowers bear a resemblance to cattleya orchids.

B. blakeana. HONG KONG ORCHID TREE. Zone 10 and warmer parts of Zone 9. The smaller of the two bauhinia species, this tree forms an umbrella-shaped crown to about 20 feet high. Some, but not all, of the gray green leaves drop off during the fall and winter bloom season. Fragrant blossoms are in the rose, orchid pink, and purple shades, often combining several tones in each 5-6 inch flower.

B. variegata. (Sometimes sold as *B. purpurea,* which is another distinct species). Zone 10 and warmer parts of Zone 9. This species sometimes needs guidance to become a single-trunked tree rather than a several-stemmed large shrub. Treelike, it will reach as high as 35 feet with a dome-shaped crown. When flowering begins in January, all the light green leaves drop to leave the tree covered with light pink to orchid purple, 3-inch blossoms. When these finish (about April), new leaves promptly emerge. The best performance occurs where summers are definitely warm; it's not a seacoast tree. The variety 'Candida' has white flowers.

Brachychiton

Woody, canoe-shaped seed pods are the common bond among these Australian trees. Otherwise, their differences are more pronounced than their similarities. Growth generally is rapid. The trees can be planted in a wide variety of soils.

B. acerifolium. FLAME TREE, AUSTRALIAN FLAME TREE. Zones 9-10. Leaves are like a tropical rendition of maple: fan-shaped and deeply lobed, bright shiny green and up to 10 inches across. These are carried on an upright tree (to 60 feet or more) whose trunk is thick, smooth, and straight (but sometimes swollen at the base). Usually, the trunk is green. Foliage drops when flowers come out in late spring, but bloom often doesn't appear on all branches so only flowering limbs lose leaves. Upright bloom clusters hold small, tubular, bell-shaped flowers that are a flashy orange red to scarlet. When an entire tree blooms, it is a spectacular sight.

B. bidwillii. To visualize this tree, read the description of the preceding species *(B. acerifolium)* and then imagine it reduced in size to about 20 feet tall with a more slender trunk and a rounded crown. Leaves are of similar style but smaller and with just 3 lobes. Flowers have a brownish cast to their basic red color.

B. discolor. PINK FLAME TREE, QUEENSLAND LACEBARK. Zones 9-10. Growth, flowering, and leaf-drop habits are the same as those of *B. acerifolium.* This,

however, is even taller (to 90 feet) and summer-flowering. Blossoms are fewer in number but individually larger, rose pink instead of red, and covered with rust colored fuzz on the outsides. The 6-inch blue green (but not shiny) leaves are fan-shaped but only shallowly lobed.

B. populneum. BOTTLE TREE. Zones 9-10. A stout and often swollen trunk gives this species its common name. In contrast to the other species, it is not a flamboyant bloomer. Blossoms are modest little tannish white bells that are rusty pink inside. Foliage resembles that of poplars and flutters in the breeze as poplar leaves do. Individual leaves vary from oval to slightly lobed, and are shiny green to about 3 inches long. Moderate growth rate produces a 30-50-foot tree with a rounded crown spreading to about 30 feet. Deep roots enable the tree to withstand drought. Good in the mild-winter deserts for shade and windbreaks.

Callistemon

BOTTLEBRUSH. (Also see *Melaleuca* for other trees sometimes called "bottlebrush.") Flowers consist mostly of long stamens and are clustered tightly together along the stems to produce a bottlebrush appearance. Woody seed capsules follow the flowers and remain attached to the branches for several years; new growth continues on from the tops of flower clusters. All callistemons grow rapidly in moist, well-drained soil and full sun. They can tolerate drought (but won't turn in their best performance) and will also take alkaline or saline soils, although chlorosis (yellowing of the leaves) may occur and require treatment with iron chelates.

C. citrinus. LEMON BOTTLEBRUSH (also sold as *C.lanceolatus*). Zone 10 and warmer areas of Zone 9. Of the four callistemon species described here, this is the toughest in adverse situations and the most cold-tolerant. Trained as a single-trunked tree it grows narrow and round-headed (it's shaped like a lollipop) to about 25 feet high. It will have a less stiff appearance if you allow several trunks to develop.

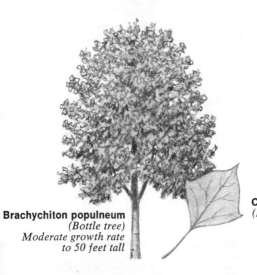

Brachychiton populneum
(Bottle tree)
Moderate growth rate
to 50 feet tall

Callistemon citrinus
(Lemon bottlebrush)
Fast growth rate
to 25 feet tall

Castanospermum australe
(Moreton Bay chestnut)
Moderate growth rate
to 60 feet tall

Casuarina stricta
(Mountain or
drooping she-oak)
Fast growth rate
to 35 feet tall

Narrow, 3-inch leaves are copper colored when they first come out and turn to bright green as they mature. Bright red flowers in 6-inch clusters come in bursts throughout the year. Foliage and flower quality vary considerably when plants are grown from seed. For best results, look for a named variety, such as 'Improved' or 'Splendens'.

C. salignus. WHITE or WILLOW BOTTLE-BRUSH. Zone 10 and warmer parts of Zone 9. Narrow, willowlike leaves to 3 inches long give this plant one of its common names. New growth is bright pink to copper colored, turning green as it matures. Flowers aren't actually white but are pale yellow to cream (sometimes pale pink) in clusters up to 3 inches long. As a tree it will be dense and fairly slender to about 25 feet high.

C. viminalis. WEEPING BOTTLEBRUSH. Zone 10 and warmer parts of Zone 9. With some attention to periodic thinning, this species makes a good-looking 30-foot weeping tree, spreading about half the height. Untended, the crown is inclined to become tangled and unkempt as well as top heavy. Its weeping habit usually is quite apparent because leaves tend to grow just at the ends of the long, drooping branches. Leaves are light green, narrow, and 6 inches long, contrasting with the bright red bottlebrush flowers primarily in spring and summer (but with scattered bloom throughout the year). The weeping bottlebrush needs regular watering. Because of this and the thick, heavy crown, it is not a good tree for hot, windy, and dry locations. The variety 'McCaskillii' is more vigorous and dense and has more colorful flowers.

Castanospermum australe

MORETON BAY CHESTNUT. Zones 9 (warmer parts) and 10. Summer-flowering trees almost always are noticed because there is much less competition at that season than in spring. And the spectacular flowers of this Australian native assure its being a garden focal point. Bright red and yellow blossoms are carried in loose spikes to 8 inches long all over the tree — even along the main trunk. Good foliage is another

asset: glossy dark leaves composed of 11-15 oval leaflets, each to 5 inches long. Mature trees are broadly rounded, growing to as much as 60 feet high. Cylinder-shaped seed pods (to as long as 9 inches) contain chestnutlike seeds.

Casuarina

BEEFWOOD, SHE-OAK. At first glance, these trees appear to be some sort of pine. But on closer inspection you'll see that the "needles" really are thin, jointed green stems with nearly inconspicuous true leaves. When these needlelike branchlets become old, they fall off and form a carpet beneath the tree of what appears to be dried pine needles. Casuarinas thrive in several situations that defeat many other trees. Because they tolerate dry soil and wind, they are good desert trees; but they also grow in wet and even brackish soils and withstand onslaughts of salt spray at the seashore. You can plant the trees to help stabilize shifting seashore sand.

They're not for close association with other plants: invasive, greedy roots commandeer more than their share of water and nutrients. All casuarinas have small, woody, conelike fruit clusters.

C. cunninghamiana. RIVER SHE-OAK. Zones 9-10. Though a fairly slender tree, *C. cunninghamiana* grows to 70 feet tall, making this species the largest of the casuarinas described here. Native habitat is in moist soil near fresh water.

C. equisetifolia. HORSETAIL TREE, SWAMP SHE-OAK. Zones 9-10. Fast, pyramidal growth reaches 40-60 feet high and about 20 feet wide. A soft, graceful aspect comes from the drooping, gray green branchlets.

C. stricta. MOUNTAIN or DROOPING SHE-OAK, COAST BEEFWOOD. Zones 9-10. Fast growth to only about 35 feet makes this the smallest of the three casuarinas. Its drooping branchlets are dark green.

Ceratonia siliqua

CAROB, ST. JOHN'S BREAD. Zones 9-10. Trained as a single or multiple-trunked

Ceratonia siliqua
(Carob)
Moderate growth rate
to 40 feet tall

To find your climate zone, see page 96

tree, the carob will give you a dense, domed crown. The heavy foliage load should be thinned periodically (and the young trees securely staked) to prevent the trees' being blown over by wind. Left to its own devices, the tree more often than not will become a tree-sized shrub with foliage to the ground. Its uses, then, extend to those of hedge, barrier, and windbreak. Young trees often produce numerous new shoots from the base. You should pull these off if you want to maintain a single trunk. Mature specimens are 30-50 feet high and wide. Dark green, very leathery leaves contain 4-10 nearly round, wavy leaflets about 2 inches across. Inconspicuous male and female flowers come on separate trees. Male blossoms have a somewhat unpleasant odor; female flowers produce thick, dark brown pods to 1 foot long that can be a litter problem when they fall (their pulp is edible and has a chocolaty flavor). Male trees have warty branches, the knobs being the spots where flowers are produced right on the stems. Established trees will tolerate considerable drought. Even in regularly watered gardens, they should be watered infrequently (but deeply) during the warm months to avoid root rot.

Chorisia speciosa

FLOSS SILK TREE. Zones 9-10. This is a tropical tree of distinct character: the tapering, green trunk is studded with broad-based spines. Young trees are arrow-straight and slender, growing several feet each year. Growth slows in later years as the tree matures at 30-60 feet tall with a spread about half the height. Technically the floss silk tree is deciduous; most or all of the leaves drop when flowering begins in autumn or early winter. But leaves reappear as soon as flowering finishes, so the tree never is totally bare. Pink to purple blossoms with white bases, resembling 3-inch hibiscus flowers, are so profuse that the tree in bloom appears to be entirely tinted. Light green leaves consist of 5-7 leaflets arranged like a fan. Fast drainage and infrequent (monthly) deep watering are musts for success. With established trees, reducing the water you provide (beginning in late summer) will encourage more flowers.

Cinnamomum camphora

CAMPHOR TREE. Zones 9-10. Although the camphor tree's growth rate is slow to moderate, don't fail to allow plenty of room for a really large mature tree. Ultimate height is 50 feet or more, and the spread is greater. Though it's a good shade tree for a large lawn, its competitive root system rules it out of association with other plants. Its structure is as mighty as that of any oak: a heavy trunk and thick, spreading limbs covered with dark brown, textured bark that looks black when moistened by rains. Contrasting beautifully with the dark skeleton are the light green, pointed-oval leaves up to 5 inches long; new growth in early spring is pink to bronzy. Old leaves drop heavily in spring and are very slow to decompose if left where they fall. Tiny yellow flowers and pea-sized black fruits are not showy. Verticillium wilt, caused by a root rot fungus, is the only serious problem. It can cause wilting and death of twigs and branches and part or all of a tree. There is no real cure, and trees often will outgrow an attack. If the wilt appears, cut out affected branches; then apply a high-nitrogen fertilizer and water deeply to promote new root growth from healthy roots. Trees in poorly drained soil are more susceptible.

Citrus

Within the citrus category fall a number of familiar semi-tropical fruit trees: oranges, lemons, limes, grapefruit, mandarin oranges (tangerines), kumquats, and various hybrids of these (limequat, tangelo, tangor), as well as the sour oranges and Rangpur lime. All are good-looking small trees or shrubby trees with glossy, oval leaves, fragrant white blossoms, and conspicuous, colorful fruits.

Hardiness of the most cold-tolerant types is about 20°, which restricts citrus plantings to Zones 9 and 10 in the Southeast, Southwest, and Pacific Coast. In order to produce quality fruit, you'll have to consider the individual variety's heat re-

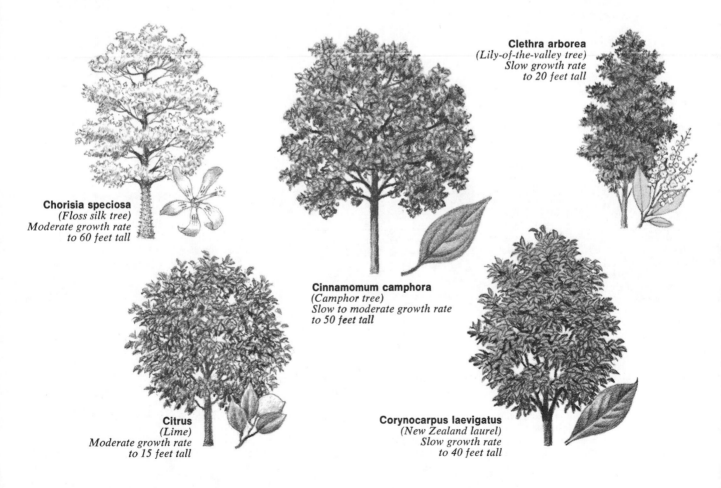

Clethra arborea
(Lily-of-the-valley tree)
Slow growth rate
to 20 feet tall

Chorisia speciosa
(Floss silk tree)
Moderate growth rate
to 60 feet tall

Cinnamomum camphora
(Camphor tree)
Slow to moderate growth rate
to 50 feet tall

Citrus
(Lime)
Moderate growth rate
to 15 feet tall

Corynocarpus laevigatus
(New Zealand laurel)
Slow growth rate
to 40 feet tall

quirement during its fruit development period, as well as the degree of winter cold it can tolerate. Remember that blossom damage by cold (for those trees that flower in winter) occurs at temperatures higher than those that damage the tree. In general, lemons need the least heat for fruit production and will bear good fruits in cool-summer regions. Oranges need more heat for best development; mandarin oranges require still more, followed by grapefruit, which needs such long seasons of high heat as the southwest deserts offer.

If you plant trees where they will be sheltered from winds and where they are against south-facing walls, winter low temperatures will be higher than in the open garden and summer heat will be more intense. This placement can somewhat expand your choices among citrus.

Different citrus types (and the varieties within any given type) have fairly definite climate requirements in order to assure good fruit production. Because citrus is an important commercial crop, this information is well documented. For the best variety suggestions for your area, consult your county agricultural agent or farm advisor.

Culturally, the first requirement is for well-drained soil; without it, citrus trees will die in time from root rot. If your soil is basically heavy and slow-draining, the best results will be if you plant citrus in raised beds. Trees need moist soil plus ample soil air (the reason for good drainage), so that means careful watering. Assuming good drainage, newly planted trees need frequent watering to establish their roots — perhaps as much as twice a week. After that, they need irrigation every other week during warm summer weather. In heavier, less well-drained soils, space waterings so that the top part of the soil dries between irrigations. Even if you have frequent summer rainfall, trees probably will need additional water: watering should moisten the entire root zone — to a depth of about four feet for mature trees. The easiest way to water thoroughly is to make a watering basin around the tree. Start the basin about 6 inches away from the trunk (so the trunk will stay dry) and, since roots extend out about twice as far as branches, build up the edges beyond the branch spread. A mulch spread in the basin will keep soil cool for those roots growing near the surface.

For best performance, citrus trees need regular fertilization; the greatest need is for nitrogen. Mature trees should have 1½-2 pounds of actual nitrogen each year; new trees should start with 2 ounces yearly, increasing that amount by ¼ pound a year in succeeding years. Actual nitrogen is the weight of nitrogen alone in a fertilizer; to figure this, multiply the percentage of total nitrogen in the fertilizer (this is stated on the package) by the weight of that package. Apply the total amount for the year in three fertilizings: ⅓ in late winter, ⅓ in June, and ⅓ in August. Spread it beneath the tree and well beyond the branch spread; then water

in deeply. Many nurseries sell packaged fertilizer specifically made for citrus.

Iron chlorosis (yellow leaves with dark veins) may result from an actual iron deficiency or from excess water. First check your irrigation practice; if the tree isn't getting too much water, then apply iron chelates to the soil to correct the iron deficiency. A zinc deficiency looks similar — its symptom is blotched or mottled yellow areas between leaf veins. Zinc foliar sprays will correct the problem.

Pests that can bother citrus are aphids, spider mites, scale insects, and mealybugs. Older trees may contract brown rot gummosis, which shows up as a brown ooze at the base of the trunk. To combat this, keep the trunk's base dry; then trim and clean the oozing wound, removing decayed bark back to a point where discolored wood doesn't show. Paint the cleaned area with a Bordeaux paste mixture.

The bark of young trees — and any wood suddenly exposed to sun by pruning — can sunburn where summers are hot. Protect the trunks (see page 11) or paint the bark with whitewash. You can encourage citrus to grow in normal tree fashion, developing a crown of foliage atop a trunk, or leave them branched to the ground as the commercial growers do. Though you can prune trees to any shape you desire, the only pruning really needed is removal of twiggy growth and weak branches from time to time.

Grapefruit. Trees reach about 30 feet high. Fruit, which ripens 1½ years after bloom, requires high heat for best quality. The best growing areas for grapefruit are the southwest deserts and the southern and southeastern states. 'Marsh' and 'Ruby' (with pink flesh) are popular in the Southwest; in the Southeast, good varieties are 'Duncan', 'Indian River', 'McCartney', and the pink-fleshed 'Foster'.

Kumquat. Forms a dense, fine-textured tree of variable height from 6-25 feet. Handsome leaves are bright green, 3-inch ovals. Small fruits are oval, bright orange, and about an inch across, with a distinctive sour-sweet flavor. Warm summers are needed for good production.

Lemon. The best climates are cool, dry summers and mild winters that are sure to stay above 25°. 'Eureka', 'Lisbon', and 'Meyer' are best in the West; 'Lisbon' is the first choice for the desert regions. 'Villa Franca' performs well in the humid Southeast, where 'Meyer' also does well.

Lime. The true limes ("Mexican") are slender, shrubby trees to about 15 feet tall and grow only in frost-free locations. The 'Bearss' lime forms a dense, rounded tree to about 20 feet and will survive temperatures down to the mid 20s. The 'Rangpur' lime is not a lime at all but an acid-fruited citrus more like a mandarin, with orange flesh and loose, orange skin. It makes a dense, bushy tree to about 15 feet high and wide and will survive temperatures in the low 20s.

Mandarin Orange (Tangerine). These are usually winter-ripening, characterized

by loose, orange skin and sweet flesh. 'Dancy' needs desert heat to develop best flavor. 'Clementine' and 'Owari' develop good flavor in cooler summer areas. Other popular varieties for warm-summer regions are 'Honey', 'Kara', 'Kinnow', and 'Wilking'. Trees are in the 12-20-foot range.

Orange. Handsome trees form dense globes of foliage to about 25 feet tall. The most widely planted variety in all but desert areas is 'Valencia', which is summer-ripening and superior for juice. 'Washington' and 'Robertson' navels are winter-ripening sorts for warm-summer (but not desert) regions of the West; 'Summernavel' is a summer-ripening counterpart. For the Southeast, some preferred varieties are 'Hamlin', 'Parson Brown', 'Homossasa', and 'Jaffa'. 'Hamlin' also succeeds in the desert, as does 'Diller'. For moderately warm summer areas in the West, look for 'Trovita'.

Sour orange. Sometimes called Seville orange, this produces bitter fruits used in making marmalade. Individual trees may reach 30 feet high and 20 feet wide but can be planted 6-10 feet apart for a tall screen or 3-4 feet apart (and pruned heavily) for a hedge.

Tangelo. These generally are hybrids of mandarin oranges (tangerines) and grapefruits. Varieties have individual flavors but tend to be sweet. Trees are somewhat smaller than grapefruits and usually not as dense. 'Minneola', 'Orlando', and 'Seminole' are popular in the Southeast; the first two are also grown in the West. 'Sampson' is a more grapefruitlike hybrid in flavor and growth habit, performing best in California's coastal valleys.

Tangor. Mandarin oranges (tangerines) and oranges are the parent material of these hybrids. 'Temple' and 'King' are the most widely planted. Both need high summer heat for best flavor, although 'King' fruit and branches can sunburn in the desert. 'King' forms an upright, erect tree, whereas 'Temple' is bushy to about 12 feet high and spreading wider. Both have large, bright orange fruits.

Clethra arborea

LILY-OF-THE-VALLEY TREE. Zones 9-10. (See *Crinodendron patagua* for another Lily-of-the-valley tree.) An elegantly beautiful distant relative of rhododendrons and, like them, easy to grow in moist but well-drained acid soil. Native to the Atlantic island Madeira, it also requires mild winters and a moist atmosphere. A dense, upright tree, this grows slowly to about 20 feet high and half as wide. Narrowly oval, 4-inch leaves are a glossy bronze green. Summer flowers resemble lilies-of-the-valley: small, white to delicate pink drooping bells in upright clusters at branch tips. Even their fragrance is similar.

Corynocarpus laevigatus

NEW ZEALAND LAUREL. Zones 9-10. Eventually this will become a 20-40-foot tree, but its slow growth keeps it in the large shrub category for some time. Foliage is its particular asset—dark green, very leathery and glossy, to 7 inches long and about 2 inches wide. Tiny white flowers are not especially decorative, but they are followed by bright orange (and highly poisonous) 1-inch-long fruits that are quite showy. Planted in moist soil, it is easy to grow in sun or part shade. Best performance is near the seacoast.

Crinodendron patagua

LILY-OF-THE-VALLEY TREE. Zones 9-10. Put lily-of-the-valley flowers (small, white bells) on a small evergreen oak and you have the general appearance of this tree. Rounded growth is at a moderate rate to 25 feet tall and almost as wide. Oval, toothed leaves are dark green above, gray green on their undersides. Quantities of flowers bloom in late spring and early summer, sometimes continuing into fall; these are followed by decorative cream and red seed capsules that can be something of a litter problem in a paved area. Because growth is good in very moist soils, *Crinodendron* is a good tree for planting in a lawn. Water it deeply about once a month to encourage deep rooting. Some early training usually is necessary to encourage it to develop into tree form: remove brushy growth in the center (to divert energy to main branches) and remove any branches that tend to hang down.

Cupaniopsis anacardioides

CARROT WOOD, TUCKEROO. Zone 10 and warmer parts of Zone 9. Wherever it can be grown, this is an excellent foliage tree for certain problem situations, as well as for the "average" garden. Among its tolerances are poorly drained soil, salt-laden wind along the seacoast and hot, dry inland winds. Neat leaves consist of 6-10 leathery leaflets, each about 4 inches long. Young trees are fairly open, but as they

age, the shade becomes very dense. Moderate growth rate produces a 30-foot-high tree spreading to about 20 feet. Roots are deep, making this a good candidate for lawn planting or a location near pavement.

Eriobotrya

LOQUAT. One species is grown strictly for ornamental foliage; the other adds a crop of good-looking, edible orange fruits.

E. deflexa. BRONZE LOQUAT. Zones 9-10. To become a tree, this species needs a helping hand to lift it out of the shrub category. But with training, it develops into a handsome, attention-getting patio tree. Long, pointed leaves (to 12 inches by 4 inches across) emerge a bright, rather shiny copper color and retain that redness for a long time before turning green. Grayish bark provides an attractive contrast to the bold foliage, and the leaves also highlight the clusters of small white flowers. The tree prefers well-drained soil and regular watering.

E. japonica. LOQUAT. Zones 8-10. Not only does this loquat provide plenty of bold foliage to contrast with the more conservative garden plants but also it gives you plenty of good-tasting fruits. The big, leathery, stiff leaves may reach 1 foot long and 2-4 inches across, showing a pattern of prominent veins. Upper surfaces are dark green; the undersides (as well as all new growth) are covered with rust-colored fuzz. In autumn, small white flowers appear in noticeable but not showy clusters. Fruits that follow the flowers are rather pear-shaped, 1-2 inches long and orange to yellow in color. If you want to be sure of high quality fruit, look for named varieties. Trees grown from seeds generally produce poorer quality fruit, often with large seeds, not much flesh, and a bland flavor. Growth habit is to 30 feet high and wide with a broadly rounded crown. Where shaded, trees are more upright and slender. Occasionally, fireblight may at-

tack part of a tree (see page 19 for recommended treatment).

Eucalyptus

EUCALYPTUS, GUM TREE. In parts of California and Arizona, eucalyptus trees have the status of an "introduced native." There they are such a familiar part of the landscape, both in gardens and in the wild, that it is difficult to believe all of them have been introduced from Australia in the years since 1856. It is difficult to describe general features common to all eucalyptus. Growth habits of the many species range from those that are shrubby and almost viny to those that are of gigantic skyline height; an equally wide variation exists in the foliage and flower forms. Yet there is a certain character that makes a eucalypt easy to spot once you've seen a number of different types. Crisp, leathery, and often aromatic foliage; fluffy flowers composed of prominent stamens surrounding the edge of a cup or chalice-like structure; and woody, rather flat-topped seed capsules are three points common to all eucalypts, even though sizes, shapes, and colors vary.

Most eucalyptus trees have two distinct types of foliage: juvenile and mature. Juvenile leaves (appearing on seedlings, on some vigorous young trees, and on new branches that grow from cut-off stumps or limbs) are softer, often broader, and bluer than the adult foliage that always is described below as "typical" of a species.

Much of their native Australia has either desert, Mediterranean (wet winter, dry summer), or subtropical climate that is reproduced exactly to the eucalypt's liking in parts of California, Arizona, and Hawaii. Some eucalypts are cold-tolerant enough to survive in the Northwest. Most species will grow well with either regular watering or little water. No pests or diseases bother them.

Typical growth is rapid, but unlike most

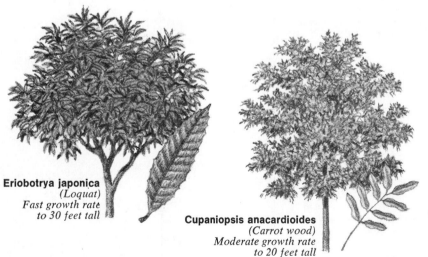

Eriobotrya japonica
(Loquat)
*Fast growth rate
to 30 feet tall*

Cupaniopsis anacardioides
(Carrot wood)
*Moderate growth rate
to 20 feet tall*

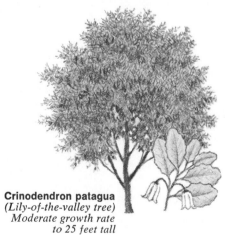

Crinodendron patagua
(Lily-of-the-valley tree)
*Moderate growth rate
to 25 feet tall*

other fast-growing trees, eucalypts usually live to a ripe old age. But because of this fast growth, you need to select and plant the trees with care. Forget all notions of size equaling health; the biggest plant is not the best. And avoid specimens with many leafless twigs or those showing evidence of having been pruned back severely. Inevitably these large, twiggy, or pruned plants will have their roots so thoroughly tangled and contorted that they will require special handling (see below) if you are to avoid serious problems later. Instead, pick out the most vigorous looking of the small plants, preferably one growing in nothing larger than a one-gallon can. If you can find in the nursery small seedling eucalypts growing in flats, set out one of these tiny specimens. (Or plant seeds of the species you want, if they are available.)

Despite your best efforts in selection, you may get a rootbound plant—or you may knowingly have to buy one if another specimen of the species you want isn't available. In either case, follow these planting procedures for best results. Wash all soil off the roots and spread them out as straight and fanlike as you can in a premoistened planting hole. Set the plant so that the stem's old soil line will be ½-1 inch below the final soil level. Fill in immediately around the fanned-out roots with moist soil; then water heavily.

Chlorosis (yellowing of leaves between the veins) may affect some species where soils are alkaline. Treating soil with iron chelates will correct this problem.

E. calophylla. Zone 10. The chief attraction of this 50-foot, round-headed tree is its show of bloom which comes on and off throughout the year. Flower color varies from tree to tree: some are white, others are shades of rose pink, and still more are red. A light pink-flowered form often is sold as *E. c.* 'Rosea'; a dark pink form is sold as *E. c.* 'Hawkeyi'. Broadly

oval leaves to 7 inches long, dark green with paler undersides, form an effective backdrop for the blossoms. Rough, fissured, corky bark sets this species apart from a similar species, *E. ficifolia.*

E. camaldulensis. RED GUM, RIVER RED GUM. Zones 9-10 and warmer parts of Zone 8. Plant this eucalyptus only if you will be able to stand back far enough to appreciate it. Its ultimate height is 80-120 feet, with a trunk that's bare of branches until about halfway up. Though its habit is somewhat variable, typical growth features a curved trunk topped by a spreading crown of gracefully weeping branches. Slender, pointed, medium green leaves reach 6 inches long; bark is tan and mottled. In its native habitats, the tree grows in lowlands subject to flooding and near rivers. So it takes well to routine garden and lawn watering; but surprisingly, it's also drought resistant. Growth is good in alkaline soils.

E. citriodora. LEMON-SCENTED GUM. Zone 10 and warmest parts of Zone 9. Tall, willowy, and long-trunked, this is the show girl of the eucalypts. Even though it may reach 75 feet high, the slender, bare trunk and well-behaved roots let you plant it near walks and walls without complications. One of its most handsome uses is as a grove planting. The powdery white to pinkish trunk, usually straight and bare for ½ to ⅔ of its height, is crowned by feathery billows of foliage. Narrow, golden green leaves reach 7 inches long and, when crushed, smell like lemons. Young trees are weak-trunked and so need secure staking until they put on some girth. Adaptable to varied amounts of water.

E. cladocalyx. SUGAR GUM. Zone 10 and warmer parts of Zone 9. As with the red gum *(E. camaldulensis),* you need to stand back a distance to appreciate this tree's beauty. Straight trunks support a crown of foliage that may top off at 75-100 feet in the air. But despite its size, the

sugar gum is something of a lightweight: puffy clouds of foliage on widely separated branches create beautiful patterns against the sky. Shiny, red-tinted leaves are oval to lance shaped and about 5 inches long. Tan colored bark peels away to reveal cream colored patches beneath. A much shorter form is the variety 'Nana', which grows about 25 feet tall. Both it and the larger species are quite drought resistant.

E. cornuta. YATE. Zone 10 and warmer parts of Zone 9. Toughness, adaptability, and good shade put this species high on a list of desirable eucalypts. A dense, spreading crown of foliage that reaches 35-60 feet high is composed of shiny, lance-shaped leaves to 6 inches long. Summer brings out greenish yellow flowers in 3-inch clusters. Growth is good in many kinds of soil (including alkaline), with much or little water.

E. ficifolia. RED-FLOWERING GUM. Zone 10 and warmest parts of Zone 9. This tree usually appears compact and round-headed, growing to 40 feet high. Often it's planted as a street tree in warm-winter communities. Dark green, leathery leaves are broadly oval to 7 inches long. Against that polished background come spectacular 1-foot-long clusters of flowers throughout the year, with the biggest display in midsummer. It is most famous for forms that have bright, light red blossoms, but flowers in orange, salmon, pink, or cream shades are possible.

E. gunnii. CIDER GUM. Zones 8-10. Unusual hardiness is the most important attribute of this species. Aside from that, it's a tall, vigorous tree good for shade or windbreak plantings. Dense and upright, cider gum may reach as high as 75 feet. It's clothed in oval to lance-shaped leaves 5 inches long. The smooth bark is green and tan to green and white. Small, creamy white flowers appear throughout spring.

E. leucoxylon. WHITE IRONBARK. Zones 9 and 10 and warmer parts of Zone 8.

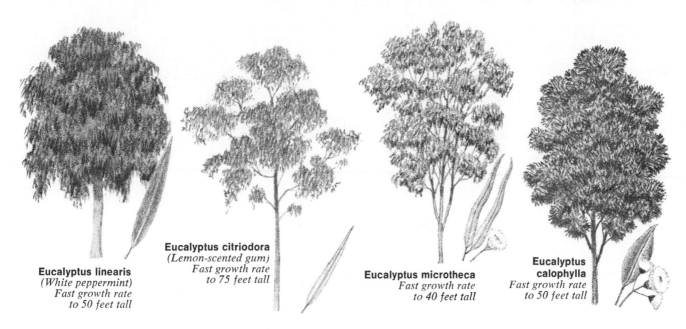

Eucalyptus linearis
(White peppermint)
Fast growth rate
to 50 feet tall

Eucalyptus citriodora
(Lemon-scented gum)
Fast growth rate
to 75 feet tall

Eucalyptus microtheca
Fast growth rate
to 40 feet tall

Eucalyptus
calophylla
Fast growth rate
to 50 feet tall

To find your climate zone, see page 96

Winter flowering trees are somewhat out of the ordinary, but this eucalyptus produces a good show of bloom from winter into spring. Normally the flowers are white, but the variety 'Rosea' bears pink blossoms. The species has slender, upright growth but drooping branches. Height ranges widely from 20-80 feet. Growth habit and size make the trees good candidates for planting in small groves.

Gray green, sickle-shaped leaves are to 6 inches long, combining attractively with the mottled white, tan, and yellowish trunk. This tree takes many adverse conditions in stride: heat, wind, and heavy, light, or rocky soil. Differing from the species in flower color and plant size is *E. l. macrocarpa* 'Rosea'. A many-trunked, shrubby tree to about 25 feet, it has a gray to pinkish trunk and clear, vivid crimson flowers.

E. linearis. WHITE PEPPERMINT. Zones 9-10. The combination of long, very narrow, drooping leaves and weeping branches give this 20-50-foot tree a graceful, swaying appearance. Leaf color is dark green, contrasting with light tan colored bark that peels in strips to show white inner bark. Creamy white blossoms appear in summer and early fall. This species grows well even in light, sandy soils with little water.

E. maculata. Zones 9-10. A broad crown of dark green leaves tops an attractively mottled trunk. Smooth bark is pearly gray spotted dark red to violet; the amount of mottling varies from tree to tree. Overall height range is 50-70 feet. Best growth is in well-drained, sandy soils.

E. maculosa. RED-SPOTTED GUM. Zone 10 and warmer parts of Zone 9. Tall, slender growth up to 50 feet supports gracefully drooping branches that sway in the wind. Narrow, 6-inch leaves are light grayish green. On young trees the bark is brown and gray, but as trees mature this bark flakes off in summer to show a powdery white surface beneath.

E. melliodora. Zones 9-10. A dense crown of slightly weeping branches and grayish green leaves casts good shade and provides good windbreak. Growth is upright, anywhere from 30 to 100 feet; sickle-shaped leaves are up to 6 inches long. White flowers in late winter are not especially showy but have the odor of honey; a pink-flowered form is the variety 'Rosea'.

E. microtheca. Zones 8-10. Bushy, round-headed growth to 40 feet high consists of 8-inch, ribbonlike leaves of a nice blue green color. Grow it either as a single-trunked specimen or a many-trunked clump. A good species for the desert, it easily withstands strong winds without breaking and tolerates drought.

E. pauciflora. GHOST GUM. Zones 8 (best in warmer parts)-10. Here is a eucalypt to grow as a striking accent and garden conversation piece. Trunk and branches are entirely white, complemented by narrow, 6-inch, gray green leaves. As the common name implies, its overall whiteness is "ghostly." Height and width are about equal (to about 40 feet), but growth

is so open you can easily see through it. Growth is good in nearly all soils, and the tree is especially tolerant of heavy, wet soils. It is a good tree for lawn planting.

E. polyanthemos. SILVER DOLLAR GUM. Zones 9-10. Its nearly round, gray juvenile foliage accounts for the "silver dollar" in its common name. But because seedling trees vary in their grayness and roundness, you'd better select carefully if juvenile leaf color and shape are important to you. Mature foliage is lance-shaped, and the bark is attractively mottled. Slender, upright growth reaches as high as 60 feet, with either a single trunk or several. Performance is poor in wet soils.

E. robusta. SWAMP MAHOGANY. Zones 9-10 and warmer parts of Zone 8. Swamp mahogany's dense, rounded crown is good for casting shade and fending off strong winds. Ultimate height is 80-90 feet. The tree is clothed in especially attractive, shiny and leathery leaves to 7 inches long. Branching begins about halfway up the rough-barked, red brown trunk. Masses of pink-tinted white flowers may appear at any time during the year but are especially profuse during winter. Good growth occurs in most soils and in soils that are alkaline or saline.

E. rudis. DESERT or SWAMP GUM. Zones 9-10 and warmer parts of Zone 8. This eucalypt is nearly failure-proof, tolerating desert conditions, coastal climates, winds, much or little water, and any soil (even saline ones). Habit is upright and spreading, 30-60 feet high, and often somewhat weeping. Dull, grayish green leaves are lance-shaped to 6 inches long. The rough bark is gray.

E. sideroxylon. RED or PINK IRONBARK. Zones 9-10. The difficulty with this species stems from its great variability. Habit may be tall to 80 feet or short to only about 20 feet. Growth ranges from weeping to upright, open to dense. Flowers usually are light pink to nearly red (occasionally white), the darker-colored trees generally having the darkest flowers. The strongly furrowed, blackish brown trunk forms a striking contrast with slim blue green leaves that take on bronze tints in winter. Pendulous clusters of showy flowers are most conspicuous from fall to late spring. Its beautiful color combinations of trunk, leaves, and flowers make it a handsome specimen tree, but it is equally good as a screen or grove planting. Chlorosis can be a problem in heavy, wet soils.

Ficus

FIG. Included here are the ornamental fig trees from the world's tropics and subtropics. For the fruit-producing fig tree, see *Ficus carica* on pages 40-41.

F. benjamina. WEEPING CHINESE BANYAN. Zone 10. Without a doubt this is the most graceful fig, but because it is damaged by frost, most people know it only as a house plant. Outdoors it may reach 30 feet tall and become broadly spreading if

planted where sheltered from strong winds. Growth is arching to drooping, featuring shiny green, leathery, 5-inch leaves that are oval and tapered to a distinct point. Because the foliage tolerates salt air of ocean winds, this is an excellent candidate for frost-free seashore gardens.

F. mysorensis. MYSORE FIG. Zones 9-10. Quick growth gives you a 20-foot tree with equal spread. Young trees bear leaves that have a fuzzy texture and are bright green or nearly yellow green, but as trees mature, the foliage becomes darker green with glossy upper surfaces. Individual leaves are rounded ovals 6-10 inches wide, covering the tree densely. The tree is tolerant of salt-laden winds at the seashore.

F. retusa. INDIAN LAUREL FIG. Zones 9-10. The nursery trade has to some extent confused this species with its form *nitida* (sometimes sold simply as *F. nitida*), but there are easily recognized differences in growth. The species (*F. retusa*) grows moderately to 25-30 feet with long drooping branches that may weep nearly to the ground if not trimmed back. These are densely clothed in blunt-tipped, 2-4-inch-long, oval leaves. New growth, produced throughout the year, is light pink to pale yellow green. The lustrous, graceful crown is supported by a slender, smooth-barked gray trunk. In contrast, *F. r. nitida* has upright branches that form a more formal, rounded crown. Leaves are about the same size as those of the species but are more pointed at both ends. Both the species and its variety have made good as city trees. Unfortunately, both are highly susceptible to a thrips that attacks new foliage, causing it to curl and drop.

F. rubiginosa. RUSTYLEAF FIG. Zones 9-10. The dense, broad crown of this tree may reach 50 feet high and wide from a single or multiple trunk. Deep green leaves — each a 5-inch oval — generally have rust colored fuzz on their under surfaces. The variety *F. r. australis* has less fuzz than the species; the variety *F. r. pubescens* has much more. Rusty leaf fig grows well in sandy beach soils and salty wind.

Fraxinus uhdei

EVERGREEN ASH. Also known as Shamel ash. Zones 9-10. Sharp frosts will cause some or all of the leaves to drop, but where frosts are light or absent, this is an entirely evergreen specimen similar to the deciduous ashes on pages 41-42. Fast growth gives you an upright and rather narrow tree for a while, but with age the branches become more spreading so that mature trees are round-topped to around 70 feet. Leaves are divided into 5-9 glossy, dark green leaflets with toothed edges, each one to 4 inches long. In youth, some branches may grow too long and lanky; if this happens, cut them back to strong side branches to promote a stronger structure. The variety 'Tomlinson' grows at a moderate rate. Young trees are denser and more upright than is the species; their leaves are a deeper green color and more leathery. 'Sexton'

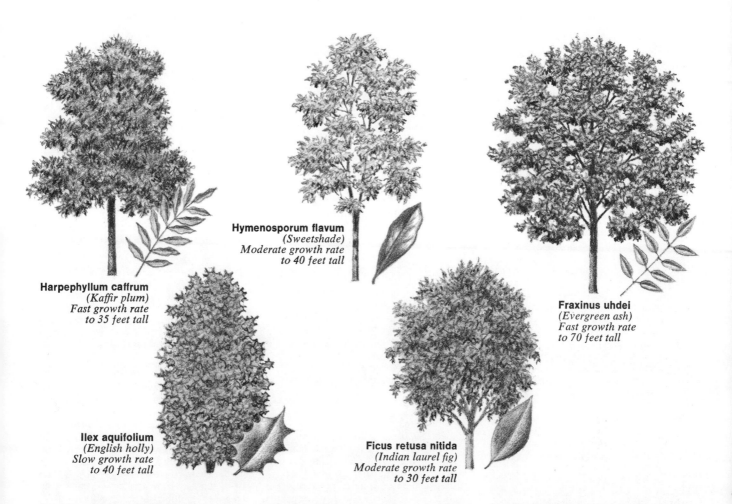

Harpephyllum caffrum
(Kaffir plum)
Fast growth rate
to 35 feet tall

Hymenosporum flavum
(Sweetshade)
Moderate growth rate
to 40 feet tall

Fraxinus uhdei
(Evergreen ash)
Fast growth rate
to 70 feet tall

Ilex aquifolium
(English holly)
Slow growth rate
to 40 feet tall

Ficus retusa nitida
(Indian laurel fig)
Moderate growth rate
to 30 feet tall

has larger leaflets of a darker green color than the species and forms a very compact rounded crown. The root system is shallow; lawn is about all that will grow easily beneath these trees. To encourage deeper rooting, water deeply. Foliage will burn in hot winds, but otherwise evergreen ash performs well in low desert regions.

Harpephyllum caffrum

KAFFIR PLUM. Zone 10 (frost-free). Fast growth and neat appearance recommend the Kaffir plum for a prominent spot in the garden. Glossy, leathery leaves are a rich red when they unfold, later turning to dark green; each leaf consists of 13-15, 2½-inch oval leaflets. Small and inconspicuous flowers produce olivelike, edible dark red fruits that can be a litter problem in paved areas. Natural growth habit is round-headed with a single trunk, although it is easily guided into more eccentric forms or multiple trunks.

Holly (see Ilex, pp. 71-72)

Hymenosporum flavum

SWEETSHADE. Zones 9-10. Don't plant this tree for shade, windbreak, or screening: it's a lightweight see-through tree, useful for giving height without a feeling of mass. Single trees sometimes look rather lonely, but a grove of several can be delicately

effective. Moderate growth rate produces a high-branching, 40-foot tree with a spread of about half the height. Shiny, dark green leaves are up to 6 inches long and 2 inches across, often clustering toward the ends of branches. Small, yellow flowers in early summer have a delicious orange-blossom fragrance. Plant this tree in well-drained soil where it won't receive routine watering but can be watered deeply at well-spaced intervals.

Ilex (Holly)

Although hollies often are used as shrubs, many species will grow, in time, to tree size — often branching to the ground unless trimmed up to reveal the trunk. Best growth is in slightly acid, good garden soil, regularly watered and well drained. Hollies will grow in sun or shade, but best berry production and most compact growth occurs in sun. High summer temperatures and persistent drying winds rule out most hollies in the lower midwest and southwest states. Those that will grow there need wind protection, regular watering, and partial shade. Most holly plants are either male or female, and both must be growing near one another for the female to produce berries. One male plant will insure berry set of up to 10 female plants of the same species. A male plant of a different species from the female can be used only if it flowers at the same time as the

female. (Sometimes you may be able to buy a female plant that has had a male branch grafted onto it, assuring enough pollen for berry production.) Scale, mealybug, and leaf miner are pests to watch for; in the more humid areas of the Northwest, leaf and twig blight can be problems.

I. altaclarensis 'Wilsonii'. WILSON HOLLY. Zones 7-10. The original hybrid plant (*I. altaclarensis*) bore no berries but was grown for its foliage. The variety 'Wilsonii', or simply Wilson holly, is from the same parents but is a heavy producer of bright red berries. Very adaptable, it will take sun, shade, wind, and almost any soil.

Trained to a single stem, it will grow at moderate rate into a 20-foot tree. Leaves reach 5 inches long and 3 inches across. They're thick, leathery, and rich green with evenly spined margins. Planted in a group, specimens will make a high screen or hedge. Trees must have sun and wind protection in the lower Midwest and Southwest.

I. aquifolium. ENGLISH HOLLY. Zones 6-9. Slow growth eventually produces a 40-60-foot tree with a 25-30-foot spread, but for many years it functions as a bigger and bigger pyramid-shaped shrub. Best performance is in regions that have a fair amount of moisture in the air during the growing season; in hot, dry areas it should be sheltered from sun and wind. This is

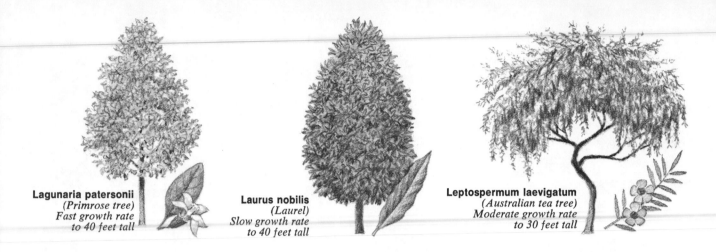

Lagunaria patersonii
(Primrose tree)
Fast growth rate
to 40 feet tall

Laurus nobilis
(Laurel)
Slow growth rate
to 40 feet tall

Leptospermum laevigatum
(Australian tea tree)
Moderate growth rate
to 30 feet tall

the species with the typical spine-edged holly leaf, but nurseries offer a large selection of varieties — some without spines and some with beautifully variegated leaves. Not all named selections produce berries (some are male plants).

I. latifolia. LUSTERLEAF HOLLY. Zones 7-10 (in Zone 7 young plants need winter protection). Leaves that are 4-6 inches long give this species the largest foliage among the hollies. Texture is thick and leathery, and leaf edges are finely toothed rather than spiny. Large, showy berries are orange red to dull red in dense clusters. Growth is slow and shrubby when young, but eventually the tree reaches 60 feet tall.

I. opaca. AMERICAN HOLLY. Zones 6-9. This native species introduces the spine-edged English holly type leaf into a colder zone than the English holly will survive in. The other significant difference between the American and English holly species is the dull — rather than shiny — leaf surface of the American holly. Eventually, American holly will develop from a dense, pyramidal young tree to a round-topped, more open specimen of about 50 feet tall and about 20 feet wide. It makes a splendid hedge. Berries come singly or in small clusters. There are even yellow-fruited varieties: 'Xanthocarpa' and 'Canary'. Leaf miners can be a problem.

I. vomitoria. YAUPON. Zones 7-10. An ability to withstand some drought and grow well in slightly alkaline soils sets this species apart from the other hollies. But even so, it requires protection from summer sun and winds in the lower Midwest and Southwest. Its leaves, though, are the least hollylike of the species listed here: they're narrow, 1-1½ inches long, with lightly scalloped edges. Growth habit is narrow to as much as 25 feet high. Its small foliage and compact, slender growth make it an excellent hedge plant. Weeping forms are offered by some nurseries. It's a heavy producer of red berries.

Lagunaria patersonii

PRIMROSE TREE, COW-ITCH TREE. Zone 10 and warmer parts of Zone 9. Fast-growing, primrose tree is especially useful in certain stress situations — ocean wind and salt spray, desert heat and alkaline soils. Young trees are pyramidal but become more spreading in age as they reach an ultimate 40 feet. Foliage is dense: leathery, olive green ovals (gray on the undersides) to 4 inches long. Summer flowers are 2-inch replicas of tropical hibiscus, pink but fading to nearly white. Seed capsules that follow the flowers hang on for a long time and are covered with short, stiff hairs that irritate the skin.

Laurus nobilis

LAUREL, SWEET BAY. Zones 8-10. Although it eventually will reach tree height and bulk, the slow-growing laurel spends many years in the shrub stage, forming a compact, broad-based cone of polished green foliage. In fact, many laurels never get the opportunity to become 30-40-foot trees because they are among the most popular plants for formal, clipped hedges and for all sorts of decorative plant sculpture. The dark green, leathery leaves are 2-4-inch ovals and have a distinctive, pungent odor when crushed. This is the traditional bay leaf used in cooking. The tree is also the laurel that furnished wreaths for the ancient Greeks and Romans. Its only soil requirement is good drainage. When plants are established, they require little water, although in hot summer climates they appreciate filtered shade or shade in the afternoon. The creamy yellow flowers and small purple to black berries are not showy.

Leptospermum laevigatum

AUSTRALIAN TEA TREE. Zones 9-10. Irregular trunk and branch patterns place this tree into the "picturesque" category. Its trunk (or trunks) are covered with shaggy, gray brown bark, becoming gracefully curved and gnarled with age. In contrast to the rugged trunk and limb structure are the fine-textured, gray green leaves — to 1 inch long but only up to ⅜ inch wide. Some branches tend to be pendulous, enhancing the contrast of strength and grace. In spring, ½-inch flowers appear like single white roses in great numbers along the branches. Tea trees must have good drainage — even nearly pure sand — and full sun. Neutral or slightly acid soils are best;

chlorosis is likely where soils are alkaline. After the trees are established, they can get along with only infrequent watering. Should you prune to shape a tea tree, cut back to a side branch; if you cut bare wood with no growth lower down, no new growth will sprout on the branch.

Lyonothamnus floribundus

CATALINA IRONWOOD. Zones 9-10. Although this species takes its name from the best known of southern California's offshore islands, the *Lyonothamnus* form native to Catalina has simpler foliage and rarely is sold; the fernleaf Catalina ironwood (*L. f. asplenifolius*), found on the other channel islands, is more popular. Its 4-6-inch leaves are divided into 3-7 deeply notched or lobed leaflets; color is deep, glossy green on the upper surfaces, gray and hairy beneath. Moderate-rate growth is upright to 60 feet and about 40 feet across. Good-looking, redwood colored bark peels off in long, thin strips. Large clusters of small white flowers 8-18 inches across are attractive but not really showy. The only soil need is good drainage.

Macadamia

MACADAMIA NUT, QUEENSLAND NUT. Zone 10 and warmer parts of Zone 9. Usually, macadamias are sold as the species *M. ternifolia*, but there really are two other species slightly different from one another that are sold erroneously under that name: *M. integrifolia*, the smooth-shell macadamia; and *M. tetraphylla*, the rough-shell macadamia. The true *M. ternifolia* is rare. Both *M. integrifolia* and *M. tetraphylla* have many similarities. They grow to 30 feet tall by 20 feet wide, with a clean, neat appearance and slender trunks. Leathery, glossy green leaves may reach 1 foot long but are narrow, no more than 2 inches wide, and are carried in whorled clusters. In winter and spring, the trees produce hanging clusters (to 1 foot long) of small white to pink flowers. Differences are that the smooth-shell macadamia has smooth-edged leaves, bears nuts that ripen from late fall to May, and performs best close to the coast. The rough-shell macadamia bears spiny-edged leaves on a more open

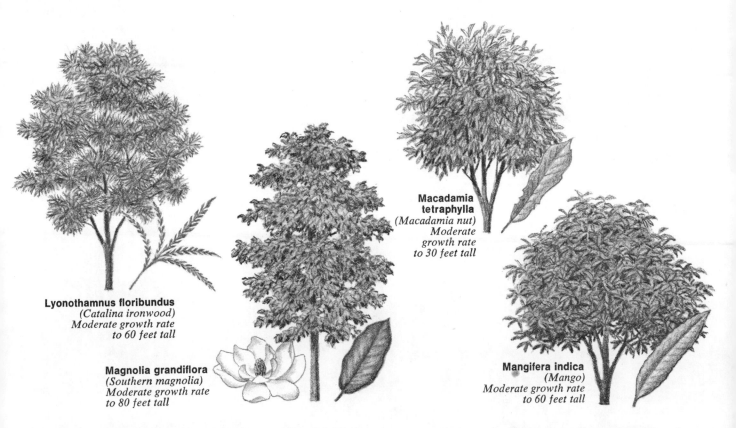

Lyonothamnus floribundus
(Catalina ironwood)
Moderate growth rate
to 60 feet tall

Magnolia grandiflora
(Southern magnolia)
Moderate growth rate
to 80 feet tall

Macadamia tetraphylla
(Macadamia nut)
Moderate growth rate
to 30 feet tall

Mangifera indica
(Mango)
Moderate growth rate
to 60 feet tall

tree, has a shorter bearing season (from fall through February), and produces best nuts when grown away from the coast. Named varieties, as opposed to seedling trees, assure you of good quality nuts. Established trees tolerate some drought, but growth will be slow without regular watering.

Magnolia

These two flowering evergreen natives of the southern states are the magnolias that evoke images of moonlight, plantations, and Spanish moss. Both grow best in good soil that is moist but well drained and neutral to slightly acid. In regions that have alkaline soils and/or alkaline water, the trees may suffer from iron-deficiency chlorosis — yellowing of the leaves between the veins which remain green. Application of iron chelates to the soil will help correct this. Plant the trees where you won't have to disturb their roots by any cultivation or digging. Both species are excellent for growing in a lawn. If you make the mistake of removing lower limbs from young trees in areas where sun is intense, a sunburned trunk will almost certainly result.

M. grandiflora. SOUTHERN MAGNOLIA, BULL BAY. Zones 8-10 and Zone 7 in the Northwest, and in the lower Midwest and Southwest if sheltered by a high wall or building that protects the tree from winds. Dense shade is cast by beautiful, lacquered-appearing dark green leaves — broad ovals, thick and leathery, to 8 inches long. Trees raised from seed are somewhat variable; most have leaves with a rust colored down on the leaf undersurfaces as well as on new twigs. Some trees raised from seed may wait up to 10

years before flowering. Plants with a heavy coating of rust colored down on the leaf undersides are more decorative than plants without it, and they usually begin to flower at an earlier age. Pure white, waxy blossoms contain about a dozen boat-shaped petals that open to a bloom that's about 10 inches across and emits a strong and pleasant fragrance. Conelike fruits that follow flowers may be up to 4 inches long and are studded with red seeds. Growth is at a slow to moderate rate, reaching up to a possible 80 feet tall and about half as wide in the most congenial climates. Growth is shorter, almost shrubby, in hot, dry regions. In areas where it's marginally hardy, the southern magnolia can be grown as an espalier against a south-facing wall where it can reach great height if the wall is high. Nurseries offer a number of named varieties, most of which will flower within a few years after planting (if not right away) and will differ from the species in size of plant, leaf, or flower. Larger flowers and leaves are characteristic of 'Majestic Beauty' and 'Samuel Sommer'. 'St. Mary' grows more slowly, is low-branched, and remains a smaller tree (20-30 feet) than the other varieties, but it blooms at a younger age.

M. virginiana. SWEET BAY. Zones 6-10 and the warmer parts of Zone 5. Another common name for this species is "swamp bay," which gives an idea of its ability to grow in very moist soil, as well as in average, well-drained garden soil. Where frosts are light or absent, it will remain evergreen. But in the colder parts of its hardiness range, it will lose part or all of its leaves in winter. In all respects, this is a

smaller magnolia than the previous species. Its ultimate height is about 50 feet, with a 20-foot spread. Leaves reach about 5 inches long, and flowers are only about 3 inches across. Growth is dense on this usually multi-trunked tree, which is inclined to be shrubby unless lower branches are removed. Green or grayish green leaves are paler green to nearly white on their undersides. From late spring to early fall, the creamy cup to globe-shaped flowers open and release sweet fragrance. The 2-inch, conelike fruits that follow are conspicuous when ripe because of the abundance of bright red seeds that cling to them.

Mangifera indica

MANGO. Zone 10 in frost-free locations. Although the mango will grow and even bear fruit in favored areas of southern California, it reaches its best development in the world's tropics, in subtropical parts of Florida, and in the Hawaiian Islands. In these areas, it forms a round-topped and spreading tree up to 60 or more feet tall, clothed in glossy, lance-shaped, dark green leaves to 16 inches long that are pinkish to red when young. Many named varieties exist, differing considerably in size, shape, and even the color of their fruits. Generally, fruits are smooth-skinned, large, rounded to oval, and red, yellow, or green. If you plant a mango for fruit production, look for one of the grafted named varieties; trees grown from seeds often bear fruit that has considerably less flavor. Trees need steady moisture but will tolerate fairly poor, shallow soils.

To find your climate zone, see page 96

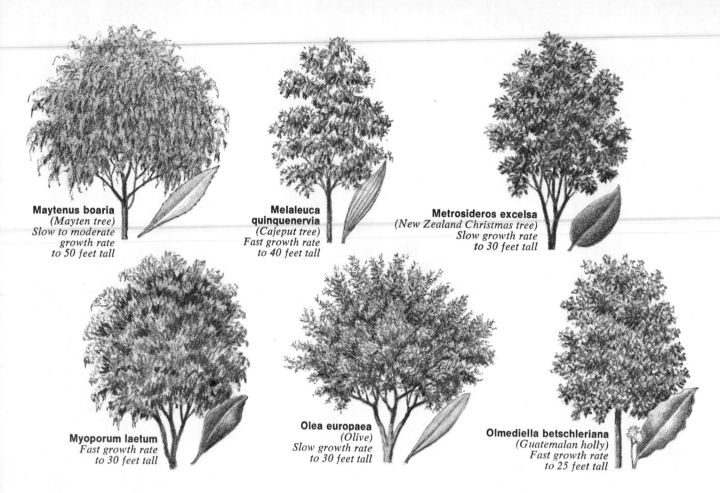

Maytenus boaria
(Mayten tree)
Slow to moderate growth rate to 50 feet tall

Melaleuca quinquenervia
(Cajeput tree)
Fast growth rate to 40 feet tall

Metrosideros excelsa
(New Zealand Christmas tree)
Slow growth rate to 30 feet tall

Myoporum laetum
Fast growth rate to 30 feet tall

Olea europaea
(Olive)
Slow growth rate to 30 feet tall

Olmediella betschleriana
(Guatemalan holly)
Fast growth rate to 25 feet tall

Maytenus boaria

MAYTEN TREE. Zones 9-10. Here is all the delicacy and charm of a weeping willow in an evergreen tree without the size and invasive root system that limit the willow's usefulness. Long, drooping branchlets hang down from all branches to give a weeping effect; these are clothed in narrow, 2-inch, bright green leaves. Although this tree will tolerate considerable drought once it is established, it grows best with ample moisture and good drainage. For single-trunked growth, you'll need to train the tree at first: stake the trunk and remove most of the numerous side shoots that, if left on, would divert energy from producing greater height.

Melaleuca

Many melaleucas are referred to as "bottle-brushes," a name also applied to the somewhat similar and related *Callistemons* (see pages 64-65). The small, clustered flowers have long, prominent stamens that look like bottlebrush bristles. New growth emerges from the tops of flower clusters. After flowers fade, they form woody seed capsules; the result is decorative cylinders of these pods around twigs and branches. Most melaleucas will turn in a good performance in stress situations of heat, wind, poor soil, drought, and salt air. Many become rather gnarled in age, with thick bark that peels in spongy or paperlike layers.

M. armillaris. DROOPING MELALEUCA. Zones 9-10. With staking and a bit of trimming up, you can coax this species into a 30-foot tree. Drooping branches carry light green, 1-inch, needlelike leaves and fluffy white flowers from spring to fall in spikes up to 3½ inches long. Gray, furrowed bark peels in strips near the trunk's base.

M. decussata. LILAC MELALEUCA. Zones 9-10. This species' natural inclination is to become a 20 by 20-foot shrub, but by removing lower branches you can get a single or multi-trunked tree. Arching, somewhat drooping branches are clothed in narrow, ½-inch, blue green leaves. The lilac to purple flowers appear in 1-inch spikes from late spring into summer. Its bark is brown and shredding.

M. ericifolia. HEATH MELALEUCA. Zones 9-10. Here's a tree whose dark green, needlelike, 1-inch-long leaves resemble the foliage of heath or heather. It forms several trunks growing up to as high as 25 feet, with tan or gray, soft and fibrous bark. In early spring it produces yellowish white flowers in 1-inch spikes. Growth is rapid, and you can expect good performance even in alkaline soil or where drainage is poor.

M. linariifolia. FLAXLEAF PAPERBARK. Zones 9-10. White is the decorative accent this species provides. The white bark of the trunk sheds in papery flakes. In summertime the tree is dotted with a profusion of fluffy spikes of small white flowers.

Leaves are 1¼-inch stiff needles, bright or bluish green in color. The tree will grow up to 30 feet tall with an umbrella-shaped crown, but young plants are willowy and need staking until the trunk firms up. Later, when the main stem or stems are strong enough, you can remove lower branches; this shapes the plant from a shrublike form into a tree. This is one of the few melaleucas not at its best directly on the seacoast.

M. nesophila. PINK MELALEUCA. Zones 9-10. If you leave this plant alone, you'll get a tree without much regularity but with plenty of character. Gnarled, heavy branches sprawl at first and then grow upward or ascend in a twisted manner. If you want more regularity, you can train the tree to a single trunk. Fast growth is to 20 feet high or sometimes taller, with thick, spongy bark. Nearly round leaves are 1 inch long, thick, and gray green. Flowering takes place during most of the year: bluish pink, 1-inch clusters that fade to white and are tipped with yellow. As a tree, screen, or high hedge, pink melaleuca will thrive with much or little water directly at the beach, in the desert, and in poor or rocky soil.

M. quinquenervia. CAJEPUT TREE. Zone 10 and warmer parts of Zone 9. Many nurseries still sell this species as *M. leucadendra*. Growing to a possible 40 feet high, it is one of the taller melaleucas (the other tall grower is *M. styphelioides*). Although young branches tend to droop, the tree's overall habit really is upright and open. Stiff and narrowly oval leaves are 2-4 inches long, pale green and shiny, although young leaves are covered with silky hairs. Flowers in 2-3-inch spikes appear in summer and fall; usually they are yellowish white but occasionally may be pink or purple. The light brown to nearly white bark is thick and spongy, peeling off in sheets. The tree is tolerant of either much or little water.

M. styphelioides. Zones 9-10. In contrast to the other 40-foot melaleuca (*M. quinquenervia*), this species is finer textured, having more distinctly drooping branches. Its bark is thick and spongy and peels off in papery layers. On old trees, bark color is light tan to charcoal. Prickly, light green leaves are narrow and less than 1 inch long. In summer and fall, the tree produces cream white blossoms in 1-2-inch clusters. Its natural habit is more often multi-trunked than single-stemmed.

Metrosideros excelsa

NEW ZEALAND CHRISTMAS TREE. Zone 10. In its native land this tree often grows by the sea, where it is drenched by salt spray. Even though it doesn't demand salt-laden air to thrive, it does perform best near the ocean. In addition, the tree appreciates an acid soil (though it will tolerate a wide variety of soils). Growth reaches 30 feet or higher, but you'll need to train it to a single trunk if you don't want a multi-stemmed, shrubby tree. Leathery, oblong, 4-inch leaves on young trees are a smooth, glossy green; older plants develop darker green leaves that have white, wooly undersides. In late spring to summer, this tree puts on a floral display that doesn't take a back seat to any other evergreen. Large clusters of dark scarlet blossoms cover the ends of the branches, coloring up the entire tree. The New Zealand Christmas tree is not at its best in parts of Zone 10 that are subject to frost or dry winds.

Myoporum laetum

Zones 9-10. These vital statistics—30 feet high by 20 feet wide—would suggest a tree; but unless you deliberately remove lower branches, this myoporum always will remain a huge shrub, usually with several trunks. Foliage forms a heavy, dense, opaque mass of dark green, each leaf a 2-4-inch-long, narrow shiny oval, covered with translucent dots. The weight of the foliage and the suppleness of young trunks require sturdy support for single-trunked trees. If you leave multiple trunks branched to the ground and occasionally thin out the growth, you'll lessen the danger of the tree's blowing over in wind.

Summer flowers are individually attractive, ½-inch white bells in small clusters, but you'd never consider them showy. They produce pea-sized, soft, red purple fruits. This is one of the finest seashore trees, tolerating salt spray and even drifting sand but not drought. An almost constant leaf drop, as well as invasive, shallow

roots, rule it out of highly cultivated and fastidiously neat gardens. The variety 'Carsonii' has larger, broader, and darker green leaves than the species, and an even faster growth rate.

Oak (see Quercus, pp. 56-57)

Olea europaea

OLIVE. Zones 9-10 and warmer parts of Zone 8. Since the beginning of recorded history, the olive has been cultivated in the lands around the Mediterranean Sea. Even today, olives are trademarks of many regions there, some of those groves having existed for perhaps 1000 years. Spanish missionaries brought the olive to the Southwest and California in the 1700s.

An olive tree's appearance is one of softness. Gray green leaves are narrow and willowlike, 1-3 inches long and silvery on their undersides; the foliage often is carried in billowy masses. The bark on younger trees is smooth and gray, but as trees age, they take on the look of great antiquity, developing dark brown, gnarled and knobby trunks and main limbs. Their ultimate size is 25-30 feet tall and equally wide. Young trees put on height fairly rapidly but are much slower to fill out, so that overall growth rate is rather slow. Olives must be planted in full sun, but otherwise they're not especially demanding, except for fairly well-drained soils. They will take much heat and dryness in summer but also grow well in the much cooler and moister coastal regions. Best and most rapid growth is in deep, rich soils with regular water, but olives will grow in soils that are shallow, rocky, alkaline, or nutrient poor and they'll survive considerable drought.

When you plant a young olive, decide whether you want a single-trunked tree branching high, one that will branch out low, or one with several trunks. Olives sucker profusely from the base, so your decision will determine how you deal with the suckers. For a single trunk, keep suckers removed and shorten side branches on the trunk below the height at which you want permanent branches. If you want a tree to branch low, leave on as many of the strongest shoots along the trunk as you want branches. Should you want multiple trunks, select as many of the most vigorous suckers as you want trunks, stake them at any angle you'd like them to grow, and remove all other sucker growth. Since crowns tend to be fairly dense, as the trees grow you may want to thin out top growth periodically to show off the branch structure.

Olive fruit is attractive (first green, then changing to purplish black), but ripe fruits stain whatever they drop on. If you plant near pavement or an area you walk through frequently, you'll have to deal with this problem. One way is to buy a so-called 'Fruitless' variety; the fruitlessness is not completely reliable, but you will not have nearly as many to deal with as you would on a fruiting variety. Or you

can spray trees with fruit-control hormones when flowers are out; such sprays can reduce the numbers of fruits that set. The most tedious but effective solution is to remove fruits by hand: knock them off the tree with a stick when they are ripe or pick them off.

Olives sometimes are bothered by scale (see page 25 for control suggestions). An olive gall may appear as knots or knobs on branches; for this, the control is to cut them off (disinfecting clippers after each cut to prevent any possible spread of the disease).

These are the varieties most often used in landscaping: 'Fruitless'; 'Manzanillo', lower and with more spreading growth than other varieties; and 'Mission', taller and more compact than other olives and more cold-tolerant than 'Manzanillo'. Other varieties grown mainly for fruit are 'Ascolano', 'Barouni' (good in areas with hottest summers), and 'Sevillano'.

Olmediella betschleriana

GUATEMALAN or COSTA RICAN HOLLY, MANZANOTE. Zones 9-10. You won't get holly berries from this tree, but the leaves could almost fool you into thinking you were looking at English holly. Glossy and bright green, they have spines that are less prominent but just as sharp as those on holly leaves. Growth is fairly rapid to as much as 25 feet tall and about 15 feet wide. Because the trees hold their branches right to the ground, one good use for them is as a high hedge or screen. With a bit of training (mostly removal of lower branches), the trees will make good single or multiple-trunked specimens. Where summers are hot and dry, plant in partial shade and give regular watering. Since dry leaves are hard and stickery, don't plant where barefoot traffic passes by. Young plants are more tender than established ones; you should plant out only after frosts in spring and perhaps protect new plantings for the first winter or two.

Palms

What evokes images of the tropics more than a palm? Palms have come to represent, in popular fancy, warm climates and romance. Found almost exclusively in the tropics and semi-tropics, these trees are important sources of oil, food, fiber, and thatch. Coconuts and dates—produced by very different palms — are two of the best known palm products.

Most palms have single, unbranched trunks topped by a foliage cluster; some naturally grow in clumps rather than individually. Most have leaves divided into many leaflets and arranged in one or the other of two ways: like a feather, with many parallel leaflets growing outward from a long central leaf-stalk; or in leaflets radiating from one point at the end of a leaf stalk like the ribs of a fan. Some palms shed their old, dead leaves; others retain them dangling from the trunk for years. Whether or not you cut off the old

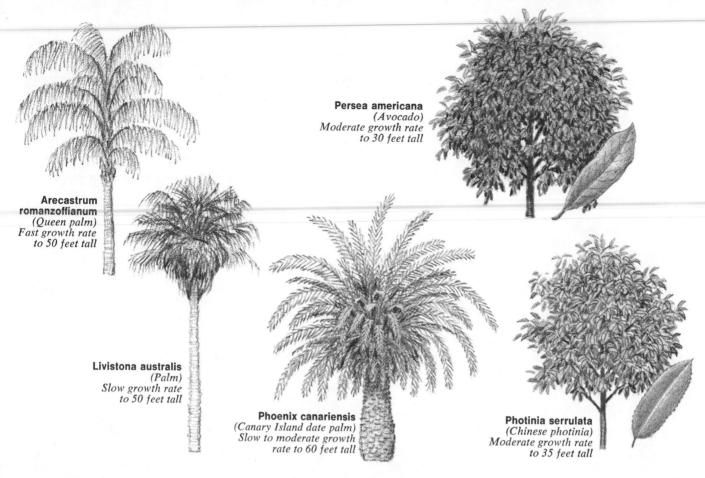

Arecastrum romanzoffianum
(Queen palm)
*Fast growth rate
to 50 feet tall*

Persea americana
(Avocado)
*Moderate growth rate
to 30 feet tall*

Livistona australis
(Palm)
*Slow growth rate
to 50 feet tall*

Phoenix canariensis
(Canary Island date palm)
*Slow to moderate growth
rate to 60 feet tall*

Photinia serrulata
(Chinese photinia)
*Moderate growth rate
to 35 feet tall*

clinging leaves is a matter of personal preference. Most feather palms look much neater with clean trunks.

Palms are not woody plants (as opposed to all other trees in this book). No growth buds form along trunks, and most palms won't sprout from the base. If the growing tip of the tree is killed or cut off, it usually marks the end of that palm.

Fertile, fairly well-drained soil and regular watering are all palms really need in order to thrive. Hosing down the leaves will "dust them off" and help discourage such sucking insects as aphids that may find refuge in the long leaf stalks.

Spring is a good season for planting palms because it precedes the growing season of many species (all tropical species do their growing during the warm months). To plant a 5-gallon palm, dig a hole 3 feet wide and 8 inches deeper than the root ball. At the bottom of this hole, spread 2 inches of manure, nitrogen-fortified sawdust, or some other organic soil amendment. Add to that, if you can, a handful of blood meal. On top of the blood meal, put a 6-inch layer of soil and finally set the palm's root ball on top of this soil layer. Fill in the hole with a mixture of half native soil and half organic soil amendment (but not manure). Water in the palm thoroughly and continue regular watering throughout summer and fall. For palms in smaller containers, scale down the planting hole described above. Since all palms will grow for a few years, at

least, in pots or tubs, they can be used as patio plants until you get ready to plant them in permanent garden locations.

The following palms are those most widely grown in the mild-winter regions of the country:

Archontophoenix cunninghamiana. KING PALM. Zone 10. A feather palm to 50 or more feet high and 15 feet across. Elegant, stately, with 8-10-foot fronds on mature trees. These fronds shed cleanly when they die, leaving a smooth, green trunk. The leaflets are quite stiff, forming a fairly flat leaf.

Arecastrum romanzoffianum. QUEEN PALM. Zones 9-10 (but is damaged at 28°, although it survives lower temperatures). The queen is a feather palm, fast growing to 50 feet, elegant and graceful. Ten to fifteen-foot long leaves consist of flexible leaflets that droop like ostrich feathers. These are damaged in high wind. You can expect fast growth, especially with water and fertilizer.

Butia capitata. PINDO PALM. Zones 8-10. A feather palm. Slow growth eventually may reach 20 feet, with a heavy trunk strongly patterned by stubs of leaves that have fallen off. Leaves are gray green, long and arching.

Caryota. FISHTAIL PALM. Zone 10. A feather palm. Three species have similar leaves: leaflets are shaped like fish tails, widening toward the tips. The effect of this tree is more soft and fine-textured than that of most other palms. *C. mitis* grows

slowly to 25 feet, sprouts at the base to grow as a cluster of trunks. Plant it only in frost-free areas. *C. ochlandra* also reaches 25 feet high and will take temperatures a few degrees below freezing. *C. urens* reaches 100 feet in its native Asia but is much shorter here. It has 20-foot leaves. *C. urens* is for frost-free regions only.

Cocos nucifera. COCONUT PALM. Zone 10. A feather palm. Probably the world's most famous palm, this majestic tree curves its long trunk over countless tropical lagoons and bears the familiar coconuts of world trade. Leaves may reach 18 feet long on a trunk up to 80 feet high. The coconut palm flourishes in frost-free, humid climates as found in parts of Florida and Hawaii. It's subject to a yellowing wilt disease for which there is no cure yet. If it has occurred in your area, you'd be wise to plant another, more disease-resistant palm.

Erythea. These trees are fan palms native to Mexico. *E. armata,* the Mexican blue palm, grows in Zones 9-10. Slow growth leads to an eventual 40-foot specimen topped with a clump of 6-foot silvery blue leaves; these are held after they die. This palm bears conspicuous cream-white flowers. It's tolerant of drought, heat, and wind. *E. brandegeei,* the San Jose hesper palm, grows in Zone 10 and parts of Zone 9 that don't go below 26°. Its growth is slow. The hesper palm's slender, flexible trunk reaches over 100 feet in its native territory. The 3-foot leaves are light gray green and fall off after they die. *E. edulis,* the Guadalupe palm, grows in Zones 9-10. Light green, 6-8-foot leaves top a stout trunk, dropping off when they die. Growth is slow to about 30 feet and is good at the beach and in the desert.

Jubaea chilensis. CHILEAN WINE PALM. Zones 9-10. This may not be the largest palm, but it's in the running for being the most massive. It's a feather palm with 12-foot leaves that arch over a tremendously thick trunk; eventually it may reach 60 feet, but growth is slow. Old leaves fall off, leaving an attractive pattern on the trunk.

Livistona. Fan palms for Zone 10 and Zone 9 down to about 22°. *L. australis* grows slowly to 50 feet, with a slender trunk patterned with scars of fallen leaves. Dark green leaves are 3-5 feet wide. *L. chinensis*, the Chinese fountain palm, grows slowly to perhaps 30 feet. Bright green, 3-6-foot leaves are composed of slender leaflets that droop vertically for about the last one-third of their length, giving an exceptionally graceful appearance. Old leaves fall off naturally.

Phoenix. DATE PALM. All are feather palms, often very large and single-trunked. *P. canariensis*, the Canary Island date palm, grows in Zones 9-10. It's a big, heavy-trunked plant to 60 feet high, spreading up to 30 feet. Slow growing until it forms a trunk, it then proceeds at a moderate rate. Dead leaves hang on for a while; usually they're cut off before they would fall. *P. dactylifera*, the date palm, is the palm of desert oases and the producer of commercial dates. It will survive in Zone 8 but its leaves will be killed; it does best in Zones 9-10. Very tall (to 100 feet) with a slender trunk topped by stiff and rather sparse gray green leaves, it will grow with a leaning trunk and often produces offshoots at the base. It grows equally well along the coast or in the desert. *P. reclinata*, the Senegal date palm, makes picturesque clumps of several curving trunks 20-30 feet high (although it can be grown single-trunked if you remove the offshoots that appear at ground level). Zone 10 is best, but it will survive even when the temperature dips to 20°. *P. rupicola*, the Cliff date palm, grows in Zone 10 and Zone 9 down to 26° before damage occurs. A smaller (to 25 feet high), more slender version of the Canary Island date palm (*P. canariensis*), it is useful in smaller gardens.

Ptychosperma elegans. SOLITAIRE PALM. Zone 10. A feather palm with bright green fronds to 5 feet long and 2 feet wide; fronds are not plentiful. Clusters of fragrant white flowers are followed by bright red fruits.

Roystonea regia. ROYAL PALM. Zone 10 (no frost). A feather palm. Graceful, rounded heads consist of 15-foot leaves that are positioned from upright when new to drooping when old and at all angles in between as they age. The tree's ultimate height may be 70 feet, with a trunk that is slightly swollen in the center.

Sabal. PALMETTO. Slow-growing fan palms. *S. domingensis*, the Hispaniolan palmetto, grows to 80 feet with bright green, 9-foot fans. For Zones 9-10. *S. palmetto*, the Cabbage palm, grows slowly to about 80 feet in the wild. It's topped by a dense, globular head of 5-8-foot leaves. Its native territory is as far north as North Carolina, and it grows in Zones 8-10. *S. texana* reaches 50-60 feet in its native Texas, bearing a dense crown of 3-5-foot light green leaves.

Trachycarpus fortunei. WINDMILL PALM. Zones 8-10, possibly even Zone 7. A fan palm. This tree gives the appearance of being somehow upside-down: its trunk is smaller at ground level than it is at the top, partly because the fibrous remains of leaf bases remain attached to the trunk and increase the appearance of girth. Moderate to fast growth will reach 30 feet. The dark trunk is topped with dark green, 3-foot leaves.

Washingtonia. Two fan palm species — *W. filifera* and *W. robusta* — are native to California, Arizona, and Mexico. Their aspect is similar when young, but one always remains shorter and stouter while the other gets skinnier and heads for the sky. *W. filifera*, the California fan palm, (Zone 9 to 22° and Zone 10) is native to desert oases. It will take intense heat but must have some water. This is the stouter of the two; thicker trunked and shorter, to 60 feet. Long-stalked, 3-6-foot leaves stand well apart in the crown; old leaves hang on to form a thatched skirt. *W. robusta* (Zone 9 down to 24° and Zone 10) has shorter leaf stalks with a reddish streak on the undersides, distinguishing young plants of this species from the California native. Older plants are easy to tell apart: this one has a more compact crown, thinner trunk, more untidy thatch, and greater height (to 90 feet), often with a slightly curved trunk.

Persea americana

AVOCADO. Zones 9-10 or Zone 10, depending on variety. The avocado tree is fairly demanding about climate and soil type. It's the sort of tree that is taken for granted in areas where growth is easy but is the object of envy (especially for its fruits) in regions where its cultivation is impossible. One necessity is well-drained but moist soil. Even a well-drained site that periodically is subject to the water table rising into the root zone won't be acceptable, for root rot is likely to set in where soil is saturated for any period of time. Because of their drainage requirement — and because of their sensitivity to frost — most commercial avocado plantings in the West are located on hillsides where both water and cold air drainage are best.

Frost protection is another avocado requirement, but this is somewhat variable. Three "races" of avocados are grown, each having a general range of frost tolerance, although individual varieties within a race will differ slightly. The tenderest are members of the West Indian race. At most, they will take only a couple of degrees below freezing. For this reason, West Indian varieties are grown only in warmest parts of Florida. Next in hardiness (down to temperatures in the mid-20s but varying by variety) is the Guatemalan race, followed by the Mexican race, whose members can take freezing to as low as 20°. These temperatures all refer to survival of the tree: most varieties form blooms in winter, and these blossoms are frost damaged more easily than the trees themselves.

Most varieties (and seedlings, if you have a young plant grown from a fruit pit) will reach at least 25-30 feet tall (sometimes much more) and can spread to 30 feet unless you prune back spreading limbs. Here again, size and habit vary according to variety, some being definitely more upright than others. All have big, oval leaves (sometimes as much as 8-10 inches long) that densely cover the tree and cast heavy shade. Old leaves fall throughout the year, requiring a continual maintenance job unless you grow trees as the commercial producers do: branched low or even growing completely to the ground, with old leaves remaining on the ground as a mulch. If you grow trees that way, you can have an unobtrusive, wide basin around the tree for most efficient watering. Since roots grow within the top two feet of soil, you should water often enough to keep that zone moist but not soggy wet. If you have a problem with saline or alkaline soil, you can irrigate deeply about every fourth watering to flush out excess salts.

Typical avocado fruit is shiny green and about the size and shape of a pear. However, this description varies among the many varieties from smaller or larger fruits with skin that may be rough and thick or have a dark purple to nearly black color. Most varieties tend to bear their fruits heavily one year and lightly the next, but a few will bear fairly consistent crops annually. Because the varieties do differ significantly in their micro-climate preferences, your greatest assurance of successful fruit production is local advice. If a close neighbor has a reliably fruiting variety, then buy the same one. If you have no nearby guidelines, consult your county agricultural agent or farm advisor, either of whom should be able to tell you what varieties have fruited well in your area and which ones would stand the greatest chances of success in your particular garden situation, taking into account its exposure, slope, and soil. All avocados appreciate periodic fertilizing, and, in areas where they grow, you usually can find "avocado fertilizer" in nurseries. If chlorosis develops (yellow leaves between green veins), treat the soil with iron chelates.

Photinia serrulata

CHINESE PHOTINIA. Zones 7-10. Basically shrubby growth is broad and dense, reaching as much as 35 feet high. For a single or multiple-trunked tree, you may have to remove the lower branches. Leaves are outstandingly ornamental: shiny deep green, stiff and crisp, to 8 inches long with prickly edges. New growth has a bright

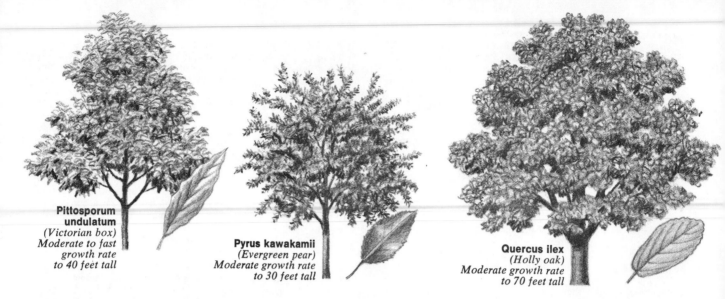

Pittosporum undulatum
(Victorian box)
Moderate to fast growth rate to 40 feet tall

Pyrus kawakamii
(Evergreen pear)
Moderate growth rate to 30 feet tall

Quercus ilex
(Holly oak)
Moderate growth rate to 70 feet tall

copper color and is produced throughout the season; in autumn, some of the older leaves turn bright red. During spring, the tree produces flat 6-inch clusters of tiny creamy white blossoms; these develop into bright red, ¼-inch berries that last into winter. Plants tolerate alkaline soils and some drought. Mildew can be a problem almost anywhere the Chinese photinia can be grown, and fire blight sometimes appears (see page 25 for suggested controls). Wherever new growth forms long, vigorous, unbranched switches, head the switches back to promote branching and greater compactness.

Pittosporum

Typical of most pittosporums are clusters of small, fragrant flowers (noticeable, but not really showy), followed by fairly conspicuous orange fruits the size of large peas. But what they all have in common is good-looking foliage: neat, clean looking, and plentiful. Growth is vigorous and often fairly rapid, but none grow rank and straggly. Established plants tolerate some drought but look better and grow faster with regular water. Locate them in full sun or part shade. Aphids and scale are the only pest problems that may occasionally require attention.

P. crassifolium. Zones 9-10. Gray green leaves (1-2 inches long with rounded ends) set this pittosporum apart from the others. Fairly rapid growth gives you a 25-foot tree, but more often the tree is used to form a high hedge or screen. Small maroon flowers appear in late spring. Since its native New Zealand territory is along the coast, it's a good choice for seashore gardens. Performance is not good in other than coastal regions.

P. eugenioides. Zones 9-10. This species makes a superior hedge or screen plant, as well as a very polished upright tree to 40 feet high by about 20 feet wide. Leaves are 2-4 inches long, lance-shaped, and glossy, with distinctly wavy edges. Their color varies according to the plant's environment from yellowish green to deep

green. Fragrant spring flowers are yellow. When the tree is grown as a hedge, you'll rarely see its trunk, but if you grow it as a tree, you can appreciate the contrast of gray bark against rippling green foliage.

P. phillyraeoides. WILLOW PITTOSPORUM. Zones 9-10. This is the pittosporum version of a small weeping willow. Only about 20 feet high by 15 feet wide, it grows slowly, with long, trailing branches. On those weeping limbs are very narrow, 3-inch, dusty green leaves. Yellow flowers in late winter or early spring are followed by yellow fruits. This is a good patio or foreground tree where it can stand alone without crowding from other trees or shrubs.

P. rhombifolium. QUEENSLAND PITTOSPORUM. Zones 9-10. Diamond-shaped (rhomboid) foliage makes this species unique among the pittosporums. The plentiful leaves are glossy deep green to 4 inches long; but growth is open enough that you can easily see the clusters of showy yellow or orange fruits that decorate limbs during autumn and winter. Slow to moderate growth rate produces a 35-foot, rounded specimen in gardens (although it's an 80-footer in its native Australia). Small white blossoms come in late spring.

P. tenuifolium. Zones 9-10. This is so superficially similar to *P. eugenioides* that if you were to see them in separate locations you might think they were the same tree. However, the distinctions can make a significant difference. The species *P. tenuifolium* has shorter leaves (to 1½ inches long) that are wider and less wavy on the margins; also its color is deeper green. Its texture is finer and its foliage a little more dense, making it perhaps even better suited than *P. eugenioides* for hedges and screens. Twigs and leaf stem are also darker, and its ½-inch flowers are purple. For gardens along the coast, it is the better choice.

P. undulatum. VICTORIAN BOX. Zones 9-10. Like most other pittosporums, this species can be kept as a hedge or screen, but its real beauty shines when you let it grow

as a single or multiple-trunked tree. In time it will become a truly handsome, dome-shaped specimen to 40 feet high with equal width; initial growth is rapid to about half the final height and then slows down. Dense foliage consists of 4-6-inch, lance-shaped leaves that are medium to dark green with wavy edges. Early spring brings out attractive clusters of highly fragrant, creamy blossoms (it sometimes is incorrectly known as "mock orange"). Fruits that follow become yellowish orange, ripening in fall and opening to reveal sticky seeds that can be somewhat of a nuisance if the fruits fall on pavement or in any spot that you walk through. Roots aren't especially deep and, on old trees, dominate the soil beneath.

Prunus

Here are the evergreen relatives of many familiar flowering and fruiting trees that are deciduous and described on pages 53-55. The following species are valued primarily for their foliage; any flowers or fruits are considered a relatively unimportant dividend.

P. caroliniana. CAROLINA CHERRY LAUREL. Zones 7-10. As a formal clipped hedge (a use to which it is well suited), the Carolina cherry laurel gives little indication of its potential tree appearance. Single or multi-trunked, the trees can reach 40 feet high with broad crowns of dense foliage. Leaves are ovals up to 4 inches long, smooth edged and glossy green. One-inch spikes of tiny creamy white flowers come in early spring, followed by small, shiny black fruits. These are not especially ornamental and can produce a litter problem if the tree is planted where flowers and fruit fall on pavement. Best growth is in good, well-drained, slightly alkaline soils. Where soils are highly alkaline, the foliage may show salt burn on the edges. Established trees are quite drought tolerant.

P. laurocerasus. ENGLISH or CHERRY LAUREL. Zones 7 (best in warmer parts)-

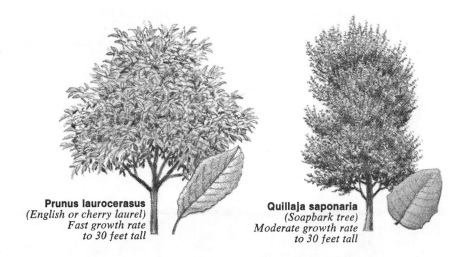

Prunus laurocerasus
(English or cherry laurel)
Fast growth rate
to 30 feet tall

Quillaja saponaria
(Soapbark tree)
Moderate growth rate
to 30 feet tall

10. This tree's reputation was made as a hedge plant—often in "difficult" situations—but when let alone, it is fast growing to about 30 feet tall and wide. The best hedge types now are various named varieties that have definitely shrubby and shorter growth. Leaves are polished, dark green ovals to 7 inches long. Tiny, cream white summer flowers in 3-5-inch spikes sometimes are so profuse that they nearly hide the foliage. These are followed by small, purple black fruits. The tree will grow in almost any soil (except soil that is poorly drained) and has a greedy root system that precludes growing of other plants beneath it. Where summers are hot, give it part shade.

P. lusitanica. PORTUGAL LAUREL. Zones 7-10. Compared to English laurel *(P. laurocerasus),* the Portugal laurel is slower growing but more tolerant of wind and hot sun. Either single or multiple trunked, it makes a spreading, 30-foot-high specimen densely clothed in glossy dark green leaves to 5 inches long with lightly toothed edges. Flowering is showier than that of the English laurel: tiny, cream white blossoms are produced in spring to early summer on spikes up to 10 inches long that stand out from the foliage. The tiny "cherries" that follow are red, ripening to dark purple or black in long spikes.

P. lyonii. CATALINA CHERRY. Zones 9 and 10. Of the evergreen *Prunus* species, this one will form one of the largest trees and is the only one with good-sized, edible (though bland) fruits. Mature specimens may be 45 feet tall with a spread greater than 30 feet. Dark, glossy green leaves are up to 5 inches long, broadest at the base and tapering to a point; edges generally are smooth or only lightly toothed, but on young plants the leaves may have distinctly spiny edges. Spring flowers are tiny and cream white, growing in spikes to 6 inches long. Then in late summer the 1-inch black "cherries" ripen and can become a litter problem near pavement. The tree is not at all fussy about soil, exposure, or amount of water.

Pyrus kawakamii

EVERGREEN PEAR. Zones 8-10. This is a highly flexible tree that can be trained in several different ways. In the early stages of growth, it almost always needs some sort of guidance. Without training, the willowy, drooping branches will produce a sprawling shrub that, in later years, may grow up into a multi-trunked tree. For fastest growth into a tree, stake one or several main stems and shorten side growth on these stems; leave the trunks staked until they thicken to the point of being able to support themselves upright without assistance. To build up framework branches and also to cure the drooping habit and get a crown you can walk under, shorten overlong, pendent branches to upward-facing growth buds or branches.

The very glossy, medium green leaves are broad, pointed ovals to as much as 4 inches long. In late winter to spring (depending on weather) come clusters of small, white flowers that on mature trees can present quite a show. Aphids and fireblight are its two possible health problems (see pages 24-25 for suggested remedies).

Quercus (Oak)

Although your selection among evergreen oaks is not as great as it is among the deciduous species (see pages 56-57), they still offer the ruggedness and majesty associated with deciduous oaks. And the same cautions and training guidelines described for deciduous oaks on page 56 also apply to the evergreen species. Gardeners in the West who attempt to incorporate old, wild evergreen oak trees into their gardens ask for trouble if they change the soil level around the trunk and root zone (see Special Feature, page 13) and especially if they include the old trees in a year-round garden watering program. Native trees have grown up receiving only winter water, and repeated out-of-season irrigation increases the danger of fatal root rot. Yet those same wild species can be planted as young trees in gardens that receive con-

tinual watering and not run the same risk. Success depends on what the tree becomes accustomed to in its early years.

Q. agrifolia. COAST LIVE OAK. Zones 9-10. Dense, round-headed or dome-shaped growth can reach 70 feet high in time, sometimes spreading even wider; young trees grow quickly if given regular watering. A typical leaf is dark green, slightly glossy on the upper surface, up to 3 inches long and 2 inches wide, and rather holly-like with toothed edges. But the leaf size and shape vary from tree to tree: some leaves are smaller and narrower, some are much spinier than others (regardless of size), some may be curved at their edges, and others are quite flat. New growth is pale green or pinkish bronze, produced in early spring at the same time the tree sheds quantities of old leaves. Wild trees often branch very low or have several trunks, but you can easily train a young tree to a single trunk. Bark on younger trees is light gray but becomes deeply fissured and dark gray brown on old trunks. Roots tend to grow close to the surface and in time become greedy, but a number of acid-loving plants (notably camellias) thrive within the root zone of this oak. (Remember, though, the warning above about watering around old oak trees.)

Q. chrysolepis. CANYON LIVE OAK. Zones 8-10 and warmer parts of Zone 7. The habit of this nearly white-barked oak is round-headed to somewhat spreading and 20-60 feet tall. Oval leaves vary from 1-3 inches long (with or without toothed edges) and are smooth medium green on upper surfaces but have grayish, whitish, or yellowish down on the undersides. A yellowish fuzz also covers the acorn caps.

Q. ilex. HOLLY or HOLM OAK. Zones 7-10. The name "holly" is slightly misleading, since other oaks have foliage that's much more hollylike. Leaf size is variable (even on one tree), up to about 3 inches long and 1 inch wide, and the edges are either smooth or lightly toothed. Upper leaf surface is glossy dark green, the underside yellowish or silvery. Trees tend to be dense and dome-shaped or rounded with a regular outline; moderate growth rate leads to a 40-70-foot height with equal spread. Unless removed to expose the trunk, lower branches usually remain healthy and continue growing for many years, so that, in effect, you'll have an outsized shrub. These trees take the wind and salt air of the seacoast in stride.

Q. suber. CORK OAK. Zones 8-10. Nearly everyone has seen the bark of this oak: it is the chief source of commercial cork. The tree's trunk and major limbs are covered with thick, corky, rugged-looking bark, giving it the appearance of massive structure. This is accentuated by small, toothed, oval leaves that are shining dark green on top surfaces, gray beneath, and no more than 3 inches long. Moderate growth rate gives you a 40-70-foot, round-headed tree with a spread that's about equal to the height. Very old specimens can become irregular and leaning. The best performance occurs where humidity is not high.

Q. virginiana. SOUTHERN LIVE OAK. Zones 8-10 but only where summers are warm to hot. Plant this species only where it will have ample elbow room: mature specimens may reach no more than 60 feet high, but the spread often is twice as wide. Trees branch low with heavy limbs spreading outwards nearly horizontally. Smooth-edged, oblong leaves may reach 5 inches long, dark shining green on upper surfaces but downy and whitish beneath. With ample water, growth is moderate to rapid. The trees prefer deep, rich soil, although they tolerate a variety of soils, including alkaline. In the coldest areas of their adaptability, they may lose some or even all of their leaves in winter.

Quillaja saponaria

SOAPBARK TREE. Zones 9 (warmer parts)-10. Old trees (about 30 feet tall, although sometimes higher) develop broad, flattened crowns, but young trees are dense columns with foliage carried to the ground. Young plants in particular have pendulous branchlets. Leaves are oval to nearly round, leathery and shiny to 2 inches long. In spring, ½-inch white flowers are followed by 1-inch brown fruits that open into a star shape. Its natural habit is bushy with multiple trunks, so you will have to do some thinning and training if you want a single trunk or specimens that are without low branches. Trees are drought tolerant once the roots are well established; but until that time they need regular watering and secure staking to prevent blowing over in strong winds.

Rhamnus alaternus

ITALIAN BUCKTHORN. Zones 7-10. More often this is planted as a tall, dense shrub for hedging or windbreak. But with just a little guidance, it will be a single or multiple-trunked tree up to 20 feet high with equal spread. Oval to oblong leaves are bright, shiny green and no more than 2 inches long. Its tiny, greenish yellow spring flowers and black fruits that follow are not important. Give it a hot climate, drought, or wind and it will thrive. (It also will grow well with regular, good garden care). The tree's major assets are fast growth and a neat appearance, combined with the ability to accept less desirable garden situations.

Schinus

PEPPER TREE. Two very different South American natives are called "pepper trees." No relation to the familiar spice, the common name comes from the resemblance of their seeds to peppercorns.

S. molle. CALIFORNIA PEPPER TREE. Zones 9-10. The common name attests to this species' widespread use in the West, but it's actually native to Peru, not California. If planted where its inherent drawbacks will be no serious problem, you could hardly choose another tree with more character and beauty. California peppers are a study in contrasts: fine-textured, light green foliage cascades downward in weeping willow style; but the trunk and branches are heavy, gnarled, and knobby, giving the impression of great strength and antiquity. Fast growth reaches as much as 40 feet high and wide. In summer come quantities of tiny, inconspicuous yellowish flowers that form pendent clusters of rose-colored berries for a fall and winter show.

Aside from sheer beauty, the tree's assets are an ability to grow in any soil (even poorly drained) and to tolerate drought once it's established. The liabilities, though, require careful consideration. Greedy surface roots preclude the growth of anything but lawn beneath the trees, and the roots will raise and crack nearby pavement, as well as seek out and penetrate water and sewer lines. The litter of falling leaves and berries is a nuisance to some people, and infestations of aphids and scale sometimes call for treatment. Many people have an al-

lergic reaction to the pollen of its flowers.

Stake young trees to establish a good, firm trunk. If you want branches to be high enough to walk under, you'll need to gradually shorten and remove lower branches up to the point where you want main limbs to begin.

S. terebinthifolius. BRAZILIAN PEPPER TREE. Zones 9-10. Trained to a single trunk, this will become a broadly spreading to umbrella-shaped tree 30 feet high and about as wide. It also looks good as a multi-trunked tree of about the same height and spread as single trunk specimens. Dark green leaves consist of 7 oval, 1-inch-long leaflets. Red fruits in winter make a bright show in time for the holiday season in December and January. Roots tend to grow close to the soil surface; to discourage this as much as is possible, water deeply and infrequently. To lessen the chance of damage during storms, shorten limbs that have grown too long and lanky and do some late summer thinning so wind can easily pass through the crown. Trees raised from seed vary in quality of foliage and fruits; winter— when trees are in fruit—is a good time to select one from a nursery, since then you can choose one with large, bright fruits. Pollen of this species may cause an allergic reaction in many people.

Stenocarpus sinuatus

FIREWHEEL TREE. Zones 9-10. Its cultural needs limit the areas in which the firewheel tree can be grown. But where conditions are favorable, this New Zealand native can be a striking conversation piece in a patio or lawn planting. The 1-foot-long, lobed leaves on young plants could almost pass for the leaves of some exotic oak. Dense and shiny, they become smaller and unlobed as the trees age. Showy flower clusters consist of 2-3-inch tubular red and yellow blossoms arranged in a circle like spokes of a wheel; their season is variable (actually trees can flower at any time), but early fall usually produces the most bloom. As well as appearing along

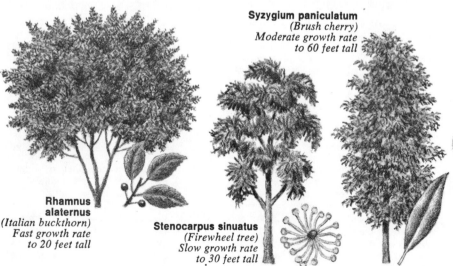

Rhamnus alaternus
(Italian buckthorn)
Fast growth rate
to 20 feet tall

Syzygium paniculatum
(Brush cherry)
Moderate growth rate
to 60 feet tall

Stenocarpus sinuatus
(Firewheel tree)
Slow growth rate
to 30 feet tall

Schinus molle
(California pepper tree)
Fast growth rate
to 40 feet tall

the branches, flowers also can develop directly on the trunk. Growth habit is upright to about 30 feet tall and half as wide. Best growth occurs in soil that is deep, rich, slightly acid, and regularly watered but well drained. Even established trees need occasional deep watering. Young trees are quite frost-sensitive but become less so as they grow older.

Syzygium paniculatum

BRUSH CHERRY, AUSTRALIAN BRUSH CHERRY. Zone 10 and the warmest parts of Zone 9. Sometimes still sold as *Eugenia myrtifolia* or *E. paniculata*. Dense upright to columnar growth combines with handsome foliage and fruits to make this tree a distinctive candidate for essentially frost-free gardens. Whether single or multitrunked, growth is narrow to 30-60 feet tall. By pruning you can limit its growth to whatever height you want. One of the most familiar uses for this tree is as a high hedge. Oblong, 3-inch, glossy green leaves are a glistening red bronze when new and often retain bronzy tints as they mature. White to cream ½-inch flowers are fluffy tufts of stamens that appear throughout much of the year and form ¾-inch rosy purple fruits that are rather showy and even edible (but bland in flavor). Fruits are fleshy and so can be messy if they fall on pavement or where foot traffic is frequent. Plants require well-drained soil in a spot where the dense and rather shallow root system won't conflict with other desirable plants. Aphids, scale, and mealybugs can bother the brush cherry (see pages 18-19 for suggested controls).

Tamarix aphylla

ATHEL TREE, TAMARISK. Zones 8-10. Here is a tree that will far outdistance most other trees in its ability to survive in difficult environments. In southwest deserts it has no equal in resistance to wind and drought, and it will grow well in alkaline and other saline soils that would kill most other plants. Similarly, it will thrive in the salt spray and sometimes saline water of direct seashore conditions. A deep tap root accounts for the Athel tree's drought resistance and is also the reason the tree may be hard to find in nurseries (it can't be kept for long periods in a container). The Athel tree grows easily from ½-1-inch thick cuttings set in place and watered regularly.

Greenish, jointed branchlets have the appearance of evergreen foliage; the actual leaves are tiny scales at the branch joints. Tiny white to pinkish flowers appear in clusters at branch ends in late summer. Where soils are saline, the tree takes on a grayish look by late summer. Fast growth reaches 30 or more feet high and wide, with a billowing, feathery appearance. A competitive root system rules it out of close association with most ornamentals in a cultivated garden.

Tristania conferta

BRISBANE BOX. Zone 10 and warmest parts of Zone 9. At first glance you might think this tree was a eucalyptus trying to imitate a madrone. Its cream to white flowers, consisting mostly of fluffy stamens, and its small, woody seed capsules resemble those of the eucalyptus. Leathery, oval, bright green 4-6-inch leaves clustered toward branch tips appear like a cross between some eucalypts and madrones; they're carried on the branches as leaves are on a madrone. Reddish brown bark that peels away from the trunk and limbs to reveal smooth lighter bark beneath is distinctly like that of the madrone.

Fairly rapid growth tends to be open and even somewhat straggly; pinching out new growth at branch tips will promote more bushiness in young trees. Although not particular about soil, young trees will get off to a better start if you plant them in fairly good soil and provide regular watering. After trees are well established, they'll withstand considerable drought. Sometimes chlorosis (yellowing of leaves between green veins) may be a problem where water or soils are alkaline. Applications of iron chelates to the soil will correct this.

Ulmus parvifolia

CHINESE ELM. See page 61 for the basic tree description and culture. The evergreen forms of this elm species are usually sold as *U. p. sempervirens* or as *U. p.* 'Pendens'. Two selected evergreen varieties are 'Brea', which has larger leaves and a more upright growth habit than the species, and 'Drake', which is more pendulous and has smaller leaves.

Umbellularia californica

CALIFORNIA BAY, CALIFORNIA LAUREL, OREGON MYRTLE, PEPPERWOOD. Zones 7-10. Mature wild trees are impressively large and shady, but you'll have to wait many years after planting time for the same effect in your garden. Fairly slow growth and a neat, dense habit make the California bay a fine small specimen tree or a good hedge candidate. And its strong wood makes it very tolerant of heavy winds. Train the tree to one or several trunks: either way it will grow dense and rounded with a regular shape to as much as 75 feet tall (after many years). Multiple trunked specimens are generally broader than single trunk forms. Glossy, lance-shaped leaves are 3-5 inches long, a deep yellowish to dark green on the upper surfaces and dull green beneath. When broken or crushed, the leaves emit a powerful aroma that is pleasant in moderation but headache-promoting in excess. Leaves can be used sparingly in cooking as a more potent substitute for true bay leaves (*Laurus nobilis*, page 72). Tiny yellowish flowers appear in spring and are followed by olivelike, green, inedible fruits that become purple in color when ripe. The tree grows best in deep, fairly good soil with regular watering, but it will live (growing slowly) in poorer soil and with infrequent watering. It even will grow in shade. Occasionally, California bay may be bothered by scale.

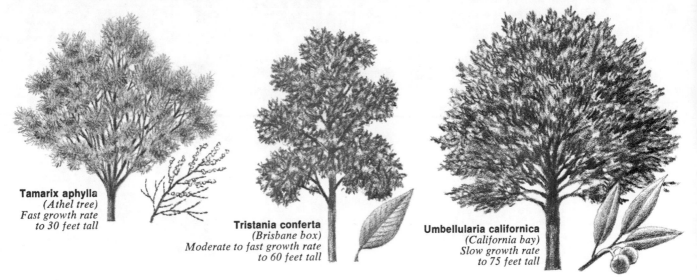

Tamarix aphylla
(Athel tree)
Fast growth rate
to 30 feet tall

Tristania conferta
(Brisbane box)
Moderate to fast growth rate
to 60 feet tall

Umbellularia californica
(California bay)
Slow growth rate
to 75 feet tall

To find your climate zone, see page 96

Needle-leafed evergreens

Are the names "pine," "spruce," and "cypress" familiar to you? They are just a few of the stately trees whose needle or scalelike leaves color the landscape throughout the year.

For gardeners in the cold winter climates that exist in over half of the United States, the needle-leafed evergreens are the only trees that provide foliage greenery all year long. Broad-leafed evergreen trees (pages 62-81) also offer year-round foliage, but they don't survive cold winters. On the other hand, most deciduous trees (pages 26-61) will grow well in cold areas but typically drop all of their leaves during autumn and remain bare throughout the winter. (Just because needle-leafed evergreens thrive in cold climates, warm winter gardeners aren't restricted from using them: many needle-leafed evergreens grow equally well in either mild or harsh climates.)

During all seasons, needle-leafed evergreens fulfill their landscape function as specimen trees, windbreaks, and screens. They are a welcome relief from the gray, white, and black winter landscapes of cold climates. And they provide a much appreciated winter haven to many birds. Though some needle-leafed evergreens do have blue, yellow, or variegated foliage which may be quite striking, as a group the trees are never flamboyant garden showoffs. They don't produce spring flowers or blaz-

ing autumn leaf color as so many deciduous trees and broad-leafed evergreens do. Instead, they offer dignity, restraint, and a feeling of sturdy permanence.

Unlike the broad-leafed evergreens that generally have wide and flattish leaves much like deciduous trees, needle-leafed evergreen trees feature leaves that are typically narrow and thin, shaped much like a needle. Classic examples are the "needles" of the pine, spruce, and fir trees. But not all of the needle-leafed trees have "needlelike" leaves. Juniper and cypress leaves are small, flattish, and scalelike, overlapping each other (somewhat like the scales of a fish) on thin twiggy stems. Podocarpus does have needlelike leaves, but they are so flattened and broad as to appear much like leaves of some deciduous or broad-leafed evergreen trees.

Botanically, the common factor shared by all needle-leafed evergreens is that they all bear cones — which accounts for the general term "conifers," meaning cone-bearing. But just as their leaves aren't all strictly needlelike, not all of their cones resemble the classic pine cone. Junipers, for instance, have cones so modified that they look like and are often referred to as berries.

Three needle-leafed trees are deciduous rather than evergreen. Described with the other deciduous trees, they are *Larix* (larch), pages 45-46; *Metasequoia glypto-stroboides* (dawn redwood), page 50; and *Taxodium* (bald cypress), page 60.

The trees described in this section are listed alphabetically by botanical name. Following each botanical name is the tree's common name (or names) and the climate zones in which it will grow well. The climate zones were prepared by the United States Department of Agriculture; a map of their locations is on page 96. Each tree's common name (along with its botanical name) is listed in the index on pages 94-96 with a cross-reference to its correct botanical name and the page of the book on which it is described. At least one representative of each kind of tree is illustrated.

Abies (Fir)

Symmetrical is the word for firs. Nearly perfect cone-shaped trees with dense foliage are created by evenly spaced branches that radiate, layer upon layer, around straight, single trunks. In overall appearance firs might be confused only with spruces *(Picea),* but the differences are easy to spot: firs have softer needles that fall directly from the stems (without leaving short pegs behind), and their cones grow upright rather than hang from the branches. With few exceptions, firs grow best where there's moisture in the air and the climate is cool. This tends to limit the popularity of some species to areas only within their native range. Another limitation is firs' ultimate size. In the wild, most of these charmingly geometric plants are timber trees. Even though they rarely reach their forest height in gardens, they still eventually take up considerable space. Most firs prefer well-drained but moist soil that is on the acid side. No firs are well adapted to the air pollution of cities. Because growth is so symmetrical, usually there's no need to prune these trees. Pruning is necessary only if a branch departs from the basic regularity, if a second leader begins to develop, or if you wish to remove lower branches on an old tree. Firs are not bothered by many pests, but spider mites or aphids may occasionally appear and need control (see page 24).

A. amabilis. SILVER or CASCADE FIR. Zones 5-9. Dark, glossy green needles have silvery white bands extending the length of their undersides, and the needles curve upward to show off the silver. Rather than being stiffly horizontal, the branches have a graceful droop. Garden height reaches about 50 feet, although trees in the wild shoot to 200 feet or more. Native from Alaska to Oregon in the Coastal and Cascade mountain ranges, this species performs best within that region and in the cool, moist air of the California coast.

A. cephalonica. GREEK FIR. Zones 5-9, 5-7 in eastern regions. Coming from the mountains of Greece, this species will grow well under conditions that discourage most other firs (except *A. pinsapo*): dry atmosphere and soils that are not acid and not moist during most of the year. The stiff, prickly, 1-inch-long needles are shiny dark green with two narrow white bands running the length of the undersides. Slow to moderate growth produces a broad cone-shaped outline eventually reaching 90 feet.

A. concolor. WHITE FIR. Zones 5-8. Although native to drier mountain locations in the West and Southwest, this species is quite at home in the North and Northeast where warm, humid summers are the rule. It is fairly drought tolerant; best growth is in areas with a distinct winter chill. It will succeed in the lower Midwest if planted where it is protected from dry summer winds. In the wild, white fir easily tops 100 feet, but in gardens it grows at a moderate to fairly rapid rate to 50-75 feet tall and about 25 feet wide. (Its highest and fastest growth is in its native area and in the Northwest.) Typical needles are bluish green to 2 inches long, but the degree of blueness varies among trees raised from seed. The variety 'Violacea' has silvery blue needles.

A. grandis. GRAND or LOWLAND FIR. Zones 6 through colder parts of 9, 6-7 in eastern regions. For Northwestern and coastal northern California gardens, this is a fast growing, majestic fir that fits nicely among other garden plants when it is young but later begins to tower above them as its growth shoots skyward. Forest height is to 300 feet, but the trees grow lower in gardens (though still tall — in the 100 foot range within a gardener's lifetime if planted as a young specimen). The deep green, glossy needles to 1½ inches long are lined white on their undersides and are arranged horizontally along the branches. Although the trees do need coolness and moisture, acid soil isn't a must. This isn't a good tree in city conditions.

A. homolepis. NIKKO FIR. Zones 5-8. Moderate growth rate gives you, in time, a broad, dark green, conically shaped tree to about 80 feet tall and 20 feet wide. Sometimes the trees appear quite silvery because needles angle upwards to reveal silver white banding on their undersides. This is one of the better fir species for Eastern and Northern gardens (as long as they aren't in a city).

A. nordmanniana. NORDMANN or CAUCASIAN FIR. Zones 5-8 but into the colder parts of Zone 9 in the West. From the mountains of Armenia, Asia Minor, and the southern Mediterranean comes this dense, dark green, and vigorous fir. Though much higher in the wild, Nordmann fir will reach about 50 feet high by 20 feet across in gardens. It grows slowly at first but picks up speed to a moderate rate after it is well established. Nordmann fir has a better chance of healthy success in warm regions than do most other firs. But it thrives better with regular watering.

A. pinsapo. SPANISH FIR. Zones 6-8. In warm, dry regions without acid soils (as well as in cooler, moister, acid soil regions) this fir flourishes, growing slowly into a narrow cone shape that's up to 50 feet tall after many years. The warmer and dryer the region, the slower the tree will grow. Stiff, short, dark needles densely clothe the branches. The varieties 'Argentea' and 'Glauca' have blue gray needles.

A. procera. NOBLE FIR. Zones 6-8. Formerly called *A. nobilis*. This species grows rapidly in the hills and mountains of its native Northwest and northern California. It also will grow in the East. It produces a narrow, conical crowned tree over 100 feet tall. In gardens within its native range, it will eventually reach nearly as great a height. But even within its own territory it shows poorer growth at lower elevation. Needles are blue green and about 1 inch long.

A. veitchii. VEITCH FIR. Zones 4-7. Fairly rapid growth matures into a broad, 50-75-foot tree with dark green needles, each banded with white on the undersides. It will thrive in the East and West, wherever it can have moist, well-drained acid soil.

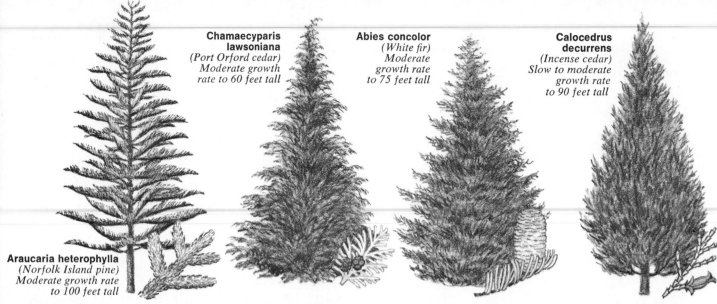

Chamaecyparis lawsoniana
(Port Orford cedar)
Moderate growth rate to 60 feet tall

Abies concolor
(White fir)
Moderate growth rate to 75 feet tall

Calocedrus decurrens
(Incense cedar)
Slow to moderate growth rate to 90 feet tall

Araucaria heterophylla
(Norfolk Island pine)
Moderate growth rate to 100 feet tall

Araucaria

From three widely separated points in the Southern Hemisphere come these three unusual species. Plant them, if you have room to spare, as garden conversation pieces rather than as plants of outstanding beauty or grace. Only one could be called really handsome. After many years these trees may bear large, heavy (10-15-pound) cones that can be hazardous when they come crashing down.

A. araucana. Monkey puzzle tree. Zones 7-10, 9-10 in the East. Perhaps the common name reflects the attitude that it's a puzzle that anyone would monkey with it. This is an arboreal oddity that at least one writer has termed "reptilian." It does look like a refugee from prehistoric forests: heavy, spreading main limbs branch into secondary branchlets that are curving and ropelike, closely set with overlapping, sharp-pointed, large triangular dark green leaves. The young plant is slow growing, but it picks up some speed as it ages and can become a grotesquely picturesque 70-90 feet tall. It grows best in moist soil. This is one of the crashing-cone models (each cone being about the size of a softball). Be sure to plant it where people and automobiles won't spend any time beneath it.

A. bidwillii. Bunya-bunya. Zones 9-10 and warmer parts of Zone 8. Narrow young trees become broadly rounded in age, casting dense shade. A moderate growth rate carries them up to as much as 80 feet. Until the tree is quite large it will continue to bear its juvenile foliage: dark green, glossy leaves to 2 inches long, narrow and stiff with sharp tips, mostly in two rows (one on each side of the stem). After many years, trees begin to produce mature leaves that are oval and only ½ inch long, almost woody in texture and arranged spirally along the branches so that they overlap one another. Heavy cones up to 10 inches long resemble pineapples.

A. heterophylla. Norfolk Island pine. Zone 10. Because of its absolutely symmetrical growth pattern, this tree is often

sold in florist shops or nurseries as a plant for container growing. Planted out in the garden in its zones of adaptability, it eventually will become a rather narrow pyramid up to 100 feet tall. Branches radiate from the trunk in a series of tiers resembling the layers of a wedding cake, branches and branchlets all very regularly spaced. For many years it will bear narrow, ½-inch juvenile foliage, each nearly needlelike leaf curved and sharply pointed, and arranged densely around the branches. Later in life the mature leaves appear; they are somewhat triangular and also densely overlap on the branches.

Calocedrus decurrens

Incense cedar. Zones 5-10, 5-8 in eastern regions. (Sometimes sold as *Libocedrus decurrens.*) In warm weather, the foliage of this tree adds a distinctive, pungent fragrance to the garden. Neat, dense, narrow pyramids of foliage in time may reach 75-90 feet tall; young plants grow slowly but pick up considerable speed after they become well established. The rich green foliage consists of tiny, scalelike leaves that overlap one another and are arranged in flat sprays that are held vertically. You won't see much of the good-looking, red brown, and furrowed bark unless you trim off the lower branches. Trees growing in the open and left alone hold their branches right to the ground. Red brown cones up to 1 inch long look like ducks' bills when they open.

Incense cedar is not only a handsome specimen tree but is good for planting as a windbreak or high, hedgelike green wall. If you water young trees deeply but infrequently, they will become quite drought tolerant. Performance is good even in the dryness of the lower Midwest and Southwest.

Cedar (see Cedrus, below)

Cedrus (Cedar)

Needles that are grouped together in tufted clusters distinguish true cedars from other

somewhat similar, cone-bearing trees (chiefly species of *Abies* and *Picea*). Like the firs, cedars carry their barrel-shaped cones upright on the branches. Any cedar should be planted where it has room to spread widely without crowding other plants or being crowded by them; otherwise the stately character is somewhat spoiled (for exceptions, see *Cedrus deodara*). All of the three cedars described below, when grown in the open, tend to form heavy limbs low on the trunk that in time become almost secondary trunks, arching outward and upward. In the Atlas and Lebanon cedars *(C. atlantica* and *C. libani),* this often leads to a flat-topped crown on old trees.

C. atlantica. Atlas cedar. Zones 7-10. The open, angular, and often straggly growth of young plants gives little clue to the ultimate beauty that comes as trees grow older and fill out. Horizontal branches have more of an upward tilt at their ends than do those of the other two species. On young trees the branches often grow too long and heavy unless you pinch out the tips or cut them back slightly. Growth is at a moderate rate and forms a tree less spreading than the deodar and Lebanon cedars (although you still should allow about a 30-foot circle for its branch spread). Needles are less than 1 inch long and bluish green to light green (foliage color is variable when plants are raised from seed). The variety 'Glauca', the blue Atlas cedar, is a distinct silvery blue color. Of a different growth habit, the variety 'Pendula' has branches that droop vertically.

C. deodara. Deodar cedar. Zones 8-10 and warmer parts of Zone 7. A graceful droop to all its branches and a nodding tip silhouetted against the sky identify the deodar cedar. This has the softest and lightest texture of the three cedars. It usually gives the impression of great density — due in part to the semi-pendulous growth and the needles that may be up to 2 inches long. Fast, pyramidal growth carries it to 80 feet or even higher, with a 40-foot

Cedrus deodara
(Deodar cedar)
Fast growth rate
to 80 feet tall

spread at ground level; lower branches tend to sweep down to the ground and then curve upward. Foliage color is green to gray green, blue green, or bluish gray; color varies somewhat in plants grown from seed. Lighter colored new growth in spring makes a striking contrast against the older, darker needles. Chlorosis, whose symptom is yellowed needles, can sometimes be a problem in alkaline soils. Unlike the other two cedars, this one can be manipulated to an extent. You can control its spread and increase density by cutting back halfway the new growth of side branches. That way a specimen tree won't take up so much room (at least at ground level), allowing several to be planted in line as a very high hedge or screen. Grove plantings are especially good looking. Nurseries may sell a few named varieties: 'Glauca' has needles distinctly more blue gray than the average. 'Pendula' is a weeping form and 'Repandens' is shorter growing and has a stiffer appearance with horizontal branches.

C. libani. CEDAR OF LEBANON. Zones 7-10; Zone 6 for the variety *stenocoma*. Although this is the most famous cedar because of its Biblical associations, it is the least common in gardens. Slow and sometimes variable growth leads eventually to a handsome specimen of up to 80 feet high; young trees usually are dense, narrow pyramids; old ones are more open, irregular, and flat-topped, with branches carried in horizontal layers. Needles less than 1 inch long are bright green on young plants, dark gray green on old trees. Because the variety *stenocoma* is more cold-tolerant, it is the best bet for gardens in Zone 6.

Chamaecyparis

FALSE CYPRESS. Of four commonly available tree species, two are native to the United States' Pacific Coast and two come from Japan. The Pacific Coast species perform best only in their native regions and other areas of the world where climates

are cool and atmospheric moisture is high. The Japanese natives are much more satisfactory in the eastern United States. None perform well where summers are hot and dry or where they are subjected to frequent drying winds. Most false cypresses have two types of foliage: mature and juvenile. Cypresslike, the mature foliage consists of tiny, scalelike leaves overlapping one another on thin twigs. Juvenile foliage (appearing on very young plants, on some new growth on larger trees, and on many dwarf forms of false cypress) is short and needle-like. But unlike branches on true cypress, these branches are carried in flat sprays.

If you look superficially at their foliage, the false cypresses could be confused with the arborvitaes (*Thuja* species), but a check on the leaf undersides shows that those of false cypresses have white lines, whereas leaves of arborvitaes are entirely green. Then, too, false cypress cones are small and round with small protuberances, in contrast to the small but slender cones with overlapping scales of the arborvitaes.

The false cypresses have produced a bewildering number of varieties that differ greatly in size, color, form, and even foliage character. Some of the most popular dwarf and shrub-sized types have fluffy-looking, needlelike juvenile leaves instead of scales.

To avoid any problems with root rot, give all false cypresses a well-drained soil. Dead foliage toward the interior of trees can be caused by both excessive shading (by the naturally dense growth) and by spider mites. (See page 24 for suggested mite controls to apply in summer.)

C. lawsoniana. PORT ORFORD CEDAR, LAWSON CYPRESS. Zones 6-9 (see the general discussion above for limitations). The basic species is a forest giant over 100 feet tall, but its garden height may be only 60 feet high and ¼ to ⅓ as wide, growing at a moderate rate. The trees are densely columnar to conelike or pyramidal in shape and have flat sprays of foliage that droop attractively. Blue green is the typical foliage color, but it can vary considerably. The narrow habit suits grove plantings and makes the trees suitable for being planted close together as a windbreak hedge.

In wet soils the roots are very susceptible to phytophthora root rot. Because of its sensitivity to dust and air pollution, this is not a good tree for the city or for planting along a heavily traveled highway.

Of the countless varieties sold, some reach tree height. The blue Lawson cypress, variety 'Allumii', forms a narrow, 30-foot pyramid of blue and blue green foliage that is carried in flat, vertical (rather than drooping) sprays. Its slow and considerably shorter growth suits it well to hedging. Two yellow foliaged varieties are 'Lutea' and 'Stewartii'. Both are upright pyramids, 'Stewartii' having the broader base and drooping foliage sprays, whereas 'Lutea' has much stiffer foliage. Only new growth is yellow; older foliage turns blue gray in 'Lutea', dark green in 'Stewartii'.

C. nootkatensis. NOOTKA CYPRESS, ALASKA YELLOW CEDAR. Zones 6-9 (see general discussion, above, for limitations). Compared to *C. lawsoniana,* this is a coarser textured, smaller (to about 80 feet), slower growing tree that will succeed in poorer (but still well-drained) soil and colder and more exposed areas; in nature it grows farther north and at higher elevations. Where *C. lawsoniana* has drooping foliage sprays, this species often has distinctly pendulous branches. Some nurseries sell the most emphatically weeping forms as *C. n.* 'Pendula'.

C. obtusa. HINOKI FALSE CYPRESS. Zones 4-9. Because of its slow growth, you'll wait many years to get a 40-50-foot specimen, but in the meantime it functions well as a large, broadly pyramidal shrub of dark glossy green. Compared to the other Japanese species, *C. pisifera,* this is more dense and compact and will retain its lower branches longer.

C. pisifera. SAWARA FALSE CYPRESS. Zones 4-9. This species is best known for its varieties rather than for its basic wild form, which is a fairly slow-growing, 50-75-foot, loose pyramid of dark green. Leaves are small and scalelike, each with a spiny tip. Lower branches die off while the tree is still rather young, exposing attractive red brown, peeling bark. Better known are the tree-sized varieties 'Plumosa' (and its form 'Aurea' with golden new growth) and 'Squarrosa'. The plume false cypress, 'Plumosa', forms a bright green, compact cone-shaped tree with upright branches. It's slow-growing to 30 feet or more with a 10-20-foot spread. A soft, fluffy appearance comes from the leaves which are short, soft needles rather than tiny scales. Soft and feathery but silvery gray green is the moss cypress, 'Squarrosa'. It has longer needlelike leaves on a tree of about the same size as 'Plumosa' but with horizontal branches that form a much broader, pyramid-shaped tree.

Cryptomeria japonica

CRYPTOMERIA, JAPANESE CEDAR. Zones 7-9. Given deep soil, ample water, and a climate that's not hot and dry, this Japanese species will reward you with rapid growth heading toward an eventual 100 feet or more in height. Appearance is soft and graceful with branches that are slightly drooping and clothed in ½-inch, bright to bluish green needlelike leaves that take on a bronzy cast in cold weather. Overall shape is narrow and conical in younger trees, broader and with a rounded top in older specimens. Bark is an attractive red brown that peels off in long, thin strips. Small, rounded cones (each to 1 inch across) also are reddish brown when ripe. Similar to the species but more compact and of a darker green color is *C. j.* 'Lobbii'. The variety 'Elegans', the plume cryptomeria, has several features to set it apart from the species: growth is slow, creating a broad-based, dense pyramid to 25 feet high—more like a gigantic shrub than a

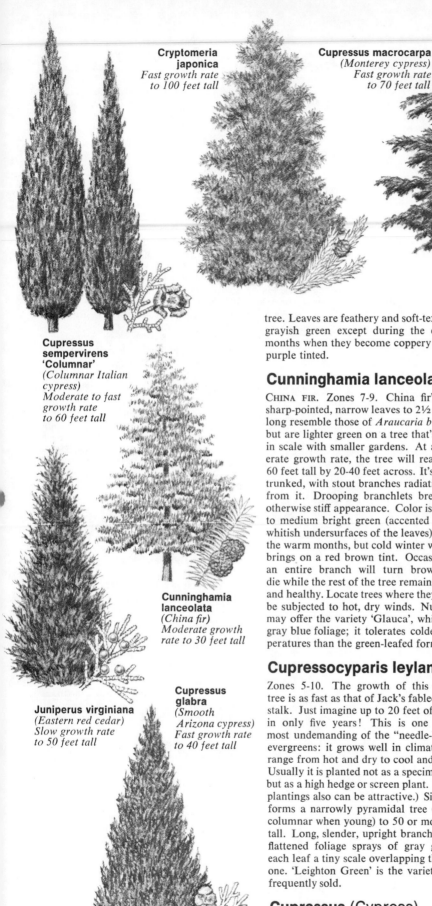

Cryptomeria japonica
Fast growth rate to 100 feet tall

Cupressus macrocarpa
*(Monterey cypress)
Fast growth rate to 70 feet tall*

Cupressocyparis leylandii
Fast growth rate to 50 feet tall

Cupressus sempervirens 'Columnar'
*(Columnar Italian cypress)
Moderate to fast growth rate to 60 feet tall*

Cunninghamia lanceolata
*(China fir)
Moderate growth rate to 30 feet tall*

Juniperus virginiana
*(Eastern red cedar)
Slow growth rate to 50 feet tall*

Cupressus glabra
*(Smooth Arizona cypress)
Fast growth rate to 40 feet tall*

tree. Leaves are feathery and soft-textured, grayish green except during the coldest months when they become coppery red or purple tinted.

Cunninghamia lanceolata

CHINA FIR. Zones 7-9. China fir's stiff, sharp-pointed, narrow leaves to 2½ inches long resemble those of *Araucaria bidwillii* but are lighter green on a tree that's more in scale with smaller gardens. At a moderate growth rate, the tree will reach 30-60 feet tall by 20-40 feet across. It's heavy trunked, with stout branches radiating out from it. Drooping branchlets break the otherwise stiff appearance. Color is a light to medium bright green (accented by the whitish undersurfaces of the leaves) during the warm months, but cold winter weather brings on a red brown tint. Occasionally an entire branch will turn brown and die while the rest of the tree remains green and healthy. Locate trees where they won't be subjected to hot, dry winds. Nurseries may offer the variety 'Glauca', which has gray blue foliage; it tolerates colder temperatures than the green-leafed form.

Cupressocyparis leylandii

Zones 5-10. The growth of this hybrid tree is as fast as that of Jack's fabled beanstalk. Just imagine up to 20 feet of height in only five years! This is one of the most undemanding of the "needle-leafed" evergreens: it grows well in climates that range from hot and dry to cool and moist. Usually it is planted not as a specimen tree but as a high hedge or screen plant. (Grove plantings also can be attractive.) Singly, it forms a narrowly pyramidal tree (almost columnar when young) to 50 or more feet tall. Long, slender, upright branches bear flattened foliage sprays of gray green — each leaf a tiny scale overlapping the next one. 'Leighton Green' is the variety most frequently sold.

Cupressus (Cypress)

Most cone-bearing evergreens are happier in cool climates or where winters are dis-

tinctly cold. The cypresses, though, form a notable exception, preferring fairly mild winters and some liking hot, dry summers. All have tiny, scalelike leaves closely set on cordlike branches, and it is the profusion of these branches that gives cypresses their look of density. Small round to oval cones are composed of "plates" that separate when the seed is ripe.

C. glabra. SMOOTH ARIZONA CYPRESS. Zones 7-10. If you need an evergreen that grows quickly and will take all the heat and dryness of a desert summer, this is your tree. Most often several specimens are planted as a high windbreak (it grows about 40 feet tall and 20 feet across), but single trees branched to the ground can also be handsome. Seedling plants vary somewhat in growth habit and in color (green to blue green to gray). In the tree's native desert, the grayish forms may look just parched and dusty, but brought into the garden to contrast with the usual green leaves of other plants, they look quite frosty and cool. To be sure of foliage color and growth form, choose one of the named varieties: *C. g.* 'Gareei' has silvery blue green foliage; *C. g.* 'Pyramidalis' is a compact, symmetrical cone; *C. g.* 'Compacta' is globe shaped. Since the roots of this species are shallow, if the soil is saturated with water the trees have a tendency to blow over in strong winds.

C. macrocarpa. MONTEREY CYPRESS. Zones 8-10. The highly irregular, wind-swept forms this tree assumes on its native Monterey Peninsula are no indication of its habit in the garden — unless you garden on a wind-battered promontory. Taken away from the constant assault of ocean wind and spray, Monterey cypress starts out as a symmetrical narrow pyramid of bright green; with age, it becomes more broad and rounded, 40-70 feet high and possibly as wide, if grown in the open. If planted in a grove, or with other trees competing for the space, its habit will be more narrowly upright and even flat-topped. It can be planted as an excellent high windbreak or even used as a clipped hedge. Unfortunately, it is very subject to an incurable canker fungus. Symptoms are yellow foliage that turns deep red brown and slowly falls off. If this strikes, there's no saving the tree.

C. sempervirens. ITALIAN CYPRESS. Zones 8-10. You seldom see the normally bushy species in gardens, but the variety 'Stricta' (sometimes sold as 'Fastigiata') is a familiar item even if only from photographs of Mediterranean gardens and hillsides. Much too big to be a shrub yet not nearly bulky enough to really be a tree, the columnar Italian cypress is almost in a class by itself. To 60 or more feet high but only a few feet across, it is the landscape's finest exclamation point. The tree's normal foliage color is a somber dark green, but its variety 'Glauca' has blue green foliage. A single columnar Italian cypress usually looks silly, but they are unsurpassed for planting in formal rows — like green classic columns. And used informally (randomly grouped as they appear on Italian and Greek hillsides and in their cemeteries) they can also be surprisingly good looking without appearing rigid.

Cypress (see Cupressus, pp. 86-87)

Fir (see Abies, p. 83)

Hemlock (see Tsuga, p. 93)

Juniperus (Juniper)

Among the junipers you'll find ground covers and shrubs of nearly any size and shape but relatively few species of tree height that look at all treelike. The tallest junipers all tend to be upright and columnar through youth and middle age, rounding out (if they ever do) only after a number of years. Usually they perform best service when grouped together to form a high windbreak or hedge. Juvenile foliage is short, needlelike, and usually prickly, but adult leaves are tiny, overlapping scales. Both juvenile and mature leaves may appear together on the same plant at any time. Male and female "flowers" usually come on separate plants, the female specimens producing small, bluish, berrylike fruits.

Junipers are valued for their toughness, as well as for their beauty. They'll grow in mildly acid to mildly alkaline soils (but never in soil that's waterlogged). The plants also tolerate hot or cool climates and both wind and drought. Several different pests can bother junipers from time to time. Controls for aphids, spider mites, scale insects, and several different kinds of worms (including a twig borer whose presence is indicated by browning and dying branch tips) are discussed on pages 24-25. A twig blight that first kills tips and then progresses to entire branches can be controlled in summer by a copper spray. Rusts that affect some members of the rose family (apples, quince, hawthorns, and cotoneaster) in the eastern United States live

part of their life cycle on junipers, where they form unsightly galls on twigs. The galls — more ugly than harmful to the plant — can be controlled by applications of ferbam or simply by cutting out the galls. Junipers are especially sensitive to weed-killing chemicals, so, to be safe, don't use weed killers near any juniper planting.

J. communis 'Suecica'. SWEDISH JUNIPER. Zones 3-10. For a narrowly pyramidal tree that borders on being columnar, this species escapes a stiff appearance because its branch tips nod gracefully downward. Growth proceeds at a slow to moderate rate up to about 40 feet. Its blue green foliage may burn during winter in the coldest zones. For Zones 3-8, where the columnar *Cupressus sempervirens* won't grow, this tree is a good substitute.

J. deppeana pachyphlaea. ALLIGATOR JUNIPER. Zones 7-10. Since this species is native to the arid Southwest, the association with alligators may seem farfetched. But one look at the strongly checkered, red brown bark discloses a strong resemblance to alligator hide. In striking contrast to the dark trunk is the silvery blue gray and waxy foliage. Habit of the tree is conical; growth is slow up to 60 feet tall.

J. scopulorum. ROCKY MOUNTAIN JUNIPER. Zones 5-10. Where summers are dry and hot, this juniper or any of its many named varieties will turn in a good performance. Where much summer rainfall is the norm, though, the Eastern red cedar (*J. virginiana*), is a better choice. With summer rain and high humidity, the Rocky Mountain juniper can be plagued by twig blight. Typically, this is a broadly pyramidal to eventually round-topped tree, 30-50 feet tall, with a short trunk that divides into several upright main limbs. More often you will find nurseries selling named varieties that have been selected for compact growth, or bluish foliage.

J. virginiana. EASTERN RED CEDAR. Zones 3-9. For the eastern half of the country, this is one of the most satisfactory tree junipers. Basically it forms a narrowly conical specimen to 50 or more feet tall, becoming reddish in cold weather. Because its native range is so extensive (from Canada down into Florida), it varies considerably from one local or regional area to another. One such regional difference is that plants grown from northern seed tend to be narrow and columnar, whereas plants grown from southern seed usually are broader and more open and have a more drooping aspect. In apple growing districts, this juniper is prohibited because it is a host of the apple-cedar rust disease. Numerous varieties have been selected. They differ in size, slenderness, and color (from deep green to silver). These varieties are also good as specimen trees and as hedges, backgrounds, and grove plantings.

Picea (Spruce)

A description of a spruce's growth habit would match that of a fir (*Abies*, page 83):

pyramidal and stiff needled, with branches arranged in precise tiers. Less immediately conspicuous details distinguish spruces from firs. Spruce cones hang downward from the branches and are produced at the branch tips (fir cones are upright and appear along lateral branches). Spruce cones also remain intact, even when they fall from the tree; cones of firs break apart on the tree to shed their seeds. Spruce needles are attached to the branches by small pegs that remain attached to the branch after the needles fall. (These pegs cause young, bare branches to feel rough when you run your fingers over them.) But more important than botanical differences between spruces and firs are their landscape uses and performance. Most spruces are tall timber trees that lose their lower branches fairly early in life as they head upward to great ultimate heights. Loss of lower branches is hastened if trees are shaded or are spaced close together (or close to other trees). As they age, the trees' crowns often thin out noticeably, leaving a skeletal appearance. As long as the tree's crown is within reach, though, you can exercise some growth control. To slow growth down and promote greater density, cut off part of each year's new tip growth on the branches to force out lateral branching. If any branches grow too long, spoiling the tree's basic symmetry, cut them back to a well placed side branch. Spruces are best planted only in larger gardens where their formal bulk won't be as likely to dominate the landscape.

Spruces are highly valuable in certain situations. Most grow rapidly and flourish in nearly any soil. And they are among the most cold tolerant of trees—increasing their value particularly to gardens in Zones 3 and 4.

Problems to watch for are aphids in late winter and spring, spider mites in summer, and a spruce bud worm on new growth in the North. With one exception (*P. pungens*), spruces are not happy with the summer heat and dryness of the lower Midwest and Southwest.

P. abies. NORWAY SPRUCE. Zones 3-8. Fast growth is the strong point of the Norway spruce, but great height and ragged appearance are the prices you pay for it. In its youth, Norway spruce is an attractive, dense pyramid of stiff, dark green needles, but its goal is 100-150 feet of mastlike trunk supporting an irregular, patchy crown. The cones reach 5-7 inches long. Plant groups of this spruce to create an excellent windbreak that will let other trees get a start in its shelter. Older specimens can be as effective as skyline trees.

P. engelmannii. ENGELMANN SPRUCE. Zones 3-8. Dense and slenderly pyramidal trees eventually exceed 100 feet in height and spread to about 30 feet across. But they grow at a slow to moderate rate, prolonging their period of garden beauty. In time, though, the lower branches will die — but not nearly as early as those of *P. abies*.

Picea engelmannii
(Engelmann spruce)
Slow to moderate growth rate to 100 feet tall

Picea omorika
(Serbian spruce)
Fast growth rate to 90 feet tall

Picea pungens
(Colorado spruce)
Slow to moderate growth rate to 100 feet tall

Blue green to gray green short needles make this species look very much like some forms of *P. pungens,* but these needles are somewhat softer to the touch and appear on a narrower tree.

P. glauca. WHITE SPRUCE. Zones 3-5. Where other spruces grow easily, this one suffers by comparison. Its chief value is in the upper midwestern states where cold winters alternate with possibly hot and dry summers. The tree is a 60-90-foot tall (to 15 feet wide) silver green cone, with drooping twigs, that grows at a moderate rate.

P. omorika. SERBIAN SPRUCE. Zones 5-8. In this species you find adaptability and beauty combined. It grows as a dense, narrow spire up to 90 feet tall and 20-25 feet wide. For many years it's branched to the ground. Shiny green needles with silvery undersides give it an air of good health. Branchlets tend to droop, lending a softness to this very upright tree. It grows in nearly any soil (as long as it's moist), tolerates city atmosphere, and generally is one of the best spruces for gardens in the northeastern states.

P. pungens. COLORADO SPRUCE. Zones 3-8. So stiff that they appear almost artificial, these are broadly pyramidal trees with rigidly horizontal branches. Even the sharp needles are rigidly unbending, sticking straight out from the branches. Slow to moderate growth eventually produces a tree up to 100 feet tall and about 25 feet wide; like most other spruces, this one will start to lose its lower branches before you'd want it to, and the once-dense crown begins to show gaps as it ages.

The Colorado spruce is the only really successful spruce in the lower Midwest and Southwest where summer heat and dryness are the limiting factors. In those areas it holds its shape longer than it does in more favorable parts of the country. Foliage color varies in trees raised from seed from dark green through all shades of blue green to icy blue. Some of the better blue-foliaged forms have been given variety names. 'Glauca', the Colorado blue spruce, is a positive blue gray color. 'Glauca Koster' (the Koster blue spruce), 'Moerheimii' and 'Hoopsii' are bluer yet and smaller growing than the species; 'Moerheimii' and "Hoopsii' are the more compact of these forms. Usually you see these trees used singly as a formal pyramid decorating a lawn or, less often, as a small group of pyramids. They're difficult to use in the garden as anything other than accent pieces.

P. sitchensis. SITKA SPRUCE. Zones 6-9 only on the West Coast. This is a fast-growing, tall timber tree, native from Alaska into California, that performs well only along the coast where the atmosphere is cool and moist. Maturing at 100-150 feet high with widely spreading horizontal branches, it is too large for most gardens unless you intend to garden under it. Narrow, prickly needles are bright green to bluish green, banded with white on their upper surfaces. Grown in the open, the Sitka spruce retains its lower branches better than many other species.

Pine (see Pinus, pp. 88-91)

Pinus (Pine)

Without a doubt, these are the best-known cone-bearing trees on earth. All of the other (more-or-less) needle-leafed evergreens bear some sort of cone or modification of one. Yet popular fancy says that it's not the "real thing" unless it's the familiar pine type. Aside from recognizable cones, pines have a common denominator in their needles and how they are carried on the branches. Although the length and even the thickness of needles vary among the species, all pines carry their needles in clusters that are distributed all around the branches. In extreme cases the "cluster" consists of a single needle, but most pines have needles in groups of 2, 3, or 5. For each species, the given number of needles per cluster is an average taken from a majority of clusters.

Pines grow best in full sun and in just about any soil as long as it is reasonably well drained. Too much water in the root zone can produce yellowed needles (older needles are especially susceptible to yellowing) and a generally unhealthy look. Rarely do pines need fertilizer; especially avoid giving them one that's high in nitrogen. You can guide the growth of pines, but they have their own set of rules for you to follow. New growth appears in spring in spikes called "candles." The best time to do any shaping is when new needles begin to emerge from the candles. If you want the tree to increase in size but grow more dense, cut the candles back halfway on major branches; you'll still keep some increase in length, and subsequent branching growth will come along the remainder of the candle. If instead you want to limit the size of the tree as well as to promote density, cut the candle back all the way; further new growth will come from secondary buds at the base of the candle. Don't cut out the leading shoot at the tree's top unless you want to limit the height.

A number of pests and diseases can prey upon pines, but which problem (if any) may trouble your pine is largely a matter of what species you grow and in what part of the country you are growing it. Scale and aphids are among the most common problems. Most species with 5 needles to a cluster are subject to white pine blister rust. In the Northwest some pines are subject to a gall rust for which there is no control other than pruning out the galls.

P. attenuata. KNOBCONE PINE. Zones 7-9. Rapid growth gives you a tree from 20-80 feet high. Young plants often are open and irregular, but older trees fill in, becoming rounded. Needles, 3 to a cluster, are yellow green to grayish green and 3-4 inches long; the 3-5-inch cones are narrow, assymetrical ovals that remain on the tree for many years. Established trees are very drought tolerant and grow well in poor soils.

P. bungeana. LACEBARK PINE. Zones 5-9. Unlike most other pines, this species regularly develops several trunks. This is no disadvantage because the trunks on older trees provide the main decorative interest. The bark almost could pass for that of a sycamore or plane tree (*Platanus*, page 52): it is dull gray and flakes off in patches to expose bark beneath that is smooth cream white to mottled red and green. Bright to dark green needles are 3 to a cluster and up to 3 inches long; the cones are rounded and 2-3 inches long. The tree grows slowly and not too densely to as much as 75 feet high and up to 50 feet across after many years.

P. canariensis. CANARY ISLAND PINE. Zones 9-10 and probably warmer parts of Zone 8. This is one of the racehorse pines: sleek, slim, and fast. Very young plants look awkward with long needles that don't begin to cover the bare spaces of trunk between the widely spaced tiers of branches. Soon, though, the tree fills out to become a graceful pyramid that heads up toward an eventual 60-80 feet tall. Mature trees are round-topped but still slender. Needles, in groups of 3, are 9-12 inches long, blue green on young trees but dark green on older specimens. Canary Island pine tolerates infrequent watering but must have some water during the dry months.

P. cembra. SWISS STONE PINE. Zones 4-8. Very slow growth to a possible 75 feet high by 30 feet wide keeps this tree in scale with smaller gardens for years. The short, spreading branches create a dense, narrowly pyramidal tree that becomes more open and rounded only after many years. Needles, 5 to a cluster, are 3-5 inches long and dark green to blue green. Oval, upright cones reach 3½ inches long. Unlike most other 5-needled pines, this is resistant to white pine blister rust.

P. contorta. SHORE or BEACH PINE. Zones 7-10 in western states. The fast growth is deceptive, for mature trees usually don't exceed 35 feet. They're dense and generally pyramidal, with dark green needles, 2 in a cluster, to 2 inches long. Oval cones may reach 3 inches long. Because the tree is native to the West Coast from Alaska into California, it does well in humid air and moist soil, though it also grows quite well where soil is poor and not moist. But it doesn't like dry, hot regions.

P. contorta latifolia and *P. contorta murrayana* (both known as lodgepole pine) are two subspecies of the shore pine (*P. contorta*) and are generally similar to one another. But they're more cold-tolerant than the shore pine because they come from western mountain ranges. They'll grow in Regions 4-9 in the West and Southwest. The difference between the two is their geographical distribution: *P. c. latifolia* grows in eastern Oregon, Washington, and the Rocky Mountains, whereas *P. c. murrayana* is native to California

mountains and extends into western Oregon. Both subspecies differ in appearance from the shore pine by being taller (in the wild) and more open in habit, with yellow green, 3-inch-long needles.

P. densiflora. JAPANESE RED PINE. Zones 5-9. Not a tailored tree, this one is suited to picturesque effects. Growth is broad and irregular, often with more than one trunk. Sometimes it is rather pyramidal but usually it becomes flat-topped. Under the best conditions it can reach 100 feet tall, but usually it ends up much shorter. Needles, 2 in a cluster, are 2½-5 inches long, bright blue green to yellow green; 2-inch cones are oval to oblong. The variety 'Umbraculifera' forms a broad, flat-topped crown about 20 feet high and often of greater spread. Numerous trunks support the umbrellalike canopy. Growth is at a slow to moderate rate. The tree is not happy in desert gardens or wherever it is subjected to regular cold wind; nor is it at its best in eastern gardens.

P. halepensis. ALEPPO PINE. Zones 8-10 but young trees will need protection for several years in Zone 8. The Aleppo is not the most handsome pine, but it makes up for that deficiency by growing in some very trying situations. It thrives in poor soils and arid regions, high heat, and the wind and salt air of the seashore. Characterized by moderate to fast growth, it forms an irregular but upright tree of rather open appearance. Some old trees are so upright as to approach columnar habit. Light green needles, 2 to a cluster, reach up to 4 inches long; the 3-inch cones are oval to oblong. The variety 'Brutia' has longer, darker needles (to 6½ inches long) and forms a fuller appearing tree.

P. monticola. WESTERN WHITE PINE. Zones 6-9. Except for its narrower habit and shorter ultimate height, this species is quite similar to the eastern white pine, *P. strobus*. In the drier parts of the country, western white pine is probably better than the eastern white pine because it doesn't require regular watering. Initially, young trees grow quickly but then slow down considerably, eventually rising to around 60 feet in the garden. The shape of young trees is generally pyramidal, narrow, and open; on older trees it is more spreading, with slightly drooping branches. Needles, 5 to a cluster, are soft-textured, blue green, and to 4 inches long; slender cones can reach 11 inches long.

P. muricata. BISHOP PINE. Zones 8-10 in western states. For a small pine (40-50 feet tall), Bishop pine puts forth an amazingly rapid growth. Young trees are dense, moderately open, and pyramidal to rounded, becoming irregular in age. Dark green needles, 2 in a cluster, reach 4-6 inches long. The 2-3-inch, broadly oval cones come in clusters of as many as 5 and typically remain on the tree for many years without opening to shed their seeds. This is an excellent tree for milder climates and small gardens.

P. nigra. AUSTRIAN BLACK PINE. Zones 5-8. This species covers a territory from

the Mediterranean to Eastern Europe, so several regional types have been identified. Most common in nurseries (and usually sold just as *P. nigra*) is the Austrian form *P. n. nigra*—a dense, stoutly pyramidal, dark green tree of moderate growth rate reaching 60 feet tall and 30 feet wide. Needles, 2 to a cluster, are 3-6½ inches long and stiff. Oval cones reach 3 inches long. Old specimens of this tree become flat-topped. The Corsican pine, *P. n. maritima*, has a more open habit, fewer branches, and gray green needles. It grows at a moderate to fairly rapid rate to a possible 90 feet tall. Both varieties tolerate city atmosphere and many types of soils and make excellent windbreak plantings.

P. parviflora. JAPANESE WHITE PINE. Zones 6-8. Often this pine is grafted onto another species to dwarf it for container growing. If you want it as a full-sized tree, be sure to get a specimen that was grown from seed. Slow to moderate growth carries it up to somewhere between 30 and 60 feet, but, unlike most other pines, its spread is about equal to the height. Young trees are broadly conical; old specimens become flat-topped. Needles, 5 to a cluster, are bluish gray to green, often twisted, and up to 2½ inches long. The oval cones reach 3 inches long.

P. patula. JELECOTE PINE. Zones 9-10 and the warmer parts of Zone 8 in western states. A fairly uncommon Mexican pine, this species grows rapidly and very regularly. Widely spaced tiers of branches form a very even, wedding cakelike pyramid, each layer decorated with 1-foot-long needles that hang straight down from the branches. For such a rigid structure, it's an extraordinarily graceful tree. The needles, usually in clusters of 3, are grass green. Oblong cones reach 4½ inches long. Chlorosis (iron deficiency) can be a problem in some of the mild winter areas in which it will grow. If needles become especially yellowed, add iron chelates to the soil to correct the problem.

P. peuce. MACEDONIAN or BALKAN PINE. Zones 5-8. Dense growth is slow and narrowly conical, making it one of the better pines for the small garden; eventual height is 60-100 feet. Needles, 5 in a cluster, are dark bluish green and 3-4 inches long; cylinder-shaped cones reach about 6 inches.

P. pinaster. CLUSTER, MARITIME, or FRENCH TURPENTINE PINE. Zones 7-10. Aside from its production of turpentine, this pine has gained fame for its ability to stabilize shifting sand dunes in Europe and America. Rapid growth produces a 90-foot tree of pyramidal habit until old age, when it becomes rounded to flat-topped. Main branches are upright, spreading, or slightly pendulous, arising from trunks covered with reddish brown, furrowed bark. Stiff needles, 2 in a cluster, are glossy green and 5-9 inches long; oblong cones reach 7 inches. Grows best where climate is influenced to some degree by the ocean.

P. pinea. ITALIAN STONE PINE. Zones 8-10 but young plants will need winter

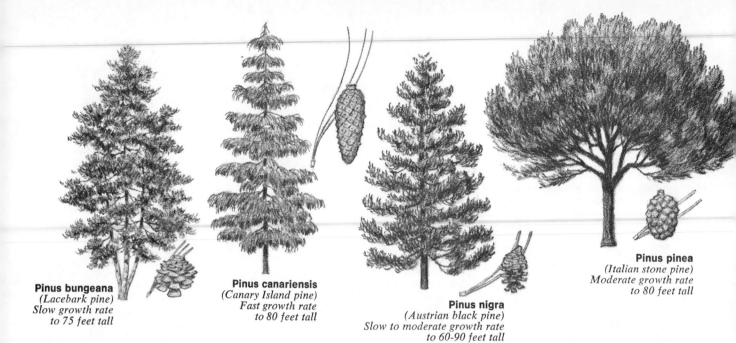

Pinus bungeana
(Lacebark pine)
Slow growth rate
to 75 feet tall

Pinus canariensis
(Canary Island pine)
Fast growth rate
to 80 feet tall

Pinus nigra
(Austrian black pine)
Slow to moderate growth rate
to 60-90 feet tall

Pinus pinea
(Italian stone pine)
Moderate growth rate
to 80 feet tall

protection in Zone 8. This probably is the easiest pine to recognize at a distance, at least after it has reached maturity. By that time it has become a flat-topped umbrella of dense foliage supported by wide-angled branches. Growth proceeds at a moderate rate to an eventual 60-80 feet tall. Young plants often are stout, bushy globes, but even then they may show heavy limbs that will lead to the ultimate flat crown. Low-branching specimens spread much too widely for the average garden; high-branching ones still spread but the crown at least is out of the way of other plants. Stiff, bright green to gray green needles in clusters of 2 are 5-8 inches long; broadly oval cones reach 4-6 inches. Established trees endure heat and drought, but best performance is near ocean.

P. ponderosa. PONDEROSA OR WESTERN YELLOW PINE. Zones 5-9 but not in eastern states; the variety *scopulorum* grows in Zones 4 and 5. The native range of this tree extends from Canada to Mexico and from the Pacific states east to Nebraska and Texas. Included in this range are a variety of growing conditions and some natural variations of the species. Basically, the ponderosa pine is a moderate to rapid grower to only about 60 feet in one person's gardening lifetime, but ultimate height can be 150 feet or more. Growth is straight up in a well formed, narrow pyramid that's dense enough to appear bushy. Needles, in clusters of 2 or 3, range from glossy yellow green to dark green and are 4-11 inches long; the 3-5-inch cones are prickly. A smaller version of the basic species is *P. p. scopulorum*. It's more cold tolerant and tends to be narrower than the species. Neither the species nor the subspecies is a good tree in the heat and wind of the desert.

P. radiata. MONTEREY PINE. Zones 9-10 and warmer parts of Zone 8 but not successful in the desert. Where it will grow without health problems, the Monterey pine becomes one of the most beautiful pines, and it does so in a hurry. Under favorable conditions, established young trees can grow as much as 6 feet a year, reaching an ultimate height of 80-100 feet. Youthful form is a broad, fairly dense cone; older trees are rounded and bare of lower branches. Bright green needles, in clusters of 3, are 3-7 inches long. The lop-sided cones, 3-6 inches long, hang on the tree for many years without opening to shed the seeds. Unfortunately, several problems — the five-spined engraver beetle, the Thermes scale, mites, and smog—limit the Monterey pine's usefulness, especially in areas with warm, dry summers.

P. resinosa. RED OR NORWAY PINE. Zones 3-8. The common name, Norway pine, is misleading, for the tree comes from the eastern United States. A moderate growth rate creates a tree 70 feet tall and 20-40 feet wide with a dense, symmetrically oval crown of slightly drooping branches. Older trees show red brown bark, which accounts for its other common name, red pine. Dark, shiny green needles come two in a cluster and are 4-6 inches long. The cones are about 2 inches long. This is a good pine for planting in poor soils and in urban areas within its zones of adaptability. Growth is not satisfactory in the lower Midwest and Southwest.

P. strobus. EASTERN WHITE PINE. Zones 4-8, best in Zones 4-7 in the East. Much well-deserved praise has been heaped on this pine's individual beauty and its contribution to the landscape.

Young trees are symmetrically cone shaped with horizontal branches; older trees are much broader and handsomely irregular but still retain a strongly horizontal branch pattern. Ultimate size is 100-150 feet tall and 50-60 feet wide. Soft, blue green, 2½-6-inch needles come in clusters of 5; slender cones reach 8 inches long. Although popular in many cold win-

ter areas, it will burn if exposed to frequent strong winds, and its need for regular watering limits its use where rainfall is scant. Its major problems are woolly aphids and white pine blister rust. Several varieties have been named; among them are 'Fastigiata' (upright and narrow in youth but broader in age), 'Pendula' (weeping branches), and 'Glauca' (with distinctly bluish needles).

P. sylvestris. SCOTCH OR SCOTS PINE. Zones 3-8. The straight, well-balanced pyramid shape of young specimens barely hints at the picturesque character that is to come. A moderate growth rate gives you a 70-foot individual with strongly horizontal, widely spaced branching that carries plateaus of blue green to blue gray needles. Overall width may reach 40-50 feet. The tree's top is flat to broadly rounded; the trunk and major limbs are covered with reddish brown bark that flakes off in thin plates. Slightly twisted needles, 2-3 inches long, come in clusters of 2; these may turn red brown during winter but green up again in spring.

P. thunburgiana. JAPANESE BLACK PINE. Zones 5-9 in western states, Zones 5-8 in eastern regions but not good beyond Zone 7 in the lower Midwest. Growth varies from rapid, where conditions are cool and moist, to slow, where the environment is arid. In favored climates it may reach 90-100 feet. In the Northeast it is valued for planting directly on the seacoast, where it thrives in the cold salt spray. At almost any age it is an irregular tree, perhaps broadly conical when young but definitely asymmetrical and sometimes leaning as it gets older. Stiff, bright green needles are 3-5 inches long and appear in clusters of two; the cones are 3-inch ovals.

Platycladus orientalis

(Sometimes sold as *Thuja orientalis*.)
Zones 7-10.

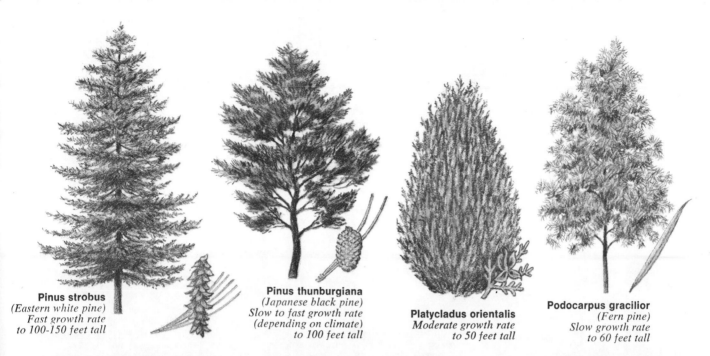

Pinus strobus
(Eastern white pine)
Fast growth rate
to 100-150 feet tall

Pinus thunburgiana
(Japanese black pine)
Slow to fast growth rate
(depending on climate)
to 100 feet tall

Platycladus orientalis
Moderate growth rate
to 50 feet tall

Podocarpus gracilior
(Fern pine)
Slow growth rate
to 60 feet tall

For warm winter regions and for the lower Midwest and Southwest, this is a good substitute for the arborvitaes (*Thuja* species; see page 93). It has the same type of flattened foliage sprays held vertically on the branches, as well as a similar conical to pyramidal growth habit. Height ranges from 25-50 feet for this tree that grows at a moderate rate. Medium green juvenile foliage is tiny and needlelike, but mature leaves are minute, overlapping scales. Small cones are fleshy when young but become woody as they ripen. They are easily distinguished from cones of arborvitaes by the small hooks on each cone scale. Growth is best in good soil with regular watering, but the trees will tolerate both drought and hot, dry summers. Many shrub-sized varieties are sold, as well as some that reach tree proportions. Among the latter are 'Excelsa', with dark green foliage on a 20-foot plant, and 'Gold Spire', a 30-foot pyramid of light green foliage sprays that are tipped with yellow.

Podocarpus

Although these Southern Hemisphere and Oriental natives often are planted out in mild climate gardens as shrubs, they can surprise their owners by growing up into definite trees. Rather than bearing woody cones, podocarpus species produce fleshy fruits after many years. The fruits come only on female trees when a male is nearby as a pollenator. Podocarpus trees grow well in most soils, although chlorosis (yellowing of the leaves between the veins) sometimes shows up where soils are alkaline or very heavy and damp. Give these trees some shade and shelter from winds in hot summer regions. Where summer temperatures are cooler and air is moist, they grow well in part shade to full sun.

P. gracilior (also sold as *P. elongatus*). FERN PINE. Zones 9-10. When grown from

seed, young fern pines will have narrow, 2-4-inch dark and glossy green leaves adequately (but not densely) covering a fairly upright plant. Some years later, when the tree has settled into maturity, it produces soft grayish to bluish green leaves about 1-2 inches long that are spaced much more closely on the branches. Plants grown from cuttings taken from this mature foliage retain the small, closely set leaves but become plants with very limber branches that often are reluctant to make any strong vertical growth. These more willowy plants usually are sold as *P. elongatus*; the larger-leafed, upright ones are labelled *P. gracilior*. Either type will make a tree to 60 feet high after many years, but the *elongatus* types will need staking and definite encouragement to assume a tree aspect. Even when staked up, they will persist for some time in drooping their feathery masses of foliage. You should stake either type until a strong trunk (or trunks) has developed. Because of their fairly slow growth, they are excellent shrub-trees for small patios, entry gardens, and any close-up garden position in association with lawn or other ornamental plants. Grouped together, they can form hedges.

P. macrophyllus. YEW PINE. Zones 7-10. The uses of the yew pine are the same as for *P. gracilior*, but its look is somewhat different and it succeeds in a colder zone. Fairly slow growth eventually reaches 50-60 feet, but this species is a little stiffer, having rather horizontal major branches and branchlets that droop slightly. It is also a narrower and more definitely upright tree. Bright green leaves reach 4 inches long, up to ½ inch wide. The variety *P. m. maki* is smaller and slower growing; best used as a shrub, container plant.

Pseudotsuga menziesii

DOUGLAS FIR. Zones 6-9, Zones 6-8 in eastern regions, Zones 4-8 for *P. m. glauca*.

Rapid growth, regular and dense form, and a soft grace that rivals that of true hemlocks put this magnificent Western timber tree high on any list of choice ornamentals. In the forests it grows from 70 to over 200 feet tall. Younger specimens are cone-shaped and foliaged to the ground; as the trees age, the conical form is retained but elevated off the ground on increasingly rugged, craggy trunks. Main limbs vary from slightly upright to slightly drooping, sometimes upright in the top part of the tree and drooping in the lower sections. The soft, densely set needles typically are dark green, to 1½ inches long, and radiate out in all directions from the branches. Their appearance and feel are soft. Springtime brings out tassels of new growth that are a conspicuously contrasting apple green. Cones are an easy identifying feature: oval and about 3 inches long, they hang from the branches. From underneath each cone scale protrudes a 3-pronged bract.

Douglas fir's native range extends from Alaska through northern California, eastward into the Rocky Mountains, and southward into northern Mexico. With a range that great, it is inevitable that the trees vary somewhat, depending on what part of the region they inhabit. Those from Alaska, from coastal-influenced northwest areas, and from northern California are the "typical" fast-growing, feathery dark green form with slightly drooping branchlets. But the growth form becomes increasingly more compact and stiff and the foliage more bluish on trees found farther east, toward the Rocky Mountains, and farther south in inland California. The inland forms also are slower growing but more cold tolerant than coastal forms, and they will grow well in Zone 4. The bluish needled form, *P. m. glauca*, found in the Rockies, extends the use of Douglas fir into the northeastern states. The basic species grows well on the East Coast in

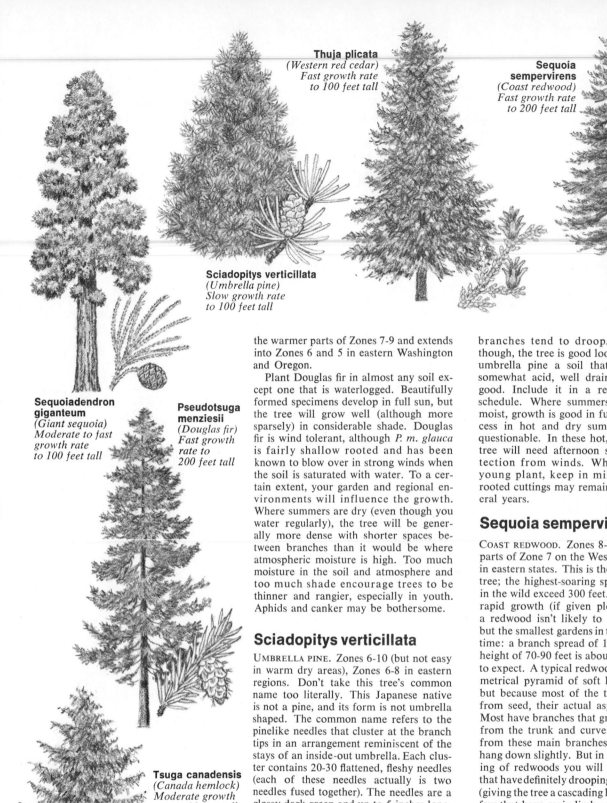

Thuja plicata
(Western red cedar)
Fast growth rate
to 100 feet tall

Sequoia sempervirens
(Coast redwood)
Fast growth rate
to 200 feet tall

Sciadopitys verticillata
(Umbrella pine)
Slow growth rate
to 100 feet tall

Sequoiadendron giganteum
(Giant sequoia)
Moderate to fast growth rate to 100 feet tall

Pseudotsuga menziesii
(Douglas fir)
Fast growth rate to 200 feet tall

Tsuga canadensis
(Canada hemlock)
Moderate growth rate to 90 feet tall

the warmer parts of Zones 7-9 and extends into Zones 6 and 5 in eastern Washington and Oregon.

Plant Douglas fir in almost any soil except one that is waterlogged. Beautifully formed specimens develop in full sun, but the tree will grow well (although more sparsely) in considerable shade. Douglas fir is wind tolerant, although *P. m. glauca* is fairly shallow rooted and has been known to blow over in strong winds when the soil is saturated with water. To a certain extent, your garden and regional environments will influence the growth. Where summers are dry (even though you water regularly), the tree will be generally more dense with shorter spaces between branches than it would be where atmospheric moisture is high. Too much moisture in the soil and atmosphere and too much shade encourage trees to be thinner and rangier, especially in youth. Aphids and canker may be bothersome.

Sciadopitys verticillata

UMBRELLA PINE. Zones 6-10 (but not easy in warm dry areas), Zones 6-8 in eastern regions. Don't take this tree's common name too literally. This Japanese native is not a pine, and its form is not umbrella shaped. The common name refers to the pinelike needles that cluster at the branch tips in an arrangement reminiscent of the stays of an inside-out umbrella. Each cluster contains 20-30 flattened, fleshy needles (each of these needles actually is two needles fused together). The needles are a glossy dark green and up to 5 inches long. Small, scalelike leaves are scattered along the branches. Bark color is dark red brown. Older trees may bear attractive, oval shaped cones up to 5 inches long. In its native habitat, the umbrella pine grows to over 100 feet, but in gardens, its slow growth isn't likely to reach more than 40 feet tall. The trees have a tendency to form multiple trunks. Young plants are very dense, symmetrical pyramids, but in maturity they become more open and their branches tend to droop. At all ages, though, the tree is good looking. Give the umbrella pine a soil that is neutral to somewhat acid, well drained, and fairly good. Include it in a regular watering schedule. Where summers are cool and moist, growth is good in full sun, but success in hot and dry summer regions is questionable. In these hot, dry areas, the tree will need afternoon shade and protection from winds. When you buy a young plant, keep in mind that newly rooted cuttings may remain small for several years.

Sequoia sempervirens

COAST REDWOOD. Zones 8-10 and warmer parts of Zone 7 on the West Coast, Zone 8 in eastern states. This is the world's tallest tree; the highest-soaring specimens found in the wild exceed 300 feet. But despite its rapid growth (if given plenty of water), a redwood isn't likely to overpower any but the smallest gardens in the owner's lifetime: a branch spread of 15-30 feet and a height of 70-90 feet is about the maximum to expect. A typical redwood forms a symmetrical pyramid of soft looking foliage, but because most of the trees are grown from seed, their actual aspect does vary. Most have branches that grow straight out from the trunk and curve up at the tips; from these main branches the branchlets hang down slightly. But in any large planting of redwoods you will see a few trees that have definitely drooping main branches (giving the tree a cascading look) and a very few that have main limbs slightly upright. Leaves, to 1 inch long, are flat, pointed, narrow, and medium green on the upper surface but grayish beneath. They grow on either side of twigs like quills on a feather. After many years — or immediately, if you cut off the lower branches — you'll have a view of the straight sided, red brown trunk and its fibrous bark. The trunk, in fact, is an indicator of health: nearly parallel sides show the tree is growing well; noticeably tapered trunks indicate more of a struggle for survival.

The coast redwood trees will grow in full sun to half shade, but they may be sparse and straggly if planted too close to other large trees or to high walls or buildings. Their best development occurs when planted singly or in a grove in an open location. Planted in a lawn, they are sure to get the abundant water they prefer. Iron deficiency (usually in alkaline soils) causes the needles — particularly new ones — to turn yellow in summer. Applications of iron chelates to the soil usually remedy this problem. You can count on the coast redwood to be essentially pest free.

Sequoiadendron giganteum

GIANT SEQUOIA, BIG TREE. Zones 6-10, Zones 6-8 in eastern regions, though best performance is limited to the West. If you have ever seen one of these trees in the wild (or even photographs of them) and read statistics of their unsurpassed total bulk (which makes them the largest trees in the world), it is hard to imagine considering one for a spot in the garden. Yet the young trees ("young" in terms of a 3,000-year life span) are neat, remarkably handsome trees for larger gardens. Foliage is gray green, each leaf a pointed scale that overlaps the next one as though it were a prickly cypress. Lower branches hang on for many years, forming an increasingly large and dense pyramid of foliage that grows as much as 3 feet in a year. Because both its foliage and roots dominate the surrounding area, the giant sequoia is a tree to plant in solitary splendor (as in a lawn, for example). Sometimes the lowest branches will take root where they touch the ground, forming secondary "trees" that blend into the original tree and further increase the amount of space it takes up. Give this tree good, deep, well-drained soil in a sunny, open location; water deeply but not too often after it is established. If you remove the lower branches, you'll expose a trunk of fissured and craggy, dark red brown bark.

Spruce (see Picea, pp. 87-88)

Thuja

ARBORVITAE. The most familiar arborvitaes are shrubs: neat, perfectly symmetrical pieces of solid geometry in globes, cones, or cylinders. Many of these are selected varieties of the tree-sized American arborvitae which is much less common in gardens. An even more surprising relation is the stunning and beautiful forest giant from the West, *T. plicata*. These tree-sized arborvitae have tiny, scalelike leaves that cling tightly to twigs and branchlets that are carried in flat sprays. Spider mites are the most serious pest.

T. occidentalis. AMERICAN ARBORVITAE. Zones 3-8 in the Northeast, 6-9 on the West Coast. (It will grow farther south on both sides of the country, but these are the best regions for good perform-

ance.) American arborvitae prefers moist soil and a humid but not hot atmosphere. The typical wild form has an upright, open habit to 40-60 feet high and up to 10 feet across, with branches that tend to turn up at the tips. Foliage sprays are bright green to yellow green but usually turn brown during cold winter weather. Most common in nurseries are varieties of the species, usually much more dwarf and compact. Two taller-growing ones are 'Douglas Pyramidal', which makes a fast-growing, green pyramid, and 'Fastigiata', a dense and narrow column to about 25 feet high, good for hedging and background plantings.

T. plicata. WESTERN RED CEDAR, GIANT ARBORVITAE. Zones 6 or 7 through Zone 9. Zones 6-8 in eastern regions. Like the Douglas fir (*Pseudotsuga menziesii*), this Northwest native ranges from the cool mildness of the Pacific Coast to the colder, dryer climate of Montana and northern Idaho. Trees grown from seeds of inland trees will get through winters in Zone 6, but coastal forms shouldn't be planted in any region colder than Zone 7. In the cool, foggy coastal forests, this tree will send up feathery spires to 200 feet; in the garden it will still be a large tree but only about 100 feet tall. The best garden use of this tree probably is as a broadly pyramidal lawn specimen, where its wide-spreading lower branches have plenty of elbow room. Gardening beneath it is difficult because of its vigorous, shallow root system and the dense shade it casts. The red cedar is an exceptionally handsome tree, with dark green, lacy foliage sprays on slender, drooping branchlets. If you have enough room, it also makes a good-looking high hedge or screen tree. Given ample moisture, it attains a fairly fast growth rate. Contrary to what you might expect, though, it doesn't demand either constantly moist soil or soil that is acid. Nurseries offer several varieties that differ either in foliage or in growth habit. 'Aurea' has golden green young branch tips, whereas 'Aurea Variegata' has patches of golden twigs scattered among the normal green foliage. The Hogan cedar, variety 'Fastigiata', forms a dense, narrow, and upright plant that takes up less room as a hedge or screen.

Tsuga (Hemlock)

If a vote were taken to determine the most graceful conifers, the hemlocks probably would win. As a group they are unanimously dense, compact, fine-textured, and at least slightly pendulous. Foliage consists of flattened needles, each under 1 inch long. Since all hemlocks need climates where there is plenty of atmospheric moisture and summer rainfall, their usefulness is generally limited to the East and Northwest. They also are best where not exposed to frequent strong winds. The two western species are successful only in their native territory. All species are rather shallow rooted and so are not drought tolerant; in addition to moist soil, they

prefer soil that is acid. The spider mite is probably the most serious potential pest; it appears during the warmest weather. Other possible problems are scale and rust diseases.

T. canadensis. CANADA or EASTERN HEMLOCK. Zones 5-9. Because it doesn't insist on acid soil, this is the most adaptable hemlock. It excels as a hedge plant of almost any height, so if you've only seen it sheared, it may come as a surprise to see it as a 60-90 foot, broadly pyramidal tree. Often it grows with two or more main trunks, but the pyramid shape remains with fairly horizontal branches and drooping outer branchlets. Growth rate is moderate. Dark green needles are banded white on their undersides and arranged mostly in opposite rows on the twigs. A number of varieties have been selected and may occasionally be found in nurseries. These differ from the species in their smaller size and varied shape or leaf color.

T. caroliniana. CAROLINA HEMLOCK. Zones 5-7. In general appearance this is a somewhat slimmer, shorter version of the Canada hemlock — to about 40 feet tall by 20 feet wide. Up close, its most noticeable difference is the arrangement of needles all around the twigs instead of in opposite rows. It is supposed to be more tolerant of city atmosphere than the Canada species, but it needs acid soils.

T. diversifolia. JAPANESE HEMLOCK. Zones 6-8. A definitely domed crown is one feature that distinguishes this species from the American hemlocks. Slow growth eventually reaches 45-70 feet. Appearance is very dense and dark green in color. Needles are banded white on their undersides, and each needle is retained for about eight years (one reason for the tree's density). Growth is good only in acid soils.

T. heterophylla. WESTERN HEMLOCK. Zones 5-9 only in western states. (The types that are hardy in Zones 5 and 6 come from northern Idaho and western Montana.) Except for foliage color, this tree appears from a distance to be a replica of the deodar cedar. It's a fast-growing pyramid to 200 feet in the wild, each of its horizontally spreading branches festooned with drooping branchlets. Even the tip of the tree bends over just like a deodar. Fine-textured, dark green to yellowish green foliage is profuse, soft, and feathery; undersides have whitish bands. Like the Canada hemlock, it will make an excellent hedge, as well as a strikingly beautiful large specimen tree. Unfortunately, it grows well only within its native range, where soil and atmosphere both are moist.

T. mertensiana. MOUNTAIN HEMLOCK. Zones 5-8 but only in its native western range. Coming from the high mountain altitudes from Alaska into California, this hemlock is accustomed to coolness at all times, although it will succeed in soil that isn't acid or always moist. In the wild it reaches 90 feet but is much shorter and quite slow growing at lower altitudes. Its customary shape is a blue green pyramid, with needles arranged all around the branches.

Index

PLANT HARDINESS ZONE MAP

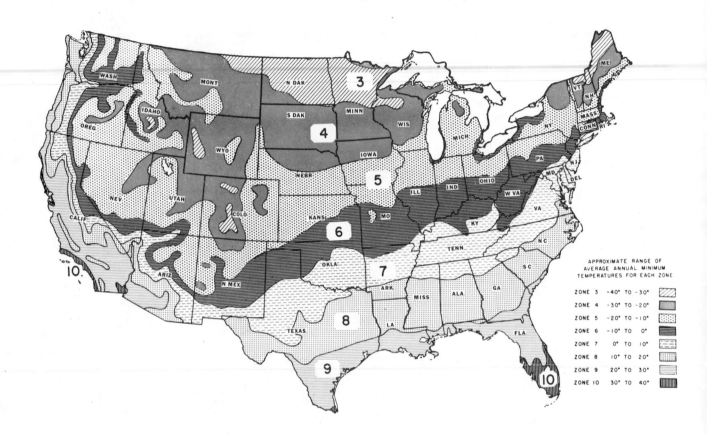

The above Plant Hardiness Zone Map—devised by the United States Department of Agriculture—is used in countless nursery catalogs and garden books to indicate where plants can be grown. In the map's original concept, the reader was to locate the climate zone in which he lived; then, if the zone number for a particular plant was the same as, or smaller than, his climate zone number, the plant was judged to be hardy in his locale.

In our listings, we have followed the standard method of hardiness rating, but in addition to indicating the coldest zone in which the plant will grow, we have considered its adaptability and usefulness in warmer zones and so indicated all zones in which the tree is generally grown.

The map's limitations are obvious. A scheme based only on minimum expected temperatures cannot possibly account for variations in soils or micro-climates within the zones. And most important, such a map fails to acknowledge other significant differences in climate that affect plant growth—humidity, expected high temperatures, and

wind, for example. Consider the differences in Zones 9 and 10 along the Gulf Coast and in Florida compared to those zones in California: the former area has high humidity and summer rainfall, while in the West, rainfall is in winter and summer temperatures are likely to be higher, but with humidity low. Zone 8 in cool, rainy, and oceanic Washington state differs greatly from warmer, steamier, continental Zone 8 in the lower South. Much of Nevada— arid and windy—falls in Zone 5 as do much of New York State and Massachusetts where summer moisture and humidity have created an entirely different environment for plants though based on the same expected low temperatures.

Fortunately for the gardener, many trees can accept a variety of climates and still turn in worthwhile performances. But where significant limitations do exist, we have noted them in such phrases as "but not for the lower Midwest and Southwest," "Zones 5-8, desert only," and "best performance in acid soils with much moisture."